STREETFIGHTERS

STREETFIGHTERS

Real Fighting Men Tell Their Stories

Julian Davies

MILO BOOKS LTD

First published in May 2002 by Milo Books Ltd

ISBN 1 903854-09-1

Typeset by Avon DataSet Ltd, Bidford-on-Avon, Warks
www.avondataset.com

Printed and bound in Great Britain by
Creative Print and Design, Ebbw Vale, Gwent

MILO BOOKS LTD
P.O.Box 153
Bury
BL0 9FX
info@milobooks.com

DEDICATED TO

The late Bartley Gorman, King of the Gypsies
and a true gentleman

Author Julian Davies (left) with the late Bartley Gorman

Contents

Acknowledgements

THERE ARE A few good friends that I would like to thank who have helped me over the past year or so. I don't think this book could have happened without them.

First, there's Anthony and Steven Thomas, who helped me right from the start. They travelled the country with me, Anthony navigating and Steven sharing the driving on the long journeys. I'm not the best of drivers and almost killed us all many times, most memorably when travelling back from interviewing Richard Horsley and one of my rear tyres decided it had had enough and commited suicide in spectacular fashion. If anyone has ever had a blow-out at 80 miles per hour in the third lane of a motorway, they will know how it felt.

My mate Dav Owens looked over my interviews and was always there when I needed him. The author Steve Richards and the fighter-writer Billy Cribb, who both said I could do this book if I put my mind to it and got up off my arse, were also an inspiration.

I owe a special debt to my new friends Richard Horsley and Vicky Simpkin (Decca's wife). I must have had about 300 telephone conversations with each of them, and their sense of humour always made paying the phone bill worthwhile.

To all the people mentioned above and to every fighter featured in this book, thank you all so very much. I regard you all as valued and trusted friends.

Preface

MY FASCINATION WITH fighters dates back to my childhood. As a young boy, I would hear tales of the heroic gladiators who met on the mountain tops of my native South Wales to fight bareknuckle. Sometimes they fought for money, more often for sheer pride. Their contests were illegal, their names whispered in the pubs and social clubs of the valleys and mining villages. The details of these "mountain fighters" have been lost in the mists of time, but the seed was sown and my love of fighting has been there ever since.

The idea of writing a book came about after I had started running an internet website (www.unlicensed2000.com) detailing the stories of a variety of fighters: not famous-name boxers (who get more than enough exposure in the media) but unlicensed boxers, martial artists, gypsy pugilists, minders, doormen and, of course, streetfighters. I was constantly being emailed by fight fans from all around the world asking where they could read more about the men I had introduced, and I realised that many of their stories had remained unknown outside their home localities until I had released them to a wider audience through the site.

After announcing my intention to write a book about them, I appealed for the names of the hardest men from the hometowns of the visitors to my website. The floodgates opened. The trail led me all over the motorway network, from Hartlepool in the North East to Swansea in the South West. I met and interviewed men whose experiences shocked me. There were sagas of appalling hardship, tragic childhoods, life-changing moments, pride and glory. In the majority of cases, the men I interviewed were strangers to me at the time of our first meeting. Just as often, when I left we had become firm friends.

And so *Streetfighters* came into being, after almost two years of research that involved travelling the length and breadth of the UK to meet each fighter and record an account of their lives and battles. I must be careful not to make this sound a chore because in truth it never was. Each of the men whose life tales you are about to read gave me the warmest of welcomes and the highest level of hospitality when I visited them. I must also say that this is not just another tome in which the deeds of "hard men" are recounted by the author. It is an insight into the lives of respected fighting men *in their own words*. Here they talk to you, the reader, direct: and you will find their words hit home with as much power as their punches.

The final selection of fighters was difficult to make, but I was adamant that certain criteria had to be met: all of those featured had to have good stories to tell, they had to be well-respected as fighting men, and, most importantly to me, they must not be regarded as bullies. These are the hallmarks of truly hard men. As with any group this size, there are different personalities involved, but the common thread is the honesty and sincerity with which they spoke. No punches were pulled and events that were sometimes very difficult for the fighters themselves to talk about were relayed to me as candidly as was possible, so that an accurate account of their lives could be recorded. Not one of the men came across as a braggart, glorying in the violence that has coloured their lives. Most have just accepted that it was the hand they were dealt in life and they had to play it the best they could. *Streetfighters* will, I am sure, have you rolling with laughter and close to tears in the space of a few pages.

Out there, even in the 21st century, are men who carve out their reputations, earn their money and define themselves with their fists. They may seem to many people brutal, a throwback to rougher times. Many of my subjects were shadowy figures, underground legends unknown to the wider public. But they exist. They are real and they cannot be ignored. I could go on and on telling you about each of them, but I won't . . . I'll let the fighters tell you themselves.

Julian Davies

RICHARD HORSLEY

Hartlepool

A well respected ex-boxer with a reputation that precedes him, Richy can be one of the nicest guys you'll meet, or your worst enemy – however you want to play it. His sledgehammer right hand has stopped many a wannabe bully in his tracks. In the North East you have to be tough to survive and they don't come much tougher than this guy.

MY GRANDAD, WHO died in 1973, was an excellent amateur boxer back in the Thirties and Forties. His ring name was Kid Morris. He held the decision over Teddy Gardner [British and European flyweight champion] three times. My grandad was a chimney sweep. Even today, when I look back I imagine him covered from head to toe in soot. You'd swear he worked down the pits.

I was born in 1964 at Cameron's Hospital in Hartlepool, which was knocked down about ten years ago. It's now a private housing estate. My mother was a housewife and my dad a roamer; he travelled all over the place working. He tried his hand at any job, from pipe-layer to working on the docks. I remember him telling me that on one of the jobs he had to sleep in the barn with the shire horses at night. In his younger days he could have a tear-up if he wanted to: he became known as "Blood Horsley" because of his fighting. He got kidney damage in the army and was medically discharged. In later years he had kidney failure, and died in 1975 before a kidney could be found for him. It was the worst day of my life.

My cousin plays in the rock band Iron Maiden. His name is Janick Gers. They called him Janick because his father was Polish. His mother was a Horsley before she married. My cousin's a tidy guy; he once told me that he thought the world of my dad. People from Hartlepool are sometimes called "Monkey Hangers". The name dates back to the Napoleonic wars. Story has it that a French galleon was shipwrecked off the coast of Hartlepool. The sole survivor was a small monkey that clung to some wreckage that drifted ashore. The monkey was dressed in a miniature French uniform and the local crofters that lived in Hartlepool were illiterate and thought the babbling monkey was a French spy. They must have got confused with the term "powder monkeys", who were small boys whose job it was to supply gunpowder to the French gunners. The crofters conducted a speedy trial on the beach and found the poor monkey guilty of being a French spy.

The monkey was sentenced to death and promptly hung (poor bastard). So there you have it: I, like everyone else in Hartlepool, am a Monkey Hanger.

I was always big as a young lad, so when it came to fighting it was always me who got stuck into it. I was never a bully and never got bullied as a kid. Whenever it came on top I'd think, *fuck it*, and bang! I'd hit the fucker and the rest would stay clear. I got into boxing as a 13-year-old kid. If I wasn't in the gym then I was out having a laugh with my mates. About this time I got my first court appearance along with four of my mates. Someone had suggested going potato picking to earn some extra money. We walk six miles and get to the farmer's field and there's nobody there. *Where are all the tattie pickers?* Not a tattie picker in sight, just this great big haystack. Well, we were only kids and this haystack looked like one of them bouncy castles that you get at fairgrounds. The guys at the bottom of the haystack were met with bales of hay dropped on their heads. We had great fun wrecking this haystack for about an hour. All of a sudden farmers and farmhands surrounded us. We made a run for it but got caught. We got taken to the local police station and got bail (no pun intended). We came back the next week to see if we had to go to court. Just our fucking luck, the farmer was a local magistrate and wouldn't settle out of court. They did us for criminal damage. When they called out our middle names in court we all laughed like idiots and the magistrate gave us a roasting. We had to pay £6 compensation and got a conditional discharge for a year.

I was going boxing on and off for a couple of years before I started fighting. I had twelve fights as a light-heavyweight and boxed some good fighters. I boxed Crawford Ashley in only my sixth fight: he was British champion at the time, and had over 40 fights. Well, he stopped me. He was a big puncher and hit me with some of the hardest punches I've ever been hit with. He was a knockout specialist. I remember he caught me with a big right hand straight to the throat; I couldn't swallow for days and my throat was sore for weeks.

At one stage of my life I did a few months in Durham Detention Centre. I was convicted of causing criminal damage. Well, I told the judge I wouldn't pay compensation, so off they sent me. Detention centres were rough, horrible places. The regime was just like an army boot camp, with physical and mental pressure. Most people would pick prison over these places. The idea was along the lines of a quick, sharp shock. Sometimes it worked, sometimes it didn't. To be employed there you had to be a pure bastard or you just weren't cut out for the job. When I turned up, the worst screw in the place marched me off to his office. He liked to push the new lads around when they first came in. He screamed at me, "Get a move on," and pushed me hard. I didn't move any faster so he went apeshit. First he banged my head against the wall, then the punches started. I just rode and rolled off his punches so they had no effect on me whatsoever. People were shocked to see that he couldn't hurt or frighten me, it was fuck all to me. I just kept answering, "Yes sir, no sir." Thing is, you couldn't fight back or things could be made really hard for you.

At one point they made us all line up. I can hear this growling in my ear and I'm thinking, *what the fuck's that?* I turn around and there's this massive lad growling at me. I nearly burst out laughing at the stupid twat. I look up at the lad and politely inform him, "Who the hell are you growling at, you stupid prick? Growl like that again and I'll rip your fucking head off, do you understand?" He nodded yes and stopped. You should have seen the look on the lad's face. I bet that was the first time anyone ever put him in his place. Within a few days and a few arguments the word went around that I was the best fighter in the place, and I got myself a cushy job in the stores. I sort of jumped the queue to get it, mind you. I loved the training and when I came out I felt so fit and strong I was unbreakable, and couldn't wait to get back to the boxing gym.

While I was learning to box there was this geezer there, he was a few years older than me. He was short, squat, powerful and covered in tattoos. He'd had a couple of fights and then packed it in. He thought he was a right Jack the Lad, a tough guy, wiseguy, etcetera. He had got a 14-year stretch for armed robbery so I didn't see him for quite a few years, just now and again when he got out. It was 1995 and a group of us were going from pub to pub and he was one of us. The more drinks he was getting down his neck the more he was getting on everyone's nerves. The guy was shouting about how hard he was, being a right pain. He shouts to me, "Oi you, outside."

Now I thought the prick was joking but he wasn't. "I'm the best fourteen stone you'll come across," he screamed. Off comes my coat and we step outside. The pub had a glass front so everyone could see us. Someone shouts out, "Go on, do him Richy." He came straight at me and BANG, I catch him with a short left hook with all my power behind it. He folded over like a ten-bob note. What an anti-climax. I bent over him and smashed him about four times with my right hand and he was on another planet. He was still sleeping when the ambulance took him fifteen minutes later with the oxygen mask on. His jaw was broke in four places, so they had to put a steel plate in with screws to fix it. I had no sympathy for him. He had brought it on himself with his big loud mouth.

I drifted in and out of boxing for a while and made a comeback as a heavyweight. Well, I fought six more times, winning five. I had too many distractions and packed in the boxing. I started working the doors and I was fighting all the time. People know me not only as a fighter but also as a tidy guy. I always treat people with respect and have never stole a thing in my life. I once got charged with theft but like I said, I don't steal. I borrowed a friend's card to get some videos out – this was back in 1985. Well, for some reason the films never got returned. The shop called the police and I was pulled in. The shop had just installed a video camera and of course I was on it. To get it all over and done with I pleaded guilty. The judge remanded me for ten days. I was gobsmacked: just my luck, locked in Durham Jail for 23 hours a day over some stupid videos. After the ten days were up, I was taken back to court and there was a different judge who couldn't believe that I had been remanded. I was also fined £300. The worst part was missing the birth of my daughter Donna. She was nine days old before I even knew she was born. I still don't know what happened to the videos. If I do ever find them I may take them back to the shop – could you imagine how much I now owe in fines!

Back in '92, '93, I was living with this girl and, of course, working the doors. There was this local geezer, a well-respected, right hard guy, who fought for money. If you had any trouble with him you knew you were going to be in a fight. He was a big powerful man and nobody wanted trouble with him. Now the girl I was with was working in a different nightclub to me, and he was coming in and trying to tap her up. After a few weeks she told me this, and that he had been saying, "What's Richy going to do to me? He can do nowt with me." I was stewing with this for a while when I went to a bar I worked at one afternoon. Now I wasn't working that day and I knew he would come in. I just wanted to get the job done with him and get out. I knew he would have a crowd with him and the bar had loads of rough guys in as well. I told my mate that when he comes in I'd wait till he goes to the bar, then offer him outside. My mate says, "Nah, just get stuck in soon as you see him." I'm thinking this over in my mind when I see them all come in, all his mates, some hard guys and some who just think they are something. In he walks, last of all. I get up and walk straight over to him. He knew I was coming over for him so as I throw a right hand he tries to slip it, but I catch him with it. Down he goes and I must have caught him a beaut because there's claret all over. I lean over him and I told him not to mess with my woman. He's all dazed as he's looking up at me, so I give him the left hook, right on the side of the jaw. His eyes roll in his head and out he goes. I look up at his mates and none of them would look us in the face. I shout out, "Come on then who wants it?" None of them wanted to know. I go out the back, and I get told now they are all up screaming and shouting what they are going to do to me.

Now this guy never had anything like this happen to him before. He may have been beat before but nothing like this, with the ambulance and all. Anyway there are rumours flying around town, shit things like I hit him from behind and that. He had this mate, a big 25-stone barrel of lard he thought he was a right handful. I'm in a nightclub and he's looking at me and he's telling people how I fought dirty with his mate. It's the end of the night and I've had enough of this; he's being disrespectful to me. I wait till it goes real quiet and I shout over, "Oi! Fat prick." He turns around snarling at me. "You're getting on my tits," I shout straight at him. Everyone can hear this and he puts his drink down and comes straight for us. Soon as he comes near me I hit him with two beauts. Down he goes on his knees. I give him some more and I know I've broke both my hands but I grit my teeth and keep hitting him because I wanted to give him some. After all that, he's in hospital with two broken legs, broken jaw and he's stitched up like a road map. So I thought, *well, that's sent the feelers out to those daft twats.* The big fat prick still told everyone that I had jumped him with friends and the reason he had broken legs was because I had done them with an iron bar. Pure lies. He never told people that he broke his knees when he landed on them on the tiled floor when I knocked him out.

There was another big lad, a friend of his as well, who had a bit of a do with me. Now this time I walked up to him at the bar and we started to fight. As he came back off the bar he's swinging back and fore like the big heavy bag. I hit him with a left-right. Down he went and he's carted off to hospital. Well he's been training for a few months and one night he phones us up like. "Richy, it was a bit fast last time," he tells me, so we arrange to meet in a car park. I had just one lad to take me there, just in case of any foul play. It was Bonfire Night and everyone was waiting for the news of the fight – seems the word had gone around the town. I go over to him and he's a big lad, he's got this white vest on and he looks impressive. We shake hands and he says, "Well, I've got to fight you now Richy, it was a bit fast last time and I want to get it out of the way." Now the pair of us square up and I'm waiting for him to come toward us, but he didn't come. I didn't really throw anything, just a light feeler, and he comes down under it and grabs me around the waist, the sneaky fucker. He's trying to pull us down but I'm too strong for him. I get him down on the floor and I'm trying to smash his head down on the pavement but his neck muscles are too strong for me to do it. "You dirty bastard," he screams at me. I get my hands free and hit him with a left-right. He shouts at me to stop but I'm not satisfied yet, so I hit him a couple of times more and he's all smashed up. I thought, *I can't hit him anymore or he'll be dead*, so I get up and walk away. As I was walking I hear him calling me "Richy! Richy!" I walk back and I look at him covered in blood. He can't even get up. "Richy, you can't leave us like this." So I thought, *fair dos*, and I pick him up and lie him in the car all bashed up. You know I'm a fair man and I don't like to take liberties; once a man is done, he's done and that's it. If I had got beat fair I'd come back to fight again, and if I still got beat I would have shaken his hand and admitted he was the better man.

I was in streetfights maybe four, five times a week. Seems people were coming from all over to have a go. I was getting so much trouble and getting locked up all the time. I never got charged, mind you. I guess it was because I had so many witnesses who came forward to say that I didn't start anything, which was always the case.

I remember once it was New Year's Eve and I'd been working since twelve in the day. This guy was trying to get into this young girl, a row broke out and I ended up hitting him. It was about four in the morning and I was very drunk. I went to the toilet and I was sitting there when I can hear all hell breaking loose outside. This big lad outside is going right berserk. He was shouting that he wanted to fight me out in the garden. I didn't want to fight him because you don't do justice to yourself when you're drunk. Anyway, soon as I get on the grass, bang, I'm down. I've been hit. My legs are like jelly and I don't know what the fuck is happening. He got on top of me and I couldn't even lift my hands up, he was punching and punching me. I remember thinking, *I wish I was sober*. I really thought he was going to kill me; he just kept smashing away and I could feel myself slipping away. I kept trying to stay awake, and after what seemed to be an eternity, he got up. Now the guy I was fighting had rings on: I was cut to bits and I could see bits of flesh cut open on the end of my nose and all. I was in a right state – all around my eyes and all were cut open.

Now it must have been a good six months gone past. I hear he's going around thinking he's King Kong, so I have to get my revenge. When things like this happen, you start getting doubts in your mind and that, you start thinking, *was it the drink or was he the better man?* When I was right and got myself sorted, I went to the club where he was drinking. Every day I had been thinking of what had happened and what I was going to do. I didn't go in but I looked through the window and the big twat's in there and he has his back to me. That's when the butterflies in the stomach start. I wait outside for him and when he sees me across the road, he shouts, "So, you want another good hiding, do yah?" He's so very confident. He comes at me, throws a big right hand but I block it and step in. I smash him twice and down he goes. I get on top of him and smash him to bits. I get back off him and I thought I'd killed him. I'd broke my hands on him as well, and he was in bits. He was rushed to hospital and it was touch and go for a while.

A good while went past and one night I was out celebrating my mate's birthday. I was just stepping out of the pub when, bang, he hits me. Now I don't know what the hell has happened. My head's spinning and he hits me again. I fly back against the pub windows and he gets me again. If it wasn't for the pub door, I would have been down, I steady up as one of my mates pushes him back. While this was happening, my head clears and I realise what's going on. My pal shouts, "Right then, let them fight." As I was walking towards him my legs are still like jelly. Seems we found ourselves in the middle of the high street, and everyone's out to watch it. All the cars stop because they can't get past. At first we both miss a few punches, then BANG. I catch him with a big hook and down he goes. I can see his eyes rolling and his head bounced off the tarmac on the road. I drag him off the road to where it started by the pub. I got on top of him and let him have it again. When I was done with him and got up and looked at him, it's like he was dying. The ambulance came and they got an oxygen mask straight on him. I could see the life draining out of him. They got him in hospital and he nearly pegged it. I was scared bloody stiff, I can tell yah. I really thought he would die. He was on some sort of machine for a while in hospital. He wanted to press charges but there were too many witnesses to say that he had started it all. Years and years later I bumped into him at a party. I guess everyone thought it was going to kick off. I looked at him and he looked at me, we both smiled and shook hands. He told me that at the time all his friends had been winding him up saying that he was scared of me and that.

A few years ago I was drinking in this nightclub and happened to be talking with this woman. Nothing in it, just talking. I notice over the other side of the room there's some guy waving his arms, threatening like, and shouting something I couldn't hear because of the noise. There were two of them, a big one and a small one doing all the mouthing. I'm thinking, *is he talking to me?* I look around and realise he is. We lock eyes and I point to myself and mouth, "Are you talking to me?" He nods yes and continues with the obscenities.

I excused myself to the woman I was talking with, put my pint down and walked over. I stopped to ask a friend to watch my back. Thing is, people like this can't be talked to, so I wasn't going to mess around. I hit the smaller mouthy one with a right, left, right, smack on his chin. Down the twat went, unconscious before he hit the floor. I turn to the big guy and off he shot like Linford Christie. I catch up with him and threw a glancing right hand. It dropped him but fear was keeping him awake. He scrambled under the tables to hide from me. As the doormen arrived I was putting the boot into him and not having much success. After about ten minutes an ambulance came for the other one. Seems the doormen couldn't revive the fucker. We were on the top floor of the club, so the bouncers had to carry him out. He looked a right mess. Turns out the smaller one had his jaw shattered. The big one said the punch that caught him was like being hit by a hammer. From what I gather the smaller one had been going out with the woman I was talking to for a couple years. The big one had a reputation as a fighter, the smaller one thought his mate would help him out of the shit, but of course the shit hit the fan.

It's not as if I start the trouble. One Sunday night I was drinking with this girl. I had been working hard on the pub and club doors and could do with a night with no trouble. We got to the pub that I had been working the door at. I got between these two guys so I could get served by the bar. One of them said, "Who the hell do you think you are pushing?" I bit my tongue, as I had promised myself a quiet night.

"Do you want a fucking chew?" he screamed at me.

I replied, "No."

"Well, you better not if you know what's good for you," he screamed again.

I got the drinks and went to the other side of the room. All the time this stupid prick kept going through my head. He kept looking over and talking to his pals, I thought, *fuck the quiet night, it's*

11

out the window now. I weighed the situation up: there was three of them and just me. I went and stood by the door – you had to pass through it to leave. After what seemed like ages, the three decided to leave. I finished my drink and stood there blocking the door. The prick with all the gob was thinking what the fuck was going on. "I've changed my mind, I do want a chew," I growled at the arsehole. I brought a big right into play and the wanker didn't know what had hit him. He was sleeping on the floor with blood coming from a deep gash. His two mates turned white and shit themselves. They didn't want it. There were women screaming like mental cases and the manager ran over and said I'd better leave before the ambulance and the police came. I slipped into the crowd and disappeared.

Now I thought it was over, even though he had lied and told people I had hit him with an ashtray. One day I had to go to this pub to sort some trouble out and who was sitting there with all his mates but the arsehole with all the gob. It was like walking into an enemy's camp. The lad I wanted to see wasn't there. As I was leaving, the wanker shouts out, "Oi, you." I turn and he's standing there. "Who do you think you are, coming here to sort chew out in my pub?" I thought, *I'm going to be killed*, so I walk off and get a few friends to watch my back. I come back and the prick is now all by himself – all his mates knew I was coming back so they up and left. Now he wouldn't come out in the car park with me because my mates were there, even just on our own. He starts raising his voice, so I thought, *fuck this*, and gave it to him. I smashed him so bad that I broke three of his ribs and he had internal bleeding. The barman told me that when they carted him off he thought the geezer was dead. He never came back. I found he had put a two grand price on my head for anyone who could do me over. Well that never happened, and no-one ever collected the money.

I never look for trouble but sometimes on the door it came my way. This bloke came in one night. He had just had a bust-up with his woman and was looking for trouble. He started to smash up all the glasses that were stacked waiting to be washed. He must have smashed about 60 glasses. I could hear all the smashing as I came from the toilet. The guy went to leave the pub but had to get past me to go through the door. The whole pub were watching him; he was marching straight towards me with a right snarl on his face. I stood in the way to block him and he threw a punch at me, I slipped the punch and snapped out a straight right smack on the button. He was on the deck groaning and covered in blood and all the fight had gone out of him. Another doorman picked him up and took him to be cleaned up in the toilets. I look down at my hand and there's this big gash and blood is pouring out. Seems I'd knocked his front teeth out and they had stuck in my hand. I still have the scar today. A few weeks later, I got banged up for it – he didn't go to the police until a fortnight later. Somebody had put him wise to getting compensation. Anyway, the Crown Prosecution Service kicked it into touch. It's amazing how many arseholes there are like that guy out there.

I started work at this wine bar, a proper place with about ten doormen. My first night there and they tell me about this bloke who comes every weekend. This guy won't see his drinks off and always makes them look stupid. You know the type: loud and loves an audience. Well it was late and practically everyone had gone. It was a bit of a headache getting everyone out, it's always like that when they have had a few drinks. There were about six lads standing around some of the doormen, they were fucking around and acting up because they had this prick with them. The doormen had asked him to drink up but he just waved and said, "Bye, bye," to them. I walk up and tell him to finish his drink or I'm taking it away. I don't like people taking the piss so you have to be firm with them. The prick just sat there smirking at me. I reached over, grabbed his pint and poured it over his huge head. Before he could move I smack him with a straight right and flatten the prick. His mates shout out that they don't want any trouble and off they go. Well they take him to hospital and they find I broke his nose, not to mention his ego. Suffice to say he never tried his little tricks again. He did consider pressing charges but thought better of it. Now, if he had done it to me I would never get the police involved. That's the trouble with working the doors: you're always in a no-win situation. In 1996 I packed the door work in, and thank God for that.

On one occasion I was sure I was going to be killed. I have this good mate known as Maori, who I have known since we were kids. He's someone I can trust and think the world of. The both of us and another friend drive over to this big estate where we arranged to meet up with some guys that we had trouble with. The three of us get out of Maori's Land Rover and walk over to the guys. Before we can say anything they pull out guns and start to fire at us. The three of us had the same idea, and that was to fuck off as fast as we could. As I'm running I can hear bullets flying all around us. We get back in the Land Rover and pull away. With that, all the windows get shot through. There were people coming out of the houses to watch us get shot at. Maori's driving and I'm ducking my head down. We manage to get away but then realise that my other mate's been shot through the shoulder. He's sitting in the back clutching his shoulder, white as a ghost, and looks like he's going into shock. We get to the hospital and dump him off in casualty. We looked a right sight driving up with all the windows shot in. Maori and myself were lucky to get away unscathed but the three of us walked around with hair like Don King for the next few weeks.

Maori's always getting involved in something or another, it's just the way he is. Life would be so boring without him around. Only the other day he nearly got himself killed again. He was living on some farmland and had a bag of gold jewellery that he had to hide, in case the police came around. Well, the daft bastard hid them on the roof of the barn where they kept the pigs, thinking nobody's going to look up there. On night he climbs up to get them so he can sell them all. He loses his footing and comes straight down through the roof, landing on his back in all the pig shit. He must have fell 30 feet and was lucky that the shit broke his fall. He told me he was stunned for a while and just lay there in the pig shit with all the porkers around him. I told him he was lucky the farmer didn't turn up and take him off to market. On the other hand nobody would buy him – too bloody ugly!

I've always loved Hartlepool and hope I never have to move. There are so many interesting people here and the town has some great history. The town itself used to be known as Little Chicago because of the amount of gangs that it once had: there was the Captain Cutlass gang, the Turquoise Gang and loads more. Loads of tough, foreign merchant seamen came to this town. They would spend their cash in a row of pubs called the Barbary Coast. I remember a story that a prostitute opened up Captain Cutlass's face with a bottle, leaving him scarred for life with a big "Mars Bar" across his face. A man I would have loved to have known would have been the town's first bouncer: he was known as "Battling" Manners, a hard-as-nails mountain of a man. He worked here in the Thirties. He was a pro heavyweight who didn't suffer fools gladly. He would literally bounce them out of the pubs.

When I was fighting all the time I got the nickname "Crazy Horse" because of my name being Horsley and my own interest in the American Indian. Well, I was a little embarrassed about it at first but got used to it. Crazy Horse was probably the greatest warrior the Indian nation ever produced. I don't get called it now but a short while ago somebody said to me, "Now then, Crazy Horse." I couldn't help but laugh, seeing as I hadn't been called it for years. I'm 37 this year [2001] and I can't say it's been the greatest of years. My sister Jackie passed away just lately, she was only 38 so it's been an emotional time for us all. I have another sister, Debbie, who is 39 years old, and I have four kids. My oldest daughter, Jill Louise, just had a beautiful baby daughter so it looks like I'm now the best-looking grandad in Hartlepool. Next in line is my daughter, Donna, she's coming up to 16 and is in her last year of school. She wants to go into nursing. My boy, Terry, is 14 and is music mad, it's music all the time with him. My youngest daughter, Ashleigh, is only ten and a great gymnast; she has just been accepted at the school of excellence. Her ambition is to be picked for her country and with our fingers crossed go to the Olympics one day. None of my kids live with me but I'm a big part of their lives and I hope I always will be.

When I think of it, I've been very lucky and only been down for three months when I was young. I've done a lot of damage to people in the past. I sometimes put it down to the way I hit. I always aim for a few inches just behind the target so my fist goes through with the punch. One thing that did frighten me was one day a clairvoyant got hold of my hands. "I can see you killing someone with these hands some day, you must pull your punches or someone will die," he told me. Now at the time I had been very lucky with some fights, people hurting their heads and swallowing tongues and that. I've moved away from the trouble and try to enjoy life a bit more these days. I've knocked loads out but never caused it, there's always been a good reason why I've done it. I help train the boys at the boxing gym now and I'm happy doing that. It's a good crack helping the lads.

MALCOLM PRICE

Merthyr Tydfil

Malcolm Price (right) with the author

A legendary streetfighter from the South Wales mining community, Malcolm built up respect by taking on and beating all comers. His work on the motorways took him the length and breadth of Britain and he stormed through the local hard men in every place he visited. His reputation soon rose from being one of the hardest men in the valleys to one of the hardest in the UK.

AS A KID, my father made me go to the boxing gym. He was a very strict man, so I had to go. I didn't want to go at first but he made me go a couple of times a week. After a while I won the Welsh Schoolboy Championship and caught a bit more interest in the sport. I went on to turn pro. I had six fights, winning four and losing two. The losses were to the same guy, "Big" Jim Monaghan. He was a big bugger, about 6ft 4in, and he gave me two really hard fights.

One day, I asked my father if he would pick up my coat, which I had left in The Swan pub the night before. When he got there, the place was wrecked. He asked for my coat and was informed that I was the one who had caused all the damage from the fight I got into. When he came home he wasn't happy, so I moved in with my grandmother for a while. Meanwhile I got six months for the offence, losing my boxing licence as well, which was the worst part of it all. I did a lot of bouncing in those days, but I didn't get into much trouble on the door. It was pretty good on the doors back then.

I don't know why I turned into a streetfighter; it just seemed to happen overnight. Looking back over my life, I can't put a finger on why I was always fighting. As a kid I was more interested in ornithology, which still interests me today. Then I seemed to change overnight, and then it was one non-stop battle. I talked about this with a friend once who told me, "Malcolm, I remember when we all would go to the dance halls together. You would always stand at the back of the hall just watching, wouldn't say boo to a goose. The old dance hall was full to the brim one night with gangs of teddy boys. I remember a fight breaking out. All the dance floor was full of lads fighting, all the girls screaming their heads off. I look over to you and you put your glass down and then start punching, and every time you punch, someone falls down. You just kept hitting and hitting all the guys fighting. In the end I had to jump on your back to stop you, just in case you really hurt someone. I kept telling you who I was until you calmed down.

18

Everyone backed away from you and we decided to leave. Malcolm, from that day forth you were always fighting. People wanted to know who was the lad who beat those guys up. Everywhere you went, people knew you as a fighter, so it was inevitable that you became what you became." I don't know if this was where my life changed but I know that it didn't help me much.

A few times in my life I had men come and see how good I could fight, try their luck. I was in The Express pub one day and this big guy from Caerphilly turned up. He had heard about me and came up to fight me, so we went outside to go to the car park. It didn't get that far because I did him in the alleyway on the way there. I smashed him up and stuck the boots in. He lost all his teeth in the process. I just left him unconscious in the alleyway and went back inside. He came for a fight and that was exactly what I gave him.

I was always getting asked to sort trouble out for other people. Sometimes I earned a bit of money out of it, sometimes I just helped out. On one occasion I got called to sort out trouble in a club down the valley. Some big karate guy and his mates were playing hell there and they were too rough for the locals to sort out. Message got back to me in Merthyr to come down and sort it out. I walk in and ask the owner, "Which one is the big troublemaker?" The owner points out this big guy sitting down drinking with all his mates. I walk over, pick up this heavy wooden chair on the way and bring it down with all my strength onto the guy's head, which splits straight open. The guy is flat out on the deck and his mates are too scared to move to help him. After that there was no trouble in the club, job done. I just wanted to be in and out of the place with as little hassle as possible.

Another time I was in The Western pub and some guy was trying to get off with my mate's wife, so I told him not to. Well, he was all dressed up and said, "I'm off out to a dance and thought I might make a kill here first." I replied, "I'll make a kill now," and

19

with that I knocked him clean out, right over the table he went. Well, Mr and Mrs Brown, who ran the pub, were very strict, so my good mate Mike Mahoney and me dragged him in front of the bar where Mrs Brown couldn't see him. Thing was, she was so short she couldn't look over the bar. As it happens, she knew we were up to something and leaned over to see him sprawled on the floor.

"What have you done?" she said.

I answered, "The man's drunk, he's fallen over a table."

"Well," she said, "he looked sober enough when he asked me for a pint just now."

When he was out we took his dancing shoes off and put them on the fire and Mrs Brown was trying to get them out, but by that time they were ruined.

One day me and Mike were out drinking in some club out of Merthyr, so I get to the bar with all the glasses in my hands when some big rugby player says to me, "Out of the way Blondie." So I said, "Look mate, I'm trying to get served by here." Well, one thing leads to another and we go outside to fight. We were heading for the alleyway behind the houses when I notice a police car watching us, and all the time this guy is ranting and raving. So I pretend to laugh so the police would think we were just messing around. We get to the alley and square up. All of a sudden I hear footsteps behind me and there's this other big bugger there both hoping to do me. I hear more footsteps and it's Mike covering my back. Well I deck the one in front of me with a straight right and Mike sorts his out. With that, the whole bloody rugby team come down the alley after us. I turn to Mike and he shouts, "It's like Custer's last stand, bugger it, let's go for gold!" There was four or five on the floor and the buggers were still coming. Anyway, someone calls the police and they were everywhere. The rugby team were fighting with the police, so me and Mike edged past them all into the street. With that, a Merthyr taxi goes past and the driver says, "Hi, Pricey." So I shout, "Wait, stop!" He stops and takes us back home to Merthyr. Now that was a close one.

I was working up in England once when the site foreman, a little Irish guy, comes up to me and says, "Jesus, a big man like yourself should be in the boxing booth earning yourself some money." So off we go to the booth to try to earn some cash. Well, I'm in this ring fighting some big guy who spends his day in these booths fighting the biggest from each town, so he was no mug. I think this guy's name was Kincaid. They give me an old pair of shorts, which left me with everything hanging out, and an old pair of daps [training shoes – JD]. I asked my cornermen from Merthyr for a drop of water to wash out my mouth. So I look for a bucket to spit in and there's none there. I indicate to them and they say, "We haven't got one." I look around me, and there's so many people there that I can't spit it into the tent, so onto the floor it goes.

Well, it goes to round two and I catch this bugger with a straight right and down he goes, flat out cold. So the little guy in charge pushes me against the ropes, saying, "Step back, step back." He keeps pushing and pushing. So I tell him, "Any further back mate and I'll be out of the ring." All the time he was giving the fighter some time to recover. Well you could have counted to 100. He wasn't getting up. I had a couple of bob for that one and off we go straight into the pub. They asked me to stay on with them and fight for them but I enjoyed my work on the motorways too much to leave it.

When I worked on the motorways, I never looked for trouble but I had one of those faces, and wherever we went, the hardest guys seemed to want to try their luck. It was everywhere I went. Once, in Liverpool, we were doing the earth-moving for the new docks there. I was in a pub, not looking for trouble, in fact I was phoning my mother, which I always did to let her know I was okay and where I was, when this guy comes up to me and tells me to get off the phone. I looked up and he was a big guy with a flat nose and a thick neck. I tell him I'm using the phone. With that he shouts, "I want a taxi," then picks up a crutch and goes to put it over my head. I step forward and butt him straight on the forehead, and over he goes on his arse. As he fell he knocked over a table and ashtrays, so the barman wasn't happy and phones the police. I leave the pub a bit sharpish and try to make it through town without getting picked up but they managed to catch me and once more I'm banged up again. I could hear my mate Schofield outside arguing with the police. When they came to see me, the sergeant said, "You know the guy you hit is in bad shape? In fact they are putting stitches in him right now. You split him open. You're in a lot of trouble Taffy." "But it wasn't my fault," I told them. With that, another policeman comes in and says to the sergeant, "Do you know who that big Welshman has done over?" and he whispers in his ear. The sergeant starts laughing his head off and shouts out, "Well he bloody deserves it. I've waited for years to see someone beat that bully up. You can go and get your arse back home Taff. I don't want to see you here again."

Another place I got banged up in was Macclesfield. We had gone to a Chinese to get a takeaway when these big Scots took our bags off the counter. I'm not going to stand for that so I told them that we had paid for them. The biggest one turns to me: "Don't worry Taff, you can have the next lot." There were six of them and three of us and they were big lads as well. My mate Tommy English goes in with the head, so I pick up this big chair and put two straight down with it. All the time this little Chinese woman is shouting at us, we can't understand her so we just ignore her. Anyways, I'd put the window through behind me with the chair as I lifted it to smash some more Scots up with it. With that the police cars came from everywhere. They surrounded us with all the sticks out and the police dogs going mad. The sergeant says, "Listen Taff, get in the wagon, one way or another you're getting in." I tell them, "I'm not getting in, it wasn't out fault so why should I?" With that, Little Mallan comes up to me and says, "Bloody hell Pricey, it's like Custer's last stand." (This wasn't the first time I heard this). So off we go, banged up for three days, then court. Fair play, the Scots said they started it but I still ended up with nine months, so off I was sent to Strangeways Prison in Manchester.

I get my head down inside and get on with doing my time. I'm working in the kitchen and this big guy walks through, all over my clean floor. There was no screw around so after a few choice words, he says, "I'll see you later Taff."

I answer straight back, "No, you'll see me now" and off we go to the toilets.

He turns round. "Right come on," he says.

"Yeah right, let's have you," I answered and with that he lets out this mighty big kick. He wasn't a mug or anything – I found out later he was a right hard bugger. I put a left and right into him and I grab him and push his head straight down the shithouse and I was trying to pull the chain at the same time. One of the screws had seen me, so the alarm bells go off. I was on the weights in those days and I was so big he wouldn't tackle me on his own. Then the entire heavy mob came and I was still holding his head down the toilet. Anyway, they booked us both. When we went in to see the governor, I find out he had told them it was his fault, which I thought was fair of him. I told them, "Look, I was to blame, you know how things can flare up in here. I started it all." They gave us three days block and we were kept apart from each other for a while. It was getting a bit stupid; with them on our cases, each of us couldn't go near the other, so that made prison life even harder. I get chatting with a screw and he tells me, "Thing is, he's like you Pricey, a hard bloody bastard who don't take telling." So I ask him, "What's the crack keeping us apart all the time? What's done is done. I don't hold a grudge. Can't I just shake hands with him?" Well they left us alone together and he says "Bloody hell, I wouldn't have walked on your floor if I knew you were such a handy fucker." We got to be big mates after that. Funny how things work out.

23

I was working away from home on the motorways again when we all decide to go out for a few drinks. Now you must remember that we were all good mates. We all stuck together, all helped each other out if needed. Well, this big guy was working with us and he didn't really fit in. He was a bit of a bully really, always pushing his luck too far. We are all in this pub and he tries his luck with me. Big mistake. He was acting the big hard man, trying to wind me up. Well, I didn't want trouble that night but as you can tell, it always seems to find me.

Out we go to the car park and he's a big guy so I don't mess with him. Bang, straight on the jaw and down he goes, broken jaw and all his teeth kicked out. The next morning I'm walking to work when the manager tells me, "Pricey, he's waiting for you and he's got an iron bar, says he's going to smash your skull in. You had better go home mate." But I decide to carry on and sure enough there's the big ape standing there with the iron bar, so I walk up to him and I tell him if he's going to use the bar he had better use it good because I'm going to take it off him and break every bone in his body. Anyway he thinks twice and walks straight off the job.

I was out drinking with big Mickey Mochan, we had been in a club out of Merthyr and were rather the worse for wear. Now Mickey was a big guy like me, in fact we often got mistaken for each other. We had just come out of a chip shop and we are walking across the forecourt when I notice these pricks on motorbikes, they were racing back and fore playing hell with people. I shout to them to stop, when this motherfucker races straight at me full pelt. I step to the side and, BANG, I hit him with a straight right hand. I catch him a good one and off comes his helmet and he disappears into the night with his head down. Mickey can see the helmet rolling towards him and says, "You've done it this time, you've decapitated the fucker!" So there we were, creeping up to this helmet, half expecting to find the bugger's head in it.

We all went to this right dive of a pub in Risca one day when this fight broke out. We laid guys out all over the shop like something out of a Western saloon brawl. Women were coming in and lifting the heads up on each guy who lay there sleeping to try and find out which was their boyfriend. Now that was a mental night.

Working away from home again, I decide to go in this pub for a few drinks and I didn't know it was a pub where all the wrestlers hung out. Well this big wrestler bumps me and his drink goes everywhere. The guy tries to get me to pay for the drink, so I tell him, "You want me to pay for your drink when it was your fault, no way." So I started to lose my head when his two friends came over and started a row. I go to put the glasses down and next thing I'm bent over in a headlock. I can't move and all his mates are trying to kick me between the legs. I lean down and grab him between the legs and twist like hell. Well he lets me go and I start fighting with them all, and they were big guys. I smashed a glass and sliced one of them across the face and a piece of flesh flies across the room and hits the wall.

Well, he said, "So it's with a glass is it?"

I tell him straight, "I'm outnumbered here, so it is."

He says, "Well it's my argument, not theirs, so let's me and you have it."

He ended up in hospital that night in a right state. I had put the boots into him as well.

I was always fighting in every town I travelled through, with working on the roads. I fought the hardest in a place called Kendal once, a big guy called Glen. He was about 6ft 3in, 18 stone and very fit. He offered me out so we went outside. He came at me like a big bear. I caught him with a straight right hand and he comes crashing down. So I stuck the boots in as well to keep him down but after that night we became good friends, so it's a pity we fought really.

I must have had hundreds of street fights in my life and sometimes I've come close to being killed myself. One close call came in my hometown of Merthyr with a friend of mine called Carl. We had a run-in and I went to his house. I put a Bowie knife straight through the front door, kicked the door in and climbed the stairs. Now I didn't realise Carl's wife and kids were in the house or I wouldn't have gone there, that's something I just wouldn't do. Well up the stairs I go and Carl was a big bugger and he's got this hatchet swinging around. Fair play, he put it in my head and there was blood everywhere. I kept on climbing the stairs until the loss of blood made it impossible to carry on. Well I talk to Carl these days. I must admit I do like him, in fact you could say we buried the hatchet . . .

ALEK PENARSKI

Chesterfield and Bolton

Born in May 1953, Alek was raised to fight, and as a boxer became Central Area light-heavyweight champ. A man you would not want to cross, he is always prepared to go the limit. When the odds are stacked against him, this man will shape the fight his way – anything goes. Losing is not an option.

I'M FROM CHESTERFIELD originally, from quite a big family of three brothers and two sisters. My old man was a sergeant in the Army, he came here [from Poland] after the War and met my old lady. My mum was only 18 at the time when she met my father. She was engaged to this other man. Turns out the other man and my father fought, ended up with my father being done for manslaughter.

As kids we were always fighting each other, sometimes there would be three on to one, with lots of punches and blood each time. My father would encourage this. I think he wanted us to be able to defend ourselves. He would take us all in to shops and we would all come out wearing new coats, which of course we never paid for. If we went to the cinema he would have us all looking for half tickets outside on the floor. Then he would tell whoever was in charge that he had just taken us out to get some sweets, and show them the half tickets as proof. He never let us eat sweets, we would all sit in the cinema with lumps of Polish bread and salami. He would even file down washers so they would fit in the electric or the gas meter, that way he could use the money he saved to get beer.

He was a very strict man, never swore in front of my mother and Sunday dinner was always like a ritual thing with him. At Christmastime he would break us holy bread. I think this all came from his childhood in Poland. We couldn't leave food on our plate – if we did he would go bananas. Even today, at the age of 48, I still eat everything that's put in front of me, sometimes even off other people's plates. Force of habit, I guess. For some reason my father sort of chose me from my other brothers, he would walk around with me on his shoulders, everywhere he went.

I can remember when our local boxing contender Peter Bates fought Brian London for the heavyweight title. The whole of Chesterfield and Derbyshire were up, listening to the fight on the radio. It was great, even though he lost the fight. Peter had a pub in Chesterfield called the Red Lion and on Sundays my father would take us there. At the back of the pub was an old stable where Peter would train. This is where I really learnt to fight. We were matched up to fight the boys from other families. If we won, then the loser's father would pay for all my dad's drink for the day, or my father would pay for the other guy's. Sometimes I'd win, sometimes I'd get battered.

My father would go to the fairgrounds and fight whoever was in the boxing booth. He always took my mother to these fights. Once he had just beat a good fighter called Morris and when he got out of the ring he started fighting with these teddy boys. All the time he was fighting, my mother, would be hitting the teddy boys over their heads with her brolly.

Back in 1968, he had been drinking this one night and he stole loads of chickens from a farm and brought them home. He killed all the chickens, and put them all in my sisters doll pram wrapped up in blankets, just before the police turned up. My sister pushes the pram away from them and it looks like he was going to get away with it. The police find all the feathers and blood so it was obvious to them that he had done it. How they tracked him down was because he had dropped his bingo ticket with his name on at the farm. Well, there were not many people called Penarski so they had him.

My father taught us to do anything to survive. I follow him in so many ways. One day we would be selling puppies at Chesterfield market place, the next we could be working on the rag and bone. I was always fighting as a kid, very seldom getting beaten and if I did get beaten it was by a few of them, not one on his own. This was because my dad had made us used to fighting. Every school I went to I was the best fighter there.

My father went away for beating two coppers up. When he came home my mother locked him out, she no longer wanted anything to do with him. I can remember him knocking the door and we weren't allowed to open it to him. That was a bit hard for us kids. I loved both of them just as much as the other. I myself have sort of become a black sheep of the family over the years, maybe it's because I take after my dad so much, I'm like his double. He's made me into a survivalist like himself.

In school there were a few teachers who never really liked my family, probably because we were always in so much trouble. What didn't help us much was when our science teacher asked the whole class what we wanted to do when we left school. Well, we told them we wanted to be gangsters. I know its wrong now but we used to take all the money off the "rich kids" in school. This other teacher took a particular dislike to us and would always pronounce our surname wrong. He would try to take the piss out of me at every chance he got. On the very last day of school, I had just come off the football field and I think the teacher threw something at me. I always said I was going to do him and seeing as this was my last day of school I let him have it. I can't tell you just how good it felt to give it to him. There's always someone who you hated at school and he was the one for me.

As I grew up I was getting more and more involved in fighting, whether it was in a disco or on the street, I just loved it. I started going around with other lads who wanted it as well, so we would get gangs come looking for us. Other days we would go looking for them. We used to get involved in some right scraps. Then there was this book published about "Joe Hawkins" [the *Skinhead* series by cult author Richard Allen – JD] and it really changed our lives, I can't stress the effect this book had on us. It was all about this skinhead who was always fighting. Next thing, I and all my mates were skinheads. We were living our lives just like the character in the book. I could introduce you to at least 20 guys today whose lives have been changed due to that book.

On one occasion we had all come back from a weekend in Skegness battling with various football fans. We supported Derby County and would love fighting guys from clubs like United, Forest or Leicester, we would hunt each other down in the bars at night-time. The fights were ferocious, with bottles, knives and

30

even ripping off parts of fences to use on each other. We came home on the train and it stopped at Grantham. We got off and when we look across the track, there on the other platform were loads of Forest fans. We were all drunk and up for it, so after we exchanged insults, I decided to run round and fight with them.

Now I always had this reputation as being the first one in, maybe it's because I was the maddest one, I don't know. Anyway, I get to the Forest fans before my mates can turn up and I wade into them. I was tooled up with a cosh in my hand. As I was fighting, some guys were on me and my arms were trapped so I couldn't use them. I can remember this one guy pulling out a knife and it's as if he was in slow motion as he stabbed me in the stomach. Even though this happened, I was still fighting with them. The blood was everywhere, all over my jeans, Ben Sherman shirt and my Doc Marten boots. After a while I started to get really hot and my stomach felt like it was a balloon that had deflated. I fought on for a while like this and then, with all the blood loss, I dropped to the floor. A few of my mates got stabbed as well, one in his head and another one in his back. The police turned up with the ambulance, they took me across the railway lines. I looked down to see this big slit, with some of my intestines hanging out. The blood was pumping out of me. I could see the ambulance man push my intestines back in and put some sort of bandage on and hold it tight against me. I had to have an emergency blood transfusion and spent four hours being operated on. The doctors told me that I would never be able to fight again, but I proved them wrong with that one

My brother phoned the house one day, he was having trouble with a few karate guys. I was sat here having my tea when he phoned. Don't get me wrong, my brother can fight, in fact I taught him how to box. The difference with me is that I'm more "streetwise" than he is and can switch when needed. Within the hour I'm down where my brother lives and I track down the karate guy's house. I kick the door in and whack him one, I take his teeth out and fracture his skull. That's the way it's been with me, I will hunt someone down if I feel they have crossed me or my family in some way.

I once got a two-year suspended jail sentence for beating up these two rugby players. I was just taking a ride in my brother's new car, he had just bought a new Cortina GT. My brother turned the car without indicating, this other guy's car came around the corner, and he spun his car around my brother's car. One of the two rugby players in the first car started shouting and sticking his fingers up. The other car pulls up and this big rugby player gets out. My brother runs over and the guy gets back in his car. My brother bends down to look through the driver's window, when all of a sudden the door is kicked open. The glass in the driver's door smashes in my brother's face, cutting him open. I get out of the car and run across, at this moment all I can see is red. I always take things like this to the extreme. I guess that's why I'm always the last to know when anyone in the family gets any trouble. They try to keep me out of things because of the way I react. Anyway, I smash both the guys up, really going to town on the pair of them. One of them keeps getting back up, but each time he does I smash him back down. I break his jaw and smash all his teeth in. Some others come at me from across the street and I lay into them as well.

I knew it wouldn't be long before the police came looking. On the way home I tell my brother that if he gets pulled by the police, to tell them I was a hitchhiker. I make my way to my father's caravan. When I get there I realize that I had broken two of my fingers fighting. I made a phone call the next day and found out that the police had sussed out that I had beaten up the rugby players. Turns out one of them had to be rushed to hospital. I was always fighting so it wasn't very hard for them to work out that it was me. I decided to turn myself in and take whatever comes.

When it came to court the guy who I did the most damage to turned up wearing glasses and carrying his umbrella, looking like

32

a right wanker. There was me standing in the dock, with skinhead written all over me. To make things worse the police had all these photos of all the damage that I had inflicted on them. I knew I was in trouble so I informed the court, "Look, I know I'm no angel. The guys said I kicked them. Well, I didn't, my father always taught me not to kick a man in a fight, just use my hands. I'm a boxer and I've never kicked anyone in my life. I did the damage with my hands because of what they did to my brother." I think that little speech got me off with that one, and I count myself lucky.

By this time I had left home. I was doing various jobs, from putting rings up for wrestlers like Big Daddy to working the doors at night clubs. I was sharing a home with a Tongan heavyweight boxing champion for about two years. I used to eat the same food as he did, which was usually boiled cabbage with corned beef covered in Libby's milk.

The skinhead movement was fading out in Britain but me, I was still fighting. Since becoming a skinhead I had changed my whole outlook on life. I just needed to fight. I was always up for a fight no matter what the odds were. It wasn't long before I got signed up to fight as a professional boxer. I can't say I was a dedicated boxer in those days. I just wanted to get straight in the fight and slug it out. I just wanted to fight and earn money, taking loads of fights on very short notice. There was talk at this time of me fighting Dennis Andries [the future British and WBC world light-heavyweight champion]. Now I had been to see him fight and felt I could beat him. Other boxers were a bit wary of him but we were similar fighters and I felt I had the edge on him. When we fought I kept the fight in close, tying him up. I was always looking for openings right from the bell. Apart from Tommy Hearns, I'm the only guy to put Andries down. I hit him with a shovel punch under the heart and down he went on one knee. The fight was a close one and I lost it by one round. I received a caution in the second round for head-butting. I was a fool to myself with that one, even the referee told me if it weren't for the caution I would have won. I met Andries a few years later and we shook hands. He seemed a nice guy; tidy family man as well.

I never, ever said no to a fight. I'd get in the ring with anyone, no matter if I hadn't trained or if they phoned me the night before the fight. I was clean out of money and was desperate to earn cash and by this time I had a family to feed as well as myself. Things were so bad that I would go to fish shops, order loads of grub and after they wrapped everything up, I'd complain that I had left my money at home. Nine times out of ten they would tell me to bring the money in later and take the food for now. For one fight I had to lose six pounds in one hour. The only way to do it was to have a sauna. It's a lot of weight to loose so fast but I did it, I weren't supposed to do it and was told not to say anything about it. I fought some well-known boxers over the years on short notice, guys like Tim Witherspoon and Henry Akinwande [who both held versions of the world heavyweight title]. I've had my ups and downs in boxing, and like I always said, if it meant my family getting fed then I'd fight ten bloody Vikings if I had to!

I was in the car park of a club I was working at called the Aquarius one night when I felt something dig into my back. I had been seeing an ex-girlfriend of another doorman and turns out he had shot me in the back. Police forensics had the bullet that they pulled from my back and told me it was shot by a .22 rifle. Strange thing was that my mate, who was living with me, went to see about getting access to his kid, and gets into an argument. The brother of the girl he had split up with gets hold of the very same gun that shot me. Then he decides to shoot my mate in the stomach. This of course nearly kills him. Shootings in those days were so very rare: to get two boxers shot in the same week was a big thing back then.

I spent a few weeks on remand over an armed robbery once. Two lads came to my house with shooters, two good friends who I used to train. They had pulled an armed robbery on a jeweller's shop. They were on the run and didn't know they were being followed. I give them a lift in my Mercedes and we all get pulled by the police. I'm remanded in Strangeways "Cat A" Prison for a crime that I didn't do. I couldn't say anything at the time but thankfully my mates owned up to it and I got my charges dropped. Now I had been doing quite well for myself, I had become a minder and had good contracts watching some famous people. I was getting £4–500 a day, and I lost it all when it was reported that I was involved in the robbery. I was in charge of various club doors around the place and I lost them all as well. My name has become tarnished for a crime that I didn't commit.

I'm 48 now and still training for fights. I fight on unlicensed boxing shows. In the last few weeks I've gone through loads of sparring partners. I train six days a week, twice a day. If I'm not in the gym then I'm on the roads or out with my dogs. I don't believe in all this fancy training that some people do. The rougher it is, the better it is for me.

I'm often asked when I will quit fighting. Well, my dad's 74 and he's still fighting, so there's hope for me yet.

BARTLEY GORMAN

Uttoxeter

The greatest ever bareknuckle champion and undisputed King of the Gypsies. Not only did Bartley take on all comers – he went looking for them. Prepared to fight anyone anywhere, be it at a gypsy horse fair, in a pub car park or even down a coal mine, if the challenge was issued, the challenge was met. An intelligent man who lived life to the full, the great Bartley Gorman was truly an inspiration.

I COME FROM a big fighting family. It all started with my great-grandfather Bartley Gorman the First. He was an Irish tinker who travelled around in a horse-drawn gypsy wagon. He would travel all over Ireland earning his money mending pots and pans. He was a very religious man who didn't use to fight. His caravan was full of pictures of the Virgin Mary and he wouldn't let a man who didn't believe in God into his wagon. How he got into fighting was through his brother Jim, who was blind since birth. Jim was in Dublin and he sold a man called Jack Ward a horse which had a gammy leg; it was lame but Jim, being blind, didn't know this. A lot of travellers buy things on sight without checking, just on a handshake and trust. Now, Jack Ward was the "King of the Tinkers", he was a good fighting man. Jack leaves the pub and takes a good look at the horse, only to find it has a gammy leg. He came back into the pub and set about Jim, dragging him outside and beating him unmerciful. It didn't even bother him that Jim was a blind man. He was beaten so bad that they had to wheel him home in a barrow. My great-grandfather couldn't believe his eyes and asked who had done this terrible thing to a blind man. He was so bad that he couldn't answer him but after a while he manages to tell him that it was Jack Ward. Immediately, my great-grandfather walks down to the pub in Dublin to fight Jack Ward.

My great-grandfather beat Jack Ward, which nobody had ever done before, so everyone wanted to know who this Bartley Gorman was. My great-grandfather now became the champion of all Ireland, from beating Ward. The famous bareknuckle fighter Jem Mace, the world heavyweight champion, came to Ireland to fight a man named Joe Coburn. Well, my great-grandfather and some other travellers told him he should be fighting my great-grandfather because he was the Irish champion. He was reluctant at first but then agreed to fight on the cobbles outside a pub in Dublin. Well, the fight went well but the *garda* [police] stopped the fight. My great-grandfather claimed the title because he had had the beating of Jem Mace. After moving to England, my great-grandfather beat the toughest Romany fighting man in England – he was called Mo Smith – and then he went on to beat a man named Wenman from London. He went on to have many bare-knuckle fights in England and was renowned for his fighting skills.

His son was, of course, my grandfather. He was named Bartley Gorman the Second, who I think I follow because he had red curly hair like me. He travelled all over the country to fight. Most of the time he would walk to a fight. He was an immaculate dresser with his checked cap, long coat with leather buttons and a walking stick. If a man or woman tried to touch him he would push their hands away. He was a real fighting man, who fought the likes of Tom Daley in Anglesey, Chasey Price on Brynmawr mountain, Black Martin Furry, again in South Wales, but the police stopped that fight, Wiggy Lee in Yorkshire, Black Walter Lee, Will Rosamount in North Wales and Andy Reilly in Ireland, which ended in a draw.

He once fought Matt Carroll, who was one of the greatest fighters in South Wales. Carroll was living in Ireland at the time but before leaving for America he waited so he could fight my grandfather first. When my grandfather was getting off the ship in Ireland, Carroll saw him and shouted, "I'm the best man in the thirty-two counties of Ireland, Bartley." My grandfather shouted back, "Yes, you are, until I get off this ship and my foot touches the floor." They fought over 75 rounds with the *garda* watching. My grandfather beat Carroll and, after the fight, Carroll left for America.

When I myself was about 20, a man called Davey Stephens told me that he had once watched my grandfather fight in Cheshire. Now Davey was about 85 when, in his Welsh accent, he told me, "There was this big travelling man who had a load of sons and one of the sons was a giant. Your grandfather was about sixty-five at the time. They fought on the cobbles and this giant lad was giving your grandfather some hammer because your grandfather had been drinking that day and was the worst for wear. Your grandfather stopped the fight and went over to a horse trough and put his head into the cold water. You should have seen him after that Bartley, he was like lightning, making mincemeat of the guy."

From an early age, I listened to tales of my family and friends bareknuckle fighting. The stories got passed down from generation to generation. People would look at me as a child and say that I looked like my grandfather and would grow up to be the champion fighting man like he was. It was something that I was expected to be and I believed I would be, so it's a good job I grew up to be over six foot tall and 16 stone. As a little lad of nine, I was fighting for the title of "King of the Gypsies". It was always on my mind even back then when I started fighting other kids bareknuckle for money.

My father took me to the Bedworth Boxing Club in Warwick-shire as a small lad. I would go in the ring with the bigger, more experienced lads. They would hurt me and sometimes make me cry. All the time I was crying, I was still fighting. I guess that's why I'm a fighter, because of my dad. I had about 20 amateur fights with that club, travelling all over the Midlands fighting. From there I went to other boxing clubs, learning all the tricks of the trade. I was asked to turn pro but I refused.

I went on to fight Jack Fletcher for the vacant King of the Gypsies crown. I was recognised as the King of the Gypsies even before I had fought for the title. I always thought I could have won the title years earlier but was kept waiting to have my shot. I remember Fletcher coming down for the fight in his big mobile home, pulling into the car park. I was a very powerful fighter, awesome in fact; I didn't know my own strength. To be honest, I knocked Fletcher out quite fast and became the King of the Gypsies.

Now I was travelling up and down the country fighting for money and for honour. If I heard someone was good then I would travel to find them and seek them out. It didn't matter if they lived in England, Scotland, Ireland or Wales, in fact anywhere; if there was a fighter, I would find him. Most of the fights were held against other gypsy fighters, within the gypsy community.

I travelled to fight a man over pit ponies once. Bob Braddock and Reg Martin had gone down to buy horses and they got talking about me. Bob came back and told me he had found a man for me to fight, a man called Jack Grant, and would I fight him down a mine for 25 pit ponies. I thought I'd like to see the ponies freed because they were going blind down the mine. I could give them to the children. I asked him what he was getting out of it all and he said there were 50 altogether, 25 for me and 25 between him and Reg. The guy I was fighting was a mine fighter. He fought down some of the South Wales mines. Now, I know he wasn't a travelling man, but I wanted to get those ponies out of there so I agreed to the fight down the mine.

We found a place to fight, it was a mine in Derbyshire, a lead mine in fact. We had to go down to the mine in a little bucket off some crane device, which I just did not like at all. All his mates had come up from Wales for the fight, as well as the few I brought with me. We shook hands and I could see when he stripped his top off that he was a fighting man: he was muscular and a strong-looking, hard man. Now I was fighting this miner in his own environment because he wouldn't fight where the police could arrest him. I was fighting in an alien environment, a place where I didn't want to be. The fight started well but all the miners around us had their hard hats on their heads with all the lamps turned toward us for light, so we could fight. Well it dawned on me that his mates were shining their lamps into my eyes to blind me in the fight.

However a fight comes, I have to take it. The only way to win was to keep punching and punching and ignore the light in my eyes. He hit me with some real good shots. My height was also a disadvantage because the mine was very low and we were fighting across the rail track. The fight was hard and rough. I took a few head-butts which nearly put me down. I threw one punch that missed and I broke my knuckles on the side of the mine. This was going to be one of the hardest fights of my life; it went on for a good while, each of us determined to win. At one stage they pulled us apart to put water over us, which I found unusual, but I was glad of it. Even today I still have the image of him coming towards me with big square shoulders, two teeth missing in the front, coal dust marks on his face and his eyes glinting with the lamplight. I put him down in the end but it was a close one. I had to really deck him to win, he was such a tough man. We shook hands after the fight and he told me I was the best fighter he ever fought. I'd love to know more about this man; he fought under the name Grant but later I found out his real name was Preece.

I never liked to fight a friend or someone I liked, but sometimes it just turns out that way. I knew this fifth dan karate expert, he was a big man with jet-black hair, a square jaw and very powerful. He even went to China or Japan to train with them as well. He was always training to fight, always practising some move or other, a dedicated man. On this day I'm lying down in the caravan watching the television. Outside, he has some travellers to hold breezeblocks so he can smash them. I didn't really want them broke, as I wanted them to build a shed at the time. The men shouted to me to come out and hold the blocks, as they couldn't hold them because he was kicking that hard. I didn't want to come out – I'd rather watch the television – but out I come and I hold the block and the karate man smashes the block to bits with his head.

"Okay lads, put the blocks back now, I'm going back in the caravan," I tell them all. Now, I always told this karate man not to mess with me in front of people, because I won't have it. If he wanted to show me a move, like a throw or a punch, he could do it in private but not to show me up in front of people. I tried to walk to my caravan and he steps in front of me. I step to the side and he's there again. No matter which way I went, he was in front of me, blocking my way. He was making an idiot of me. I didn't want to hurt him, I just kept asking for him to move, but he wanted to make me look a fool. He wouldn't even speak to me, just this karate stance and silence.

I said, "Okay, if that's how you want it," and moved straight in on him. I never stopped punching until I finished it. I broke my knuckles and hands on his head. During the fight he did this move on me called, I think, "the tiger's teeth", where he bit my arm and dragged it like a zip all the way up, ripping me open. But I wasn't a breezeblock that was going to stand still for him to hit. I just kept on smashing him up, not giving him a chance to use a useful move on me. He was all beaten up and I was standing there with my hands bashed up, with all the flesh hanging off my knuckles.

He said later, "Bartley, we must never fight again."

I answered him, "Yes, that's what I told you before this started." I never wanted to hurt him, it was just that I'm a fighting man and he just kept pushing me to the limit in front of travellers. I was put on the spot.

I've been is some terrible fights in my life but the one that nearly killed me was when I went looking for Bob Gaskin. He and a band of travellers were taking the north of England by storm. Any travellers who stood in their way were in trouble. I sent out a challenge to him but heard nothing about it. Then one day I was painting this barn and came back home covered in black tar and worn out from working all day. I got told then that my brother John had been looking for me. He had got six stitches put across his eye by Bob Gaskin. He was playing the melodeon at Doncaster when Gaskin hit him and John was only 16. I didn't know that Doncaster was Gaskin's hometown at the time. Hitting my brother was meant as a message to me. I was furious, so angry that I kicked the door of the house off the hinges.

I jumped in the old Transit van that I had and drove all the way to Hinckley, near Coventry, to see my brother Sam, almost turning the van over as I drove. I told our Sam what Gaskin had done and that I had by now arranged to fight Gaskin the next Saturday. Sam said that he would deal with it tomorrow and went off to sleep. I was just going to go to sleep myself when up comes my other brother John with a gang of men. I went to my friend Frank's house and while I was upstairs lying in the bath I could hear them talking about the up-coming fight. They were saying that travellers from all over were coming to watch it. From Scotland and all over the UK, word was spreading. I had to go to Doncaster racecourse on the day of the St Leger race and get the fight over with.

Sam had hired a Vauxhall Ventura, so we drove up with a few men with us to the Park Royal Hotel looking for Gaskin and his men. There were men everywhere and they all knew what I was coming for, they were expecting me. The word of the fight was spreading out ahead of me. I met Hughie Burton [King of the Gypsies before Bartley – JD], who told me not to go down amongst the trailers or they would kill me. I should have taken his advice but off we go all the same. As we travelled down to where the trailers were, we could see the heat coming off them, there was that many there for the races. They had come from all over the world just for the Doncaster St Leger and here was us coming down to fight amongst them all.

When we got amongst the trailers, we found that hundreds of travellers were waiting for the fight to start but there was no Bob Gaskin. I didn't know that he was out recruiting men, paying them money to stand by his side. I was stripped to the waist waiting for Gaskin. I was just going to leave when all these trucks turned up just like the army. They had all weapons; there was about 200 of them all told. I fetched a crowbar out of the car and gave it to my brother Sam. "Here you are, see me fair play in this fight, Sam," meaning he should make sure the fight is fair and if needed use the crowbar. Sam says, "I don't need that Bartley," and throws it on the floor. He was a brave man our Sam, and a good fighter. I just knew that it wasn't going to be fair play and Sam always said he should have kept the crowbar.

I'm standing there waiting for the fight, stripped to the waist with my boxing boots on. Every one of them knew who I was with my head full of red hair. The men who came towards me looked like a Walt Disney film with tall men, short men, fat and skinny men all marching towards us. I can honestly say I wasn't scared, I was now in my environment – I'm a fighter, therefore I must fight. I had a chance to take a way out which would have at that time got me away but I couldn't do that, it was against everything I stood for.

"Where's Bob Gaskin?" I shout to them all.

With that, about ten men shouted back that they were Bob Gaskin. Well, I saw the one who fitted his description move towards me. I was so determined to hurt Bob Gaskin that when I threw a punch at him I put him down straight away, his feet went up in the air first before he went down.

Next minute, there were men all over Sam, kicking him to pieces. There must have been 40 around him, all fighting to kick him. Before I could do anything I get smashed over the head with a car prop shaft. I drop to one knee but get back up with my head smashed up on one side. I then take another blow on my hands which busted them open. I run straight into them, trying to get through them to the car to get Sam and me away. As I'm fighting to get to the car, I have at least eight men trying to hold me and bring me down. I was that strong that they couldn't stop me.

I got into the car as about 50 men surrounded the car, smashing every bit of it, ripping the doors off. The car was a write-off. An iron bar comes through the windscreen and hits me between the eyes, blood dripping down my face. They had me trapped but I wouldn't leave go of the steering wheel because they would have dragged me out and killed me. The steering wheel was buckled with me holding it. They were coming in through the doors and windows all the time, smashing me with bars and other weapons. They push a bar right down my throat, breaking my Adam's apple as the bar went from side to side.

At one time things went a little silent and I spot a Gaskin coming towards me with a broken cider bottle in his hand. I was sure I was going to die. I was so weak from the hiding and the loss of blood from where they had stabbed me, I was convinced that this was the end. I scream out, "I came for a fair fight, no bottles and that, just a fair fight." They hold me down and this Gaskin starts to saw off my leg with the broken bottle. I'm screaming in pain, bent back in agony while he is cutting me below the knee. The reason my leg was getting cut was because I kicked out to stop them getting my throat with it. I know I later had 400 stitches and micro-surgery on it but I still came off better than if they had my throat. The blood poured all over this Gaskin; I remember him standing with my blood all over him.

Somebody took the bottle off him, but I'm still getting hit. A baseball bat smashes me in the head about four times and I have to stay awake because if I left go of the wheel I would be dead. My brother Sam gets in the back of the car. How he did it I don't know. They drag him out and put him under the car's wheel, hoping that I would reverse over him. Sam got away in someone's Mercedes. It was every man for himself – I couldn't help Sam and he couldn't help me.

They are on me now and they are really giving it to me. There's so much blood in my eyes that the whole world looks red to me. They were also fighting with each other over who was going to do me. They were having terrible fights over it. Someone smashed me again over the head and I pretend to go down but still I hold the wheel, I thought they would leave me be but they increase the damage. All blood was pouring out of my mouth as I'm lying there, I'm getting weaker and weaker. I tell them, "You're hurting me too much my brothers, too much," but they didn't care, it didn't bother them. I notice my godmother's husband, my Uncle Peter, and I shout, "Help me, Peter." He runs in to get me out – like Rocky Marciano he was, 48 years old – and he's amongst them with all his teeth knocked out. He ran to Bob Gaskin and told him to stop it all. With that I manage to start the car. Thank you God, for that.

I just drove off, shot through them all. I didn't care who I knocked over. I had been attacked 200 yards from the Royal Box; I could have had millions for my story if I had drove up and stopped the St Leger race. There was dustbins flying everywhere, I drove so far up in this car with the doors pulled off, windows smashed in and bumper torn away. I couldn't drive any more, I was too weak, then I stop the car and I see this man all bashed up. He was covered in blood and his skin was bruised purple.

I ask him who he was and he tells me, "I'm Sam Gorman. Who are you?"

"Sam! It's me, your brother Bartley." We were so beaten that we didn't know who the other was.

There were hundreds of people all around us now, women screaming, children being sick. I call to a friend to help me hold my head up but he was too scared to move and help me. I look down and I see my leg. While I was getting beaten and trying to get away, I had forgotten about it, but now I could see blood gushing out of it. I pick up a rag and tie it around my leg. A policeman took off his jacket and held it onto my leg. I'm on the stretcher being taken away and I can see all the Gaskins looking at me. I roll off the stretcher and I stand on one leg and shout, "Still King of the Gypsies! Come and fight me now Bob Gaskin, with all these police watching, fight me man to man." Of course, he didn't come but I made sure they all heard me.

While I'm in hospital there are about 200 trailers in the car park waiting for me to get out. For two weeks they waited there. There were hundreds turning up to see how I was. I was in bed not able to move, in a critical condition. They rushed me down to have an emergency operation. While all this was happening, there were travellers there with shotguns to protect me. The drawers in my room were stashed full of well-wisher money, the room full of bottles of Guinness and various drinks. Later on I had men from

Scotland Yard standing in my room armed, watching over me after I received death threats.

My mother came to see me. She held my hand and informs me, "Before two months today, the man who did this will be lying in the same bed as you." When I'm out of hospital, my brother Sam phones me and says, "Guess who's in intensive care in the same bed as you Bartley? Bob Gaskin." Turns out someone had shot him. He had been shot in the stomach while in an argument with other travellers.

After years of rehabilitation and walking with crutches, I was back fighting fit. I had many fights after the Gaskin battle and was never put down. I never look to cause trouble when I go out. I just like to talk with people and have a drink and maybe sing a few songs. The trouble with being a fighter is that everyone knows you as one and there's no escaping from it. There was no escaping the fighting. Even years after at my brother's funeral [Sam Gorman died in 1991], someone had wrote to the papers saying I could fight all the gypsy fighters one after another and beat them all on the same day. Everyone took this as a challenge but I hadn't said it, it was a stupid thing to say. There's no way I wanted to fight just after my brother Sam's funeral, but in the night when we all were having a drink, I got into an argument with Ned Rooney [an Irish traveller]. He wouldn't believe that I didn't put the article in the paper. I explained that I didn't but we both kept arguing back and forth.

Now, I didn't want to fight, I had just buried my brother and was dressed up in my suit with my rosary beads on. I just did not want to fight. Well, one thing led to another and my blood started to boil. Thing about me is, once I'm started and had a few drinks, then there's no turning back. We kept arguing and I was getting wound up. Then all of a sudden, his brother, big John Rooney, smashes me straight in the face. He was wearing a big saddle ring at the time and it busts my face open. I didn't go back or fall down after the punch though. Another thing about me is that I have

BARTLEY GORMAN

always been ready in case I have to fight; call it instinct but I'm always on my guard, even now when I'm sitting here telling you this story.

Anyway, I went to the corner and stripped off to my waist. Even up to this stage, I hadn't taken the fight serious, but then big John throws a big right and his fist with the ring on busts my eye open. I thought, *right, no more clowning with him.* I just threw body shots at him and he went down five times and I picked him up five times. Not once did I go for his head. The police came to stop the fight but they knew they couldn't and the fact that our own community controlled the fighting made them just stand and watch.

Another fighting man shouted for John to take off the ring, but I said, "No leave it on, give him a chance." In the middle of the room was a big pillar that you could put your drinks on. Well, I took him straight through it. I bent down to finish him off but he gave in, so I thought the fight was over. Well, he gave me a punch in front of the police. I walked over to the bar, ordered lemonade and thought about how I had been punched at my brother's funeral. I walked back to John and then I really hit him and he goes back into the wall. The fight was now over. I have to give it to John, he was a really tough fighter. The side of my face was like liver, all red where the ring had hit me.

With bareknuckle fighting, you must be able to take pain. I mean real pain. If you can't take it then you can't be a fighter. I've had men stand before me trying to kill me, wipe me off the face of the earth, with men behind them shouting, "Kill him! Kill him! Kill him!" You must understand, there's no referee going to jump in and say, "Oh he's got a cut above his eye." They wouldn't stop it, not if they rip out my heart they wouldn't stop it.

I went on to have many bareknuckle fights after that one with John. Once I fought another travelling man called Bugsy Price. When I knocked him down and beat him, his wife came out and pointed a twelve-bore shotgun to my body to blow me away. I

49

hear the gun click twice, the safety catch was on, and so I was able to take it off her. She wanted me dead and I came very close to it. I found out later that her father had done 15 years for shooting a man and now Bugsy Price is inside doing life for shooting someone. It looks like someone was watching over me that day.

When I tell people that I'm retired from fighting, they don't realise that there's no such thing as retirement with the gypsies. Even if I am using two sticks or a frame to walk, then they will say I look reasonable to fight. As long as I can be beaten it won't bother them what condition I'm in, it would be a feather in their cap to say they have beat Bartley Gorman. Sometimes I feel it has become a burden on me, heartache. A man can have pain in his heart as well as his body from so much fighting. A lot of things have happened in my life, some things that I wouldn't wish on a dog, but as my father used to say, "My back is big enough to bear it all."

I feel that nobody knows me but myself and God. He knows all about me, and that's what matters. I'm not bothered by what people say about me or what title they give me. Fighting is like being on stage and I myself must play my part. I was born to play it and that's my destiny, or die.

Bartley Gorman sadly died of cancer on January 18, 2002, at the age of 57, just a few months after this interview. His autobiography, *King of the Gypsies*, is also published by Milo Books, priced £15.99.

RAY HILLS

London

You have to be tough to earn a fighting reputation in the capital, and this is exactly what Ray has achieved. He freely admits that his life has not always been lived on the straight and narrow. From time served in Wormwood Scrubs to the shady world of bareknuckle fights, Ray's life has been a blood and guts struggle all the way.

I WAS BORN in 1951 and come from Acton [West London]. I came from a good family but my dad died when I was about five years old. I was always fighting when I was young, even as an infant the teacher made me wear slipper gloves, which was like a bag glove that boxers wore, reason being that they couldn't stop me fighting, so with the gloves on I couldn't hurt the other kids when I hit them. It wasn't long before they expelled me from there. I went on to junior school and still they couldn't stop me fighting all the time. Looking back now, I guess it may have been that I was assaulted by a relative when I was young. He got seven years prison and it just changed me, making me the way I am. There are no fighters in my family, just me, they were just a normal family. I was the only one who needed to fight.

A friend in school was a good welterweight boxer. His dad taught me how to fight, he was a good fighter and he trained us well. I had a job as a night porter in the fruit market. I shouldn't really have been working there, as I was only 15 at the time. Some of the lads there would fight bareknuckle fights. We didn't fight for money back then, it was just to see who was the hardest in the market. What gave me an advantage over some of the lads was that I could fight and was very mature for my age, with a good punch. The fights were hard and one guy called Colin was the guv'nor of the fruit market, he was always bashing someone up, he was a big tough fighter back then. He was always trying to prove himself. He was a lot older than me and I suppose he made a man out of me with all the fights we had.

Things were going well for me, I was training to be a pro boxer, but I went and threw it all away. I got done for armed robbery and attempted murder of a police officer. The van we were doing over pulled up, I jumped out and a have-a-go-hero's car came around the corner and rammed me up against the van. My gun flew away from me, and myself and two accomplices run off. I make the mistake of running straight toward the car that rammed me. It hit me again, right up in the air. I rolled off the bonnet, dragged myself up and got in our getaway car. The other car is following us as we drive away, it rams us and I'm thrown through the windscreen. I don't know how I found the strength to get away but I do. I'm hiding out in an alleyway as the police helicopters are flying overhead. I'm covered in blood so I rub all sand on my head and over my body. I step out and a copper spots me, they stop and take a look at me and drive off. They must have thought I was a workman or something. Two days later I get nicked. I got grassed up, so they had me. I got sent down, all told, for 22 years and I did 14 years and two months out of it.

First time I went away I was only young and they sent me to the Scrubs. I was approached at some stage by a Taffy screw. Seems these two Asian guys had raped his daughter. He asked me to sort things out for him because the two guys were in the prison. This guy knew I didn't like sex offenders and because I was always fighting as a young prisoner I was the man for the job. In the morning before they let everyone out of their cells they let me out first. I went up to where the first Asian was getting water. Now in prison the first water that comes out of the tap would be white hot, you couldn't believe how hot it was. Soon as this guy turned up I done him with a bucket of the scalding water and smashed him to bits. I got back to my landing before the alarm went off. What I forgot was that someone had drawn a red heart on the back of my shirt just for a laugh one night. The screws were told that the guy who burnt and did the first Asian over had a red heart on his shirt. I was then walking around the exercise yard when I spot the second Asian going off to the toilet. Now, some off the screws were on the lookout for the prisoner who had the red heart on his shirt, but even so they still left me alone for a while when I followed the guy into the toilets. Now, he's in the cubicle when I come in with a heavy wooden toilet brush and beat the shit out of him with it. I run out and while I'm walking around the exercise yard, some of the screws grab me and drag me off to the block unit.

In the block I was kept away from regular prisoners. Upstairs were all the sex offenders like Ian Brady, the Moors Murderer. I could hear him typing some days, and would have loved to have gotten my hands on him. There was a guy a few cells away from me who was a well-known poisoner at the time, I can't recall his name but I remember he was famous for doing his whole family. While walking on the exercise yard I get talking with him, not knowing who he was. The screw later on tells me and informs me not to take anything off him. The next night he gets the screw to take me a bun from him. The screw informs me that it was okay because the guy hadn't touched it. Later he shouts for me to lend him some tobacco, which I did. When he returned what he owed me, the screws told me not to touch it, no way! Thinking about what he had done, I'm glad now that I didn't touch it.

They shipped me out to the Isle of Wight. First I was in "A" wing, then later on I was sent to "C" wing, which was known as "married quarters" because some of the older guys were getting hold of the younger guys and shacking up together. Thank God I was a pro boxer and was big and fit because there were loads at it. I met some right hard bastards in there as well. I had four or five fights in there. I had to make myself known so I was left alone.

One of my hardest fights there was with this big coloured bully who I would see training in the gym, he was a big strong guy. He worked in the kitchens the same as me. I was working on the hotplate on this day and once a week we were all allowed a fry-up, eggs, beans, bacon and that. Well, this was fry-up day and there were four eggs left over, two for the bully and two for me, great stuff. I went to get my two and he had taken three, leaving only one for me. This may seem silly now but when you're in prison things like this mean a lot. After arguing about it we agree to fight it out in the toilets, the screws turning a blind eye to all of this, which the screws used to do in those days. I put my tray on the floor and he tries to kick me in the face. I move, stand up and throw a straight right, which puts him on his arse, splitting his

54

nose wide open. Now, in this prison there were metal cages around the staircases. Well, when he stood up I threw a left hook and it connected with the metal cage busting my hand to bits. The fight got broken up and I was put in isolation for a while.

It was a while before I saw him again, then one day I was in the gym and I'm training with my hand all busted up when I spot him. He's come in to play basketball, his face is smashed up and all. Nothing happens so I forget about it all. Now, in this prison we all had wedges to put under our doors, like doorstops, everyone has these to stop people coming into your cell to get you. I'm lying on my bed when the door opens only a few inches because of the wedge. It was the geezer I bashed up. His arm comes through the door with this big blade in his hand, he puts it into my bed missing me by inches, and I was lucky he couldn't get through the door or I'd be dead. I get out of my cell and chase him back to his cell, where he locks himself in. He gets moved out later on to a section where I can't get at him. This all sort of got me a name in the prison, people knew not to mess with me because I wouldn't have none of it.

One day I'm in my cell and this guy called Billy, who we all called Mary for obvious reasons, calls me. Seems his boyfriend George was giving him trouble and could I help? I didn't really want to get involved but I still told him I would sort it out. Next morning I've forgot about this and I'm in the kitchen cooking a steak for myself. With that, all the alarms went off and all hell breaks loose. I look out of the kitchen as they bring George out with 16 stab wounds from a quarter-inch wood chisel; at this time he was still alive but dies later from his wounds.

Due to the fact that in prison I was fighting all the time, they put me under a woman psychologist. She told me, "Ray, if ever you feel violent then you must do some training to calm yourself down and release your anger that way," which I found to be good advice. I would train constantly and was becoming bigger, fitter and stronger all the time. I had this little party piece: to entertain people I would snap off the prison door handles. If you ask anyone who's been inside how hard it was to snap the handles off, then you would realise how strong I was.

I had another argument with this guy in prison and the screws had to come to my cell to get me. Now they knew what I was like so they send the psychologist down to speak with me first. The talk with her went well but later when the screws came for me they crashed through my door and attacked me. I smashed one so hard that I broke his spleen and I left-hooked another. I would have put them all out but they used a tranquilliser gun on me. Down I went. I was awake and aware of everything around me but not able to move a muscle. While I was like this they steamed into me, smashing me up bad. I was moved out to Parkhurst, and put down the block with a straightjacket on. It was real bad there. All I had in the cell was a trough, and the jacket had no back to it, just fixed so I couldn't move my arms. They would come into the cell, hose me down and jab me up each day. They moved me around every prison in England, never staying long enough to settle, always in a different environment.

When I got out I got straight back into the gym. Thing was that I had lost my pro licence so I couldn't get fights. I used to look after a place called The Fox and Castle to earn some cash. I got to speak with a good boxer called Jimmy Tippett in there who put me on the road to unlicensed boxing. Following Jimmy's advice I started training down the Thomas a' Becket gym. The first day I turned up for training I saw Roy Shaw [the famous unlicensed fighter known as "Pretty Boy"] sparring with a few guys. He asked me if I would spar with him, which I did and I found him to be a good puncher. I have a lot of respect for Roy. During my time at the Becket I sparred a lot with him.

I found prize-fighting easy. You must understand that I was big, very fit and a hard puncher. I remember fighting at a social club in Woolwich, it was a barefist fight and the guy I was fighting was an absolutely massive geezer. I must admit I was a bit scared because the guy was about 25 stone, so that's a bit intimidating to say the least. He started throwing punches but I could see an opening downstairs and smashed into his ribs, breaking two of them. He went down and I jumped on top of him, smashing him to pieces, until they finally pulled me off him. That got me about £300, which was easy money compared to the way I used to earn it. I was fighting two to three fights a week, and even started promoting other fighters.

I was now training like a pro again so the prize-fights were easy money for me. I would just go in and smash them up. You could still get disqualified but were given three warnings first, so I knew I could get away with two fouls before they disqualified me. I could nut a guy or bite a lump out of his ear and still go on to win the fight. I fought this big black guy once, he had these long, big arms, so I worked my way in under his arms. I threw a punch over the top that connected, nutted him and then bit his ear lobe right off. The guy jumped out of the ring screaming his head off; I was in the ring shouting at him to come back. He just didn't realize that with bareknuckle it's the most barbaric fighting style there is, you can't be a nice guy in bareknuckle fighting.

I fought Kevin Paddock in an unlicensed bout. I found that a real hard fight, he was a good fighter and all the time he was talking to me, calling me on. He was a talented boxer and the fight ended in a draw. I later watched him beat Lenny McLean. Paddock was a lot better fighter than Lenny and he had loads of fights. I had known Lenny for years, we had words quite a few times, we sparred together many times. We trained at a pub called The Ring which had a boxing gym upstairs. Now Lenny and myself wanted to get it on but we always held back when we sparred because it could have ended in a war. It was strange that Lenny and me never fought each other because most of the guys Lenny fought I also fought. It would have been a good fight. I always felt I was the better boxer but Lenny could sell the tickets, he was good at that, he could fill the place.

If I wasn't fighting for money then I was working the doors. In London you had to be able to have a row to work on the doors because there was always trouble. I worked some of the best clubs from the Hippodrome to Stringfellows. I remember once when I worked a place in Ealing, it was called Crispin's Wine Bar and it was a really big establishment. I let a good mate at the time in and he began to cause trouble. I threw him out at first but he came back and I ended up knocking him out. I picked him up and left him outside on the pavement. Well, I thought that was the end of it all. I finish work and I'm walking home when I can hear something behind me. I turn around and there's this car following me. I look and notice there's something sticking out of the window. I knew straight away it was a gun so I ran like hell and jumped away. The gun was fired and I felt my right leg lift up in the air. I knew I had to get away before the second shot was fired. I got back on my feet, ignoring the pain, and started running across the green nearby. If I had stood still I know they would have got another shot off and I would be dead; that may be what made me keep running with my leg in bits. I got to my mum's and she cleaned it up, pulling all the pellets out and bandaging me up. I was really hurting bad with that one, very painful for sure.

I threw myself into my fight promotions and, of course, I was still fighting myself. For my second show I went to see big Colin from the fruit market, I told him I was now a prize-fighter and does he fancy a fight? He agreed and I gave him some tickets to sell. The place was a sellout. Everybody wanted to see us get it on, they all knew it was going to be a good scrap. First round and he comes straight at me, he smashes me to pieces, busting my face up. I know now that he is still a good fighter even after all these years. Round two, I start to throw him around like a rag doll, I grab him and throw him into the corner, nutting him on the top of his head, which smashed the front of my own head up.

He jumped out of the ring shouting, "I'm not getting back in that ring."

I shout back," Come on get back in, we'll have it proper this time."

He starts to get back in, I kick him straight in the face, and we had a right old fight and I bashed him up. He was my nemesis at the time. I always wanted to beat the guv'nor of the fruit market, it was always on my mind, even through all my prison years I thought about it. We laugh about it all these days. He once said to me, "God mate, you were a bit dirty!" but like I always say to people, that's what prize-fighting was all about. I just came to fight and win at any cost.

In the end I was earning £2,000 to £3,000 a fight and was finding it hard to get fights. Jimmy Tippett would take me around all the clubs looking for a fight. I would sit in the corner having a drink and Jimmy would be off talking to the doormen and fighters trying to set me a fight up. Like I told you, I found prize-fighting easy but as I got bigger paydays the fights got harder and harder. The fighters I was meeting were also hard men who could box, bite and do anything to win.

Once again I got done for an attempted armed robbery, I only got six months this time though. When I came out I thought, *fuck the prize-fighting*, I just started ducking and diving and back on the doors again. I'm working the doors again, it's not something I enjoy these days but it's work. Thing is these days, if you hurt someone on the door they often come back. You're constantly on the lookout for the knife in your back. I know if someone did me I would come back for sure. Well, I'm thinking of promoting fights again. I know so many people in the game, I feel I could really do well out of it all. There are so many kids who want to fight these days and who better to promote them than someone who can train them, look after them and knows what they are going through?

ANDRE MARTIN

Coventry

Although standing just five feet five inches, Andre is a giant amongst men. Many have made the mistake of thinking that the diminutive doorman would be an easy option when the action started but, as the holder of 16 black belts, nothing could be further from the truth. A nice guy, he would be the last person to start trouble, but the first to put an end to it.

I WAS BORN in Coventry in 1973 and I come from a good family environment. My dad worked in a factory and my mum worked for British Telecom. I had a great upbringing with them, never wanting for anything. My dad was known for his fighting. He practised judo and was an accomplished boxer. Dad was a right scrapper and strong as an ox and would fight any amount of men at the same time. When I look back to when I was about six or seven, I can remember him coming home: he had a few cuts and bruises on him, his hands were swollen and I found out he had a scrape with a large guy, who towered over my dad at six foot seven, when he was out with my mum having a quiet drink. It ended with my dad knocking the shit out of the giant that had tried it on with him; he made a big mistake. He was knocked to the floor with my dad all over him like a rash, screaming and begging for my dad to stop. You see, that's what my dad was like: he would never give in no matter what. He was known as a giantkiller because he would always make for the biggest trouble-maker and knock him out first. He was a very aggressive fighter: if he knew it was going to kick off he would make sure he was the first one in and would punch first and ask questions later. I tend to follow mum in the way that I'm more passive to people.

When you're a schoolkid there are always some kids who have all the new clothes and all the new stuff, usually these are the kids who would get bullied. I suppose it's the same in every school. Well in my school I was one of those kids and some bullies tried to make my life hell. The first one to try his luck was a big ginger kid who hit me in the stomach and winded me. This would happen again and again. Other kids wouldn't come near me because of the bully. About this time my dad was taking me boxing, I was only five and I was the smallest in the club. I hated it but he used to get me to go every week. Dad's advice was always to get into them and give them a good slap, but of course I was only a kid and felt I couldn't do that, maybe that was just my mum's passive side of me. One day the bully was chasing me with his mates and for some reason I stopped running. Don't know why I did, I had this hot feeling in my stomach and felt sick. Maybe it was the first signs of the adrenalin rush I was experiencing. I ran straight at the bully and started throwing some of the punches I had learned at boxing at his head. I got on top of him and battered him. I sometimes wonder how he felt being the one getting beat up for a change.

As I went through school I would confront loads of bullies. One was a big half-caste lad called Mohammed, he was 5ft 6in and only eleven years old. He was also built like an adult, which didn't help matters. He was the typical bully, stealing the kids' money and picking on smaller kids. One day he bullied me and I was like everyone else and felt quite scared of him. I was doing *tae kwon do* now. I didn't feel scared doing that or boxing, but it felt different fighting on the street or in the schoolyard. I had a game plan to beat this bully though. One day I brought my martial art suit to school and at dinnertime I changed into it. I walked up to Mohammed dressed in my suit. He was picking on some other small kid at the time. It's funny how the suit gave me the confidence I needed. I said some words to Mohammed and front-kicked him and beat him to the ground. The teachers tried to pull me off and even then, when I was a kid, they had to struggle with me.

Thing was, the headmaster thought I was being a bully. He couldn't get it into his head that the fights I had in school were because I was being bullied or some smaller kid was. The head-master told my father that I must stop the martial arts or I'd be in serious trouble. My dad agreed to this but told me not to worry, he wasn't stopping my martial arts and he was proud of what I did.

When I went to senior school the bullying started again. The bullies would look for a victim and I think because of my size I fitted the bill. This one bully's name was Simon and he was onto me, smashed my head against the lockers, and was on my case all the time. One day he was picking on me and smacking me around.

Funny thing, I'd remembered that a teacher had taken a baseball bat into his room that morning. I run into the teacher's room and take the bat. I'd really had enough of being the victim so I remember thinking that that was the day I would pay back Simon. Simon saw me coming so he legged it into the toilets and hid behind this heavy door. I was so angry that I kicked down the door and whacked the hell out of him. I just kept hitting him with that bat, there was blood all over the place but I couldn't stop myself. They finally pulled me off but I had done what I had wanted to do. He never picked on me or anyone else again.

After that fight I sort of had a little bit of respect from the guys, some would still tease and call me "Little Ninja" but I didn't really mind. Some of the teachers could be a pain though. One day in the changing rooms some kid wanted to fight me and he flew at me. This time there was no fear and I just bounced the lad all around the changing rooms. Well, I got pulled into the office by a teacher. Now this teacher just couldn't take to me and was an arrogant loudmouth. He would love to put a kid down and always taunted me. He didn't even want to know my side of the story, he just pushed me into the showers with all my football kit still on. He started to shake me around but I exploded again and like a madman I attacked him. I hit him in the stomach and followed that with an uppercut. He was now winded so I just kept hitting him. Another teacher pulled me off and he had some as well.

I was sent to the headmaster again and my parents called in. The headmaster accused me of being a bully but my dad was having none of it this time. My dad told them that I was just defending myself and some of the teachers were bullies. He even went as far as to threaten to knock out the headmaster, which was typical of my dad.

When I left school I went into the butchery trade. I liked the job and got my head down and did the work. When we used to have a break I'd sit and read my martial art magazines. There was this one guy there, Ammon his name was, he just took an instant dislike to me and tried to make my life hell. I didn't need the trouble, I just wanted to do my job. Again, me being small, he thought he had a victim. He would take my magazine off me or lock me in the freezer. He thought he was being funny but all the time I was thinking of paying him back.

I was sealing meat by vac-packing them one day and I dropped a sealed piece on the floor. Well he thought he'd have a go and started shouting because I'd put it back with the others. Now this was common practice, the meat was sealed and completely safe but he wanted to try his luck again. He grabs me by the hair and pushes me down. I get away and walk off, when he grabs me from behind. I'm only 16 and he's a 33-year-old, pock-faced big bully who you could see by his face had been in some wars. I try to reason with him but I get a surge of adrenalin. I turn around fast and armlock him. I push him down onto the big wood cutting block that we cut meat on. I bring down my steak knife into the wood block by his face. He was terrified, like all bullies are when they get a taste of their own medicine. I told him and the other guys in the place that I was no victim and the shit stops from now on. I felt good about sorting that out. There's a good feeling you get when you stand up to a bully.

Things were going fine but what I didn't realise was that the customers had seen what had happened and some of the staff complained. I get up one morning and there's a letter waiting downstairs for me. The firm was sacking me because I didn't "fit in". That was the end of that, I was 16 and now looking for a new job. I didn't know what sort of work I could do. The only thing I knew about was fighting. You see, all the time I was growing up I was training in different fighting arts. The only real thing I could do was fight, and then it struck me that I could be a doorman. I really fancied the idea; it seemed a natural thing for me. Not only had my dad been a doorman for years but also so had all his mates. In fact they would all come over to our house after work to eat their curries and that. I knew the ins and outs of working on the door from all their stories that I sat and listened to. You may find it strange that a little lad would enjoy the stories but they were great, each story was about the good guys beating up the bad guys. It was from these stories that I learned not to tolerate a bully, and inside each bully was a coward just asking to be sorted out.

I got it into my head that I was going to work the doors and nothing was going to change my mind. I went up to this club one night just as the place was opening up. All the doormen were at the front door, all suited up getting ready for the customers to come. Up I come to the door and I speak to the head doorman there. I explain that I wanted to work the door and needed a job. Now the doorman thought it would be funny just to turn his back and shout to his friends about my size and the fact I wanted to be a doorman. He pushed me away and basically told me to come back when I was bigger. I saw red straight away and shout to him, "You know what, you arrogant bastard, I'll fight you right now." I'm only a youngster and he was a top doorman at the time. My mate who came with me wanted me to go but I was having none of it. I'm still shouting at the doorman who has now changed his tune, in fact he looks worried and tells me, "Er, come back when you're older mate, I'll try and get you some work." He didn't want to fight and went back in and locked the doors behind him. I turn to my mate and tell him, "You know, by the time I'm seventeen I will be running most of the doors around here." Well, as it happened when I turned 17, I was running six doors and they were some of the roughest places in Coventry which most other doormen wouldn't do.

People started to hear about me and I was getting phone calls to run more and more places, things were really taking off. Out of the blue a Mr G phones me up and explains that he was the community councillor for the Hillfields area [an inner-city Coventry ward with a large ethnic minority population]. There was a drop-in centre for Afro-Caribbeans. It was a very rough place indeed and was known as the "Front Line". In fact, a police chief inspector had a meeting with us, he told us not to work there, he said the place was too rough and we could get hurt really bad. He informed us that one of his lads went in there undercover to infiltrate the drugs gangs who worked out of there. When the undercover officer was in the toilet some guys grabbed him and tried to cut his throat wide open. If it wasn't for him using the panic button on his radio he would have been dead. He escaped with just a few cuts and bruises.

I started working at the centre and also I was bodyguarding the councillor as well. Thing was, the people who came to the centre were happy when they were running things, but when the councillor was put in charge they weren't happy with him or the way things were run. At the weekend they had a reggae night and on one occasion trouble broke out. I rushed down stairs to find chairs and tables going up, bottles and glasses being thrown. To top it all, the councillor was being attacked. I got him away to his office and returned to the trouble.

Things came to a head one evening in the aforementioned club when a group of about six coloured lads threatened to "cut me up". They were giving it the big 'un in front of all their mates. I was the only guy working and because of my colour, and against six blokes as well as the other 300-odd punters that would have no doubt kicked off given the slightest chance and opportunity, I played the situation down and managed to calm everybody and later on cleared the place. The following afternoon, however, whilst walking down the street, I encountered Errol and one of his mates from the evening before. They had made up their minds that I was weak, having taken so much abuse from the evening before. They decided to have a little more "fun" with me. But this time the six were only two and the 300 others were not around.

Errol pulled a lock knife on me and the other was giving me verbal abuse telling me how his mate Errol was going to cut me up and after that he was going to kick the shit out of me. I used some psychological warfare tactics, saying I wanted no trouble, no trouble at all, pleading for them to leave me alone. Then, bang, as their guard dropped I simultaneously parried the blade arm away and followed with a lead-leg hook kick to Errol's bollocks. He hit the floor like a sack of shit, trying to catch his breath. I kicked him again and my foot connected with the side of his jaw. His head whiplashed to one side as he let out a painful cry. I had still not finished with Errol: if he had the chance and I did not act first, he would have cut me up, so he had to learn the hard way. I lifted my leg and brought down an axe kick onto his head. He was out there with the stars and Jupiter. I turned and faced his mate who was now doing the 50-yard dash in the opposite direction. I remember giving chase and grabbing him from behind, applying a rear naked choke, taking him to the ground. I'm now on top of him punching and smacking my elbow into him. I noticed he's starting to lose consciousness. Before I put him away I explain what I'm going to do to him or his mates if I ever get any trouble from them again. I leave him sound asleep on the floor covered in his own blood, and walk off as if nothing ever happened.

When I was running the door at the centre I also had the door at a pub called The R and another called The G [names changed here]. Of course, I had to get some boys to help cover the door at Hillfields when I shifted from pub to pub. Two guys who were partners ran both pubs. I had to literally fight in one pub then run through an underground walkway then fight in another. If anything, it got me really fit! The R was in those days a really violent pub and to top it off the guys who came there were huge; it was like the land of the giants for me. There was this one big guy there called Shaun, he was a big lump covered in tattoos and was known as a bully, he was about 17 stone and loved to fight. I knew that one day our paths would cross, it just had to happen. This night I'm watching Shaun and he's getting himself worked up all night, getting louder and louder, making a nuisance of himself.

My mate offered to help me sort things out but I refused; it would look better if I did it on my own.

I get him on his own and I politely say, "Listen mate, do me a favour and keep it down tonight, will you? There are people complaining and we don't want no trouble here."

"Don't you call me mate," came his response.

I carried on talking politely and put my hand on his shoulder. Why I do that is to test which way he wants to go and sure enough he pushes my hand off and marches away, giving me verbal as well. I'm weighing the fight up already, getting my game plan in my head before it starts. He goes back with his mates and things go pretty quiet. I go upstairs and the message comes up that a fight has started downstairs. I just know it's Shaun, it just had to be him. I run down and sure enough there he was battering some young student, a kid who just didn't have a fight in him. I push them apart and tell them to leave it alone. Now the kid is safe but Shaun turns his attention to little Andre; he sees me as his next victim. Big mistake for him. He's looking confident, of course, he now has an audience watching so he's playing up to it. Quick as a flash he lunges at me and tries to headbutt me. As he brings his head back I bring up my elbow and he brings down his head onto it, it catches him right in the face. I deliver a Thai kick to his leg and he falls down. As he starts to fall, I'm on him. I'm punching the fuck out of him, giving him everything I have: uppercuts, hooks, elbows and every punch hits home. There's blood all up the walls, up my arms and, of course, all over him. People are all around us shouting and screaming but what I find strange was that none of his mates jumped on me. Maybe they thought that he would beat me.

When I stopped and looked down at him lying there I knew that the fight was over and he wouldn't be coming back for more. His mate steps forward and shouts that the fight is over. At this point I'm so psyched up that I just want to fight them all. I go into them all, calling them on all the time. One steps forward and I bang him straight out. I side kick the second into the wall and the third I knock straight out. My friends pull me out and I start to calm down, I switch back to Mr Nice Guy mode and things are okay once more. The one thing that has changed was that people treated me with respect and they saw the other side of me, which sometimes has to happen. Once relaxed I find I'm covered from head to toe in blood, in fact even my socks are soaked in blood. Sometimes on the door you have to be an animal, you can't always be the nice guy because some people see kindness as a sign of weakness.

I tell my mate Wayne that I know there will be comebacks, maybe not off Shaun but I just had this sneaky feeling. It's two nights later and I'm in the pub having an active night again, I've been involved in about five fights and thrown a few out as well. What I didn't know was that three of the lads who I threw out were friends of Shaun's. I got called to The G, so I run down the underpass and get to the pub. Once I get there I spot Shaun's mates sitting there, feet up on the table, with grins on their faces, thinking I'm not going to throw them out. I walked up and told them that their sort was not wanted in the pub, so they can leave. They didn't even look up, one of them told me to fuck off and they just sat there. I grab the biggest one in a leg lock and drag him off his chair, his big head hits the floor and he's out cold, job done. I drag him to the door and throw him out, next thing his mates have jumped me. They hold me tight between them; don't ask me how I got out of their grip but I somehow manage it. I step back into the doorway and the two guys both try to grab me at the same time, this time there's no room and they both collide with each other. I throw two hooks at them, one each, and they don't know what's hit them. Funny thing was that when they both fell to the floor knocked out, they fell at the same time, just like some comedy act.

As I'm lifting them out I get a call to go to The R, so off I run back down the underpass. I turn up and there's two guys going for it. I start to get things cooled down when I feel something just miss the back of my head. One of the guys fighting had tried to smash a bottle down on my skull. I turn around and both of the guys who had been fighting were coming for me. Wayne, my mate, runs in and smashes one of them to the ground and proceeds to choke him out. I'm left with the arsehole with the bottle. A crowd have gathered around me, tables have gone up and people are screaming like mad; all the time this guy is approaching with the bottle. I'm moving back, ducking the bottle and waiting for a chance to take him out. This guy is hellbent on doing me some serious damage. All of a sudden he pulls his arm back to strike and I'm on him. I hit him straight in the throat with the back of my hand, he drops the bottle and clutches his throat. He coughs out blood where I ruptured him. I finger jab him in the eyes and deliver a full force kick to his nuts. Remember this guy wanted to hurt me bad so that's what I do to him, I think it's only fair. I axe kick him to the head and chest. A few good kicks and he's out for the night, leaving me once again covered in blood. You wouldn't believe my cleaning bill, cost me a small fortune.

Working the doors as much as we were, it was inevitable that we would get comebacks. People you had thrown out or knocked out sometimes just wouldn't leave things lie, so you would be constantly looking over your shoulder when you were out on the street. Wayne and myself stopped off one night and got some chips to take home. All of a sudden this car screeches up and this big fucker jumps out. He starts to shout and tells us what he and his lads were going to do to us. We have no idea who he was but gathered he may have been a friend of someone we had trouble with. He puts his hand into his coat and we jump back a bit, not knowing what he had under there – a knife or maybe a gun? Somebody shouts that the police are coming and he gets into his car shouting that he would be back for us and shoots off down the road. Wayne and myself are left there dumbfounded, we have no idea who he was but knew he was big trouble. After a good talk Wayne and myself decide to track him down and visit him before he visits us.

A few days go by and we finally find out where he lived and drive down to his place. His car was outside, so we gathered he was in. It's about eleven o'clock at night when we knock his door. He opens the door and stands there in shock to see we are there; they never like it when you track them down, it makes them feel so vulnerable. As he starts to speak, we both throw a punch at him and both connect, sending him to the floor. I step in and start booting the hell out of him, splattering the doorframe with his blood. After a while I stop and look down to see that he's out and in a terrible state – it's only what he would have liked to have done to us. That was the last time we ever saw him. Thing is, these people like to come looking for you but it sometimes comes back to haunt them.

At this point of my life I'm training really hard. Each day Wayne and myself work out. We did all sorts of training, from boxing through the different martial arts. People always wanted to know how I progressed so fast with each different style, well what I did was to find the best in each style and train one-on-one with each of them. Some of the styles were similar so I picked them up quite quick. The best days for me were the "animal days" where a few of us would really go for it. We would go for each other just like a street attack, only just pulling back the punches and kicks. We would attack each other with such venom but we were in the business of fighting and had to experience it from all angles. It may seem mad for people to watch us spar barefist but it's what we needed. All this training and the fact that I was using the skills on the door got me more and more work. The phone would ring each day with offers of new doors to run.

We got a call to run the door at a place in Chalk Hill, London. We had to look after this community centre where they were holding this Pakistani festival. Now I know that doesn't seem a violent situation but when you realise the centre was just across the road from an Afro-Caribbean housing estate with a history of violence with the Asian community, you can understand the pressure we were under.

The whole day is going well, we were having a good time eating food and enjoying the job but never leaving our guards down. All of a sudden the glass in the front door is blasted through with a shotgun. Glass is flying everywhere, cutting everyone near the door. We get some of the kids down on the floor to safety as a large gang of coloured guys break in to fight the Asians. They have baseball bats, hockey sticks and weapons of all sorts. I can't say this didn't scare me because it bloody well did. I had been taught gun disarmament before and was trying to work out how to get to the guy with the gun. About this time a large gang of Asian lads come running down the stairs all tooled up – don't forget there were about 650 Asians in the building and we were trapped between both gangs. Somebody makes for the guy with the gun and he almost takes his head off, he's down and beaten to a pulp. We are also being attacked by the Asians who we were supposed to be looking after, it's just one mass brawl. There were fights everywhere. We were ducking bottles, chair legs and any other weapon that they could use. I'm knocking out people left, right and centre. I've got lumps and cuts all over me. Then the police turn up. The fights stop and the crowd starts to disperse. The police take a look around at all the mess. We of course tell them nothing, and they leave. Now that was the first instance with a gun and I must admit it scared the life out of me. Any man who says a gun don't scare them is a liar.

What you must remember here is that I'm not a violent man. In most cases I try to talk people out of the fight yet I was having four to five fights each night of the week. Sometimes I would be out walking the street and someone would start and most were big-name fighters who wanted to take me out. It's like the old scenario with the gunslingers in the Wild West, someone was always waiting to see how good I was. I couldn't go anywhere with my family without having to fight. They didn't care who I was with or where I was, walking the street was just the same as running the door. I had to weigh everybody up and take on all comers. Funny thing is I can't remember one of them being smaller than me, always the big bullies who thought I would make the perfect victim.

There were also some people who though they could take the door off me, they could see how quiet the place was and would think that they could handle the job. What they didn't realise was that I may have been fighting all the hardest in that area for months to get the place that quiet. I was working this one place on my own as usual and that's the way I preferred it, I had got the place in order and earned the respect of the customers. People came to the door and spoke to me politely before entering, sometimes stopping to pass the time of day with me. Two big lads turned up one night, both wearing these big, long, crombie-type coats. I think they thought themselves as gangsters. They both stood by the door, blocking it. One asked if I was Andre and I told him I was. All the time, I'm watching them, taking into account their body language and the fact that they were very big, rough-looking fuckers.

"Come in lads, if you want to," I politely tell them.

"Nah, it's okay mate, we've come to take the door off you," the bigger of the two growled at me.

I'm a little shocked, to say the least, when the other one tells me, "We are going to take over a few doors around here and yours is the first to go."

There's no amount of training that could prepare me for a scene like this, so I reply to them, "Come on guys, I've worked hard for this door and there's no way I'm giving it up. Anyway, how the hell are you two going to take it?"

They looked down at me and the biggest says, "We aren't going to take it, he is." With that, they separate and standing behind them is what I can only describe as Frankenstein's monster. He made the other two look like little boys, he was one of the biggest men I have ever seen in my life. His face was scarred all over the shop, he was a giant of a man standing there looking down at me full of hatred, clenching and unclenching his massive battered fists. I won't kid you, I'll tell you the truth, I just didn't want to be there, I really didn't, but I wasn't walking away. The whole pub was watching all this, nobody moved, they couldn't believe what was going down, and this was straight out of the Hammer House of Horrors. As you know, I'm not a big guy but I felt microscopic next to this monster.

The monster tells me, "Little guy, I'm going to piss on you."

"Okay, I know I have to fight but let's keep it like gentlemen, let's shake first," I say to the monster.

He puts out his bear paw hand out to shake mine. I pull him forward and released a cracking head-butt and an elbow shot to the temple. He's sort of staggering, half down but still on his feet, I keep the pressure on and keep hitting him with my elbow and hands. One eye socket was bust wide open with blood shooting into the air, but he still hasn't gone down yet. I step back and hook-kick his leg, which sends him crashing down onto the pavement. I stamp on his hands until they break, his head is bust open and he is screaming for me to stop. The whole pub now comes out to back me up, and the other two drag him away as I'm being held back by the customers. Now I'm going completely berserk and I'm trying to break free to batter the other two. As they disappear around the corner I start to cool down, and I'm sane again.

I look down at the floor and I notice the whole alleyway is soaked in blood, even a trail where they dragged him around the corner. I'm thinking, *if the police turn up I'm in deep shit*, so I grab a mop and bucket and start to clean all the blood away. This was taking ages and all the time I'm thinking that if I carry on like this my life is never going to change for the better. There's only so much a man can take. I had a wife and kids to look after. If I weren't fighting I was paying the scumbags home visits, constantly in fight mode. The troublemakers even came onto my wife when I wasn't there. I was planning to get out of the game as soon as I could.

Some of the drug dealers would try anything to get me on their side. A guy comes onto me one night and tells me my dad nearly got jumped. He tells me that two scumbags tried to sell my dad drugs and were planning to do him over, seems he was lucky this guy knew he was my dad and stopped the whole thing. Well, I thank him but I do some research and find he sent the guys onto my old man just to make it look like he was a hero and I'd owe him big time. Don't get me wrong here, my dad could still fight even though he was now a lot older, but in that area if he had laid into them loads of scumbags from the flats nearby would have come out and attacked my dad.

I'm in the Vine Street Community Centre one night and I'm looking for this dread-locked druggie who said he helped my dad. I know he's in the toilets so I enter and kick the cubicle door in, to find him and two mates cutting up their drugs. Now he still thinks I'm his big mate, and he's smiling at me and greeting me as if I'm his long lost brother. I call him outside the cubicle and inform him that I know the truth and he was a liar and a scumbag. I throw a straight right and it takes his head right back, two more for good measure and he's out. I knock one of his mates out and the other is crying like a child not to be hit. On top of the toilet I find a huge pile of powder that they were cutting up. I get it all and flush it down the toilet. A few well-aimed punches and I leave the toilets. In the corridor I shout to all the other dealers there, "There's one of your men smashed up in there and if you want to know who did it, it's me, and I'll do the same to any one of you who touches my dad or who I catch dealing in here." They all stop what they are doing and listen to what I tell them: " Some of you I get on with, others I don't. Just remember, if you get me in a gang I'll hunt you down and kill you."

The reason I stopped the door work was because of my wife and kids. I had been running this really rough door and one night before I left for work my wife says to me, "Andre, before you go to work tonight would you please write a letter for the kids explaining why you do the work you do, because one night you're not going to come home and I don't want to be the one to tell them why you are what you are." Now I didn't listen at first but later on I'd got a little trouble in the club. There was this big, really nice guy by the bar and he was having a good time. Before we could react, this bunch of lads jumped him. There were so many of them jumping on this guy, we were in trying our best but there was so many of them. A new doorman had started that night and he got slashed from ear to ear. The police came and stood outside in riot gear doing nothing but watching us three doormen fight with this, by now, huge gang. We somehow, God knows how, stopped the fight and got them out. The new doorman was sent to hospital along with the first guy who got battered, and I'm looking at my wage packet, looking at the blood-stained floor and rubbing the gash on my head where I had been bottled. Then I remember what my wife said, and packed in the door work for good. I came home to the wife and told her that I was finished on the door. Of course, she had heard it all before but this time I was serious. After ten years on the door I just had to get away and spend more time with my kids.

Now, I've worked the doors for years and along the way I've collected 16 black belts in various styles, which came in handy many nights. I'm a trained bodyguard and qualified to train others as well. I've looked after loads of top celebrities, the downside being that I've had contracts put on me, death threats from major drug dealers, been shot at more than once, I've been in more life-threatening situations than I can count. A few book companies have expressed an interest in my life story, which I plan to get down on paper very soon. I sometimes travel the world teaching combat styles to various military personnel from Special Forces units. You could say I've had a full life, not always a happy one but a full one. At the end of the day I'm still here with my beautiful wife and able to watch my beautiful children grow up which, if we all get our priorities right, is the reason we are all here.

DON LEWIS

Tredegar, Wales

Truly one of the old school, Don was born in 1934 and, from the earliest age, all he wanted to do was fight in the ring. A travelling man known as the "Corring Mush"("Fighting Man"), his lifetime of fisticuffs, both in and out of the fairground booth, could not be further removed from the devotion he has for his family.

I AM FROM Tredegar originally and from a fighting family. My mother died when I was young and I never knew my father. My grandmother adopted us and brought us up. I went to one school and some kids tried to knock my sister about, so that's when I started to fight. Then when we moved to a different school, I always fought the top boys. When I left school I couldn't read or write, I just wanted to fight all the time, never wanted to do anything else but be a boxer. I went to Jack Phillips to teach me to box. He was an old-time boxer, and fought some good guys. They put me in with this kid called Rocky who I beat after three hard rounds. They said I was just lucky at the time but I told them it wasn't luck.

I was working down the pits at the time when the boxing booth came to Ebbw Vale. I went straight down to it, never knew anything about it or even who to speak to. I spoke to Ron Taylor, the owner of the booth, and asked if there was a chance I could have a go. They wanted to know if I could box, so I told them, "I can't box but I can fight and can take anything you give and still come back." Ron said, "There's a boy here you can fight and if you're any good I will give you a job." The boy's name was Johnny Arrow, a boxer from Croydon. I didn't know who the hell he was but I still beat him. Mind you, I had to put some time into him to do it.

After the fight, I said to Mr Taylor, "Well how about the job now then?"

He turned to me: "I think you were very lucky to win that fight."

I looked at him and said, "Well you've got another show, so I'll box someone else. I don't care who it is, I'll fight them."

I was told to come back the following night and fight again and if I did the same I'd get the job. I came back and fought Johnny again and he was a good boy, done the same thing again and I was in. The wages were £2 10s a week and my keep, but the money didn't bother me. I just wanted to fight, and fight I did.

I travelled around with the booth and one day it came to Sophia Gardens in Cardiff. A coloured boy called Rocky Kent came to the booth. Ron says to me, "Whatever you do, I don't want you to hurt this boy." I didn't know why he said this but I did what he said. Now when we fought there was me taking my time and he was laying into me. After the fight I asked Ron what was going on and he told me Rocky had taken a load of punches over the years and Ron didn't want him hurt anymore. Ron would always look after the boys that way. So night after night he kept coming and the same thing was happening. I told Ron I wasn't taking any more of this, I was getting banged around every night. The next fight we had I got stuck into him. Now, I didn't go all out and try to stop him but at least he knew he'd been in a fight. Ron said it was a good fight but don't do it no more.

We travelled around the country fighting each night. Some nights I couldn't sleep with my face being so bruised and my eyes puffed up. I'd lie there crying in pain and would swear that in the morning I'd pack it all in, but I would rub some witch hazel on my face to take out the bruising and the next day I would be up ready to fight again.

When we would get to Gloucester I'd fight old Johnny Melpha, the middleweight. Now there was no easy fight with Johnny. Every time he went in the ring he would try to knock you out. I'd give as good as I got but they were really hard fights with him. In Gloucester there were loads of coloured boys who would give us some real good fights.

Every year I would turn up at the May fair in Hereford to meet up with the booth and travel around fighting. I'd fight all-comers from all walks of life. Sometimes I'd be giving away four to five stones to some of these guys. This may sound funny to some people but when I'd be standing on the front looking at the crowd, I'd know straight away who the fighters were. There was something about the real fighters that made them stand out; something that I can't put my finger on that set them apart from the guy who just wanted to try you out. Remember I was fighting every night against guys who wanted to earn money by knocking me out.

From Gloucester we would go to Fairford where we would get Yanks and some Irish who would want to fight. The Yanks were all big guys, so they would fight our big heavyweight, Frankie. Now the Irish would always come into the ring half-cut; they would love a fight after a few drinks. They would get ten bob for three rounds, which they could go and have a few more drinks with. No matter what you did to them they would come straight back the next show, ready to earn some more drink money. One thing Ron always told us was, if we were fighting a boy or someone who couldn't fight, then we must take our time with them. If we hurt them, then of course we would stop having people come to the fights.

Sometimes we got the message that some boys wanted to know how much they would get if they knocked you out, so Ron would tell us what they said and then we wouldn't pull no punches with them. Everyone who put his hands up got a fight. One thing was that if someone got beat in the ring they never came to fight us outside the ring. All the fights were done fair and we treated everyone tidy. In all the hundreds of fights I had, I never once got knocked down. I got stopped with bad cuts but never knocked down.

I think it was the third year with the fair when I met my first wife. She was a traveller, a gypsy or whatever you wanted to call her. Her family were the Crowes, who came from Scotland originally. We met and got married all in seven weeks, which I know seems fast but that was the way we were then. Sometimes I'd be fighting as much as six to seven times a day. Now and again, if we had a busy week, Ron would say, "Look, you've had a busy week, so have Saturday off." Oh, and that would be good to have off!

My first wife had three brothers and they never liked the Welsh, so they didn't like me. Caroline came to the pub one night to say, "You'd better come back down and get your case packed, my brothers are going to try you out tonight, you're in trouble." I told her not to worry, "Just keep out of my way and give me plenty of room." I went back to our caravan and changed out of my suit and put my jeans and my boots on. I walked up to the big fire where they all were. Now I wasn't scared because I always believed if you got scared you lost the fight. Well the shout goes up, "Come on then, yah Welsh git." I moved Caroline out of the way as the four of them came down. Now her brother Blackie came to me first and, oh, he was a good fighter. Well I put him straight down. The others ran, so I chased after them, catching one and giving it to him. Now I didn't fight him clean, like I would in the ring. One of her other brothers ran to the fire and got this big log of wood. He lifted it up and brought it down on my shoulder. I just managed to push it out of the way. Anyway, I beat the four of them on my own. Just before this all happened, I'd asked Caroline to marry me and her mother said no because we were too young. After the fight, her mother said, "Well, if you can do that to my sons, you're good enough for my daughter." So we got wed.

Even after the fight, the boys still didn't like me. The one brother, Isaac, if ever he got into a fight and was losing or if they were too good for him, then he would tell them, "Well, if you're a fighting man come down and fight my brother-in-law. He'd lick any one of you." There I would be, in my bed, when down they would come, knock on the door, and out I'd go to fight. Isaac would be telling all who would listen what I could do, so they would bring the Davies's or the Smiths down to fight me bareknuckle. They were always getting me to fight someone. Every week there was someone new for me to fight. There was no money involved, just family pride. You see, I had to fight rather than embarrass her family.

I remember going to Worcester blackcurrant picking. There

were loads picking, students and all sorts. Well, they weren't very good, they would leave more on the bushes than they picked. I was one side and Caroline the other and this girl took her top off because she was hot and tied a scarf around her top half. Well I couldn't help but notice this. After all, you know, I was a young man and that. There I was, looking at this girl, then BANG, Caroline smashed this box down on my head.

"What did I do?" I said.

"I saw you looking up at that girl" she replied, and off she went.

Up I go to get my boxes weighed when I hear someone call me "the Corring Mush." Now I didn't know this type of Romany because it differed from the Romany used on the fair. When I went back to the caravan I told Caroline what I had been called. She laughed and said, "You know what that means? It means they are calling you 'The Fighting Man.'"

Once, my niece Caroline came running up to me, screaming, "Quick, quick, they are killing Charlie Richards." It seems Isaac and Henry were really battering Charlie. Maybe it was because of all the trouble they were causing me or just because they hated me and the rest of the Welsh that I got involved. I got an old chair leg out of my van. It was one we would use to play baseball with the kids. I marched up to where a load of them was battering Charlie. Isaac and Henry ran straight at me. I swung the bat at Henry's head just as he lifted his arm up. Well, he went down with his arm broken in two places. Isaac came at me and I sort of dropped the bat and threw a punch straight into his kidneys. Well, for someone who was known as a fighting man, down he went, and I beat hell into them. I've never used a weapon but that time I just had enough. There's only so much you can take.

[On another occasion] even though it was a summer's night, it was still cold. Isaac walked from Worcester to Stourport with no shoes or anything but his trousers on. The Smiths had given him a good hiding. The father and four boys had made a right mess of him. They had beaten him bad with barbed wire as well. Anyway, him now being family, I was forced to help out. We waited three to four days till he came around better. He went to look for them in the Live and Let Live pub in Worcester. Well, by now they didn't want to know but one was getting a bit lairy with Isaac. But as soon as I walked in they went quiet and nothing happened.

A week or so later, Isaac was out again saying how good his brother-in-law was, so the word that I was a fighter was spreading all the time. One of the Smiths, Black Harry, said to me in Stourport that he wanted to fight me for money. Well, at that time I had no money so I said I'd fight him for his lorry. Harry turned to me and said, "Its okay son, I'm pulling your leg. You've done nothing to me." Well, I said, "I've got nothing, but I'd fight you for your lorry," but he didn't want to know. There was a common there where they would all turn up to fight. Well Isaac started on me, saying what he was going to do to me. I told him to stop but he wouldn't listen, so we fought there with all the fighting families watching. It was a rough fight and in the end he just had to give up. Some of the fighters came up to me and said I should have done it years ago.

By this time my marriage had broken up and I was still travelling around with Ron. I had one weekend off and went to Luton to see my brother. I was told he was in the pub so I turned up, to his surprise. I explained I was down for the weekend. "Well, I'm glad you've come now," he said. "I had some trouble last night. Some guy put a chair over my back." The guy wasn't there that night but the following night my brother pointed him out to me. I walked up to him and said, "They tell me you're a good man with a chair. Let's see outside if you can still be good with me." There was a green outside where people would fight. Well, I tell you, it was a hard fight, a real tough scrap. I put him away in the end. Down he went and down he stayed. We shook hands and went back in the pub as friends, which was the way it always was with me.

At some of the fairs we had boxing and wrestling. I tried the wrestling once and didn't like it. I told them, "I don't mind taking a punch but I'm not putting my back down on there." Once we even did boxer against wrestler. I tried it and thought, *I'm not letting him get his hands on me.* As fast as he came forward I jabbed and stepped away from him. There was no way I would stand still to be grabbed.

Another time I had some fights with a guy called Percy Lewis from Oxford. He was a little bigger than me and could hold his hands up. Each night he would put his hands up to fight. Now he was a good fighter and each night he was getting the better of me. This one night I told everyone that I would beat him. Well I noticed that when we fought, every time I threw a right hand he would jump up a little. This time I threw a right, he jumped up and I threw a body punch, but I hit him right between the legs and down he went and didn't get up. Nobody believed it was an accident and Ron said, "Well, you did say you were going to beat him tonight." I couldn't get them to believe that I wouldn't do something like that but there you are.

Ron and Mrs Taylor would look after us well. We would always have a good breakfast and Mrs Taylor would make sure we had clean blankets and that. Ron would sometimes come into the trailer late at night with his torch to make sure some of the boys didn't have girls with them. When he found one there he would tell them to go and the boy would be sent packing in the morning. I can remember Ron catching many girls there and he would be shining his torch on them as they got dressed.

There were travellers coming from miles around to my caravan to fight me. In the end I couldn't go out for a quiet night because when I got home there would be someone waiting for me. I can honestly say with my hand on my heart that I only ever got beat once and that was when I was in school, by a boy called Ronnie Lewis. He was the most delicate boy you ever met. Now what I would do, as a boy, was go up to them and say, "Can't you fight?"

And if "yes" was the answer, we would go off to fight. Ronnie gave me the finest hammering of my life and it was my own fault. A year ago I bumped into him. "Ron," I said, "I haven't seen you for years. You're the only man to ever beat me!" He laughed. "Shh, don't tell anyone," and we laughed like hell.

I was working in the steelworks years later. I was in the lorry in the passenger seat when I saw this other lorry coming towards me on the wrong side of the road and that's all I remember. The lorry crashed into us, taking my side off. When they found me, I was stuck down between the wheels. I had a fractured skull, broken hip, my shoulder was gone and I woke up in hospital. Not long after I was cleaning my shotgun when it went off into my stomach. I walked about 30 yards to my friend's caravan covered in blood, then I fell down and that's all I could remember. Even now when I go for an X-ray, the doctors are amazed to count the 70 bits of shot still in me.

I went back to the booth after a while and soon worked off the excess weight I put on. I still fought there for years. I travelled with the fair for over 38 years, and after fighting hundreds and hundreds of booth and bareknuckle fights, I decided to call it a day. I was 52 and still fighting, so it was time to quit and take things easy.

BRIAN COCKERILL
Stockton-on-Tees, Durham

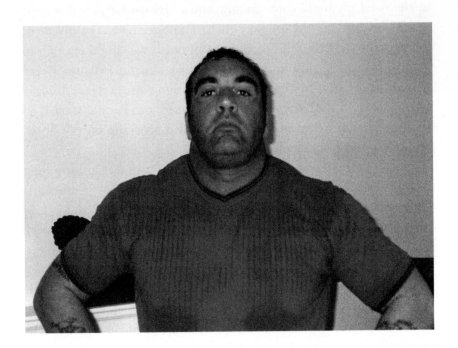

At six feet three and 23 stone, it's not difficult to understand why Brian is known throughout the hard Northern towns simply as "the Big Fella". A physically intimidating man never , ever to be crossed. Brian's reputation was earned the hard way by taking every fight to the extreme. He crossed swords with some legendary fighters and put an end to every challenger.

WHEN I WAS a kid I had asthma and I'd always get picked on. From the age of eight to 13, it was always the same. My mam and dad would always be on the move so whatever school I was going to I was always the new kid. Thing is, when you went to a different school the kids would always pick on the new boy. They made my life hell. At the age of 15, I started to lift weights – my uncle owed my mam some money and in return he gave her a set of weights and an old weight bench. The bench was the old type, a made-up one with a bit of carpet on, but it was good enough to get me started. I didn't really put much size on because I was playing football and that. I started training properly at Redcar when I was 19 and started packing the size on. People started to notice how big I was and in no time I was working on the doors and that's when I started fighting.

One lad would come in and I'd put him out and beat him, then his mate would come and I'd beat him – there was always someone else wanting to have a go. That's how I started fighting and before long I had worked every door in town. I went to work at a place called the Top Hat and it was really rough back then. One night, these guys come in, top boxers they were. One comes up to me and says, "Listen, we run this town, I've had sixty-three amateur fights and only lost two." So I give him the right hand and drop him and shout, "Well you've lost three now, haven't you?" His brother came in and I banged him as well, both brothers lying there knocked out on the floor. Now they didn't come back but they sent this big guy over for me, six foot seven, right hard, top gypsy fighter. Can't remember his name but I know they called him "The Dentist" because when he threw his right hand it would smash out all your front teeth. Now, I'm six foot two and I'm looking up to him like a schoolboy, he was massive. I know what he's come over for but I still say to him, "You can't come in mate, last orders have been called, sorry about that." He was there to fight me and had a big load of lads behind him. He threw this big heavy right hand, which I slipped, and I threw my left hook. He drops to the ground with a shattered jaw. The police come that night and the guy gets me arrested. Unbelievable. Well, the charges got dropped.

I decide to try my hand at boxing and I train for about six weeks to fight this guy who had already had six fights, so I shouldn't really be fighting him. Now, I'm the first to say that I'm no boxer, I'm more of a streetfighter and not into all this jab and move stuff. I prefer all-in fighting. I'm trying to get in on this guy and the ref keeps pulling us apart. I tell him to fuck off and he takes a point off me. All the time this guy is jabbing and jabbing me, my nose is bleeding, my lip is cut open and I'm getting really annoyed. I can't knock him out because the ref keeps pulling us apart every time I get inside. After I lost the fight, I lace him in the changing rooms instead. I went in and bashed him all over. I know I shouldn't have but I was still so wound up.

There was this big bully in Redcar who had fought and beat some of the hardest there. He was making this young kid sell ecstasy for him but he was giving the kid aspirins so the kid was getting loads of shit off the people he was selling to as well. I felt sorry for this little kid, so I go up to the bully and I tell him it's not going on any more. Well, he tells me the kid is going to keep selling for him and with that he gets out of his big fancy car. I'm standing there waiting to get it on when he dives and grabs my legs. I'm 23 stone and I'm thinking how the hell is the daft bastard going to lift me up. I grab him and ram him into this car, he jumps back up and I smash my fists into his body and forearm, smash him to the ground. I'm on top of him now and I stick my thumbs into his eyes and push them right back. Blood shoots right up my arms. He's screaming, "I've had enough! I've had enough!" All the time people are egging me on to kill him because he was such a bully. I'm glad nobody called the police. I could have been in real trouble with that one. It wasn't long after that the bully moves from the area.

I fought all the hardest from up there, then I came down to

Stockton to work the clubs. There was a big gang in Stockton called "the Wrecking Crew" who would go around 20-handed. Nearly all the pubs wanted me on the doors down there. I'd go around each one through the night, checking they were all okay. Late one night this crew turn up with the same old "we run this town" bullshit. I tell them how we are only trying to earn some money on the door and they can come in but no shit tonight. Now, I'm a fair guy and I try to get on with everyone, but when they come in, the one who spoke with me starts to roll a joint in front of the customers and, of course, the manager. I tell him to take it outside and he starts with all the mouth. Now, I'm not going to take that so I bang him out. His mate runs up and I put him out cold as well.

One night, in another club, I go outside and there's 15 or so of them waiting for me. Now I'm working on my own that night. Well, they come at me and I knock seven of them out, they are all just lying flat out when the police come. I'm on CCTV camera so I'm thinking, *I'm fucked here,* but the police are over the moon and love it.

Before I came to those clubs there would be 50 or so kids outside the clubs at night throwing stones and bottles at the doors and the bouncers. Most were National Front skinheads and that. I thought, *I'm not putting up with that shite.* One night I ran out and whacked about three of them, I put this one on his arse and he bounced back up shouting that he wasn't hurt. He ran into the road and his best friend's car knocked down the silly fucker, breaking both his legs.

Working one night, this big guy came down to the club and said, "I want to fight you."

I said, "Where, here or outside?"

"I'll fight you anywhere," he replied.

We step outside and he's got all his mates with him. We square up to each other, I head-butt him and he finds his arse. I head-butt him again and down he goes again. I lean over him and tell him,

"Look, I haven't even punched you yet and you're fucked," so that was him done. About two years later, I see him in this club. This other guy comes over and says the big guy was worried in case I was going to do him again. I says, " Fuck me! He's six foot three, about eighteen stone, what the fuck is wrong with him?" I go up and tell him that it's all forgotten with and he says sorry. I never hold grudges with them; if I beat them, I've got nothing more to prove. You see, there's no fear if I've beaten them, so I'd rather leave things lie. I'd fought every hard fighter from Scarborough to Newcastle, going through each town. I'm not being big-headed, it's just the way things were for me. It's the life I lead.

My mate John Black tells me one day that I would get on with a guy called Lee Duffy. John himself was a good bareknuckle fighter and used to train Lee. "Lee is just like you, he was bullied as a kid, then started training. He's beaten everyone, in all the jails he's been to he's beaten all the hardest there." Later on I was with my mate Kevin and we had just been to this jail to see a friend who was on a murder charge. We are walking along the street in Redcar, I've got my middle finger on my right hand in a splint because I broke it, when Lee walks up to me. Now I was only 24 and a little bit naïve. Lee is about six foot three, around 17 stone and has been fighting since he was a kid. He comes up and says, "What they call you then?" Now I think he's going to mention John, who we both know, and introduce himself. "My name's Brian," I tell him. All the time I'm watching his mate who's drinking out of this bottle. I chat to his mate and I'm always watchful of someone with a bottle.

Lee sneaks closer and hits me right on the chin, and Lee could really hit when he wanted to. I see stars and fall to my knees, dazed, disorientated. I grab hold of him and shake the punch off, lift him up and ram him into the wall. I have him trapped in the corner by a bay window. I was about 22 stone so my whole weight was on him. I butt him twice, knee him in the face, smash him with my forearm and pull him down. I hold him down and I realise there's no way I can hit him with my right hand because of the splint. As I'm holding him his mate brings the bottle down on my head. I grab his mate and smash him into a car.

I look at Lee on the floor and he's still dizzy and his mate is fucked as well. I don't want to fight the two of them with my damaged hand so I back off. I had a mate who lived around the corner, his name was Mickey, he's dead now, so I try to make it to his house thinking I'd have a better chance there. I get maybe 300 yards down the road when they both come running up. I'm keeping my head down not to get another right hand. When we are squared up, his mate is trying to come from the side. As I back off I bump into one of the metal bollards they have on roundabouts and it wobbles. I rip it up from the ground and hit Lee with it and push him right back. I run at his mate with it and he runs off.

I shout at him, "Wait till my hand's better and we will have a proper fight, you can get John Black and we'll meet in a field and sort it."

"Come down this alley here and fight us now. I just done you once," he cries out to me.

"What, so you two can jump me with bottles and that, and yes, you did put me down Lee, but you hit me from the side like. When I did you, you were screaming for your mate to get me off," I shout back.

Now time goes on and it's about nine weeks later, I'd been training and my hand is better. I go off to Lee's mate's house. I beep the horn and his mate comes to the window. "Is Lee fucking there?" I shout. He comes out with a shotgun. I go up to him and he runs off back into the house, just trying to bluff me with the gun. Now nothing happened for a while because Lee had hit some guy and snapped his neck, so he was on remand. Lee had all these guys selling his drugs for him so I went out and taxed the fucking lot, took £15,000 off all these fucking people.

Lee gets out of prison and I had this friend tell me all the time that I would kill Lee Duffy, so I was getting right wound up. I went out looking for him all day. We were driving through Eston [in Middlesbrough] when I spot this Sierra. Lee's in the car, he's calling me on, shouting things.

I scream to my mate, "Ram the fucking car, ram it!"

"No, its Lee Duffy, I can't" he tells me.

"What? We've been looking for him all fucking day!" I scream.

I get out of the car and run 40 yards down the road. Lee's calling me on but they try to drive away. I dive on the back of the car and my sudden weight stalls the car. I'm punching and kicking the car, I even pull the wipers off, but they drive off and I can't catch them.

It must have been two weeks later I'm drinking in this pub when the phone rings and the guy behind the bar says the call was for me. Don't know why, but before I took the call I told my mate that it was Lee Duffy on the phone. He looks at me strange but it was Lee.

"I was out of order that night. We are the best fighters in the area. Why don't we team up and make some money?" he tells me.

"Fair enough, I'll come and see you," I replied.

Down his house I go and he's there with his mate and his family. He's putting his boots on and he looks up to me and tells his family, "Look at the size of this fucker, and there's me trying to fight him, I must be mad, me." We hit it off really well, me and Lee. I go around with him for about three months. We used to go to all the drug dealers' houses, just the scum ones; you know, the police-informer type ones. We would tax the cash off them. They used to call us "the Taxmen". We would go all the way across Hartlepool right across to Teesside getting money.

I love to have a good night out, and one night I was out with some younger guys. I'm enjoying myself, even showing off a little. They had me picking up the front of cars and that, just out having some fun. I turn around a corner and there's all these doormen kicking some poor lad on the pavement, four of them. Now, I think you know by now that I hate bullies, I just can't abide a bully. These bouncers were big guys and one of them, Steve, was about 20 stone. I fucking run up and lay into the first two, and I'm fighting like fuck when the police turn up and grab me. While they are holding me, the big fucker, Steve, runs up and hits me in the face, so I lose it. I shake the police off me as the bouncers run into the club. Then about 20 to 30 police turn up and all hell breaks loose. They manage to get me into the van but I kick the doors straight off the hinges. I get out but I won't hit the police, you know I'm not stupid. They can't get me into the van because I'm too strong, only five or six can grab you at one time and I just throw them off. They get me into another van and I once again kick the doors off. I also kick in the doors to the club. Now I don't know if it's because of me, but all the club doors there now have locks on them on the inside as well!

The big fucker, Steve, was telling everyone how he had given me a go, which was starting to get to me. I was with Lee, we had been out taxing and we had made a few grand each. We spot this Steve guy in a kebab shop. I walk up and said to him, "Come on then, you fucking gobshite. What you been saying about me?" He runs straight at me and, like I said, he's 20 stone, right? I throw a straight right hand and you know when you've hit someone and you know if you've hit them good. I could feel the impact all down my arm and he went down with that one punch. Well, the prick grassed me up and I went away for three months. While I was away, Lee was killed in a fight. He was stabbed to death, I know for a fact if I had been out and we were together it would never have happened.

I remember being in this house one night with him and I was really drunk. He said to me, "Remember that fight we had?"

Now I don't even know what day it was, I was so drunk. "Forget about it," I answer.

"Well," he goes on, "you beat me that day, you know. I'd never do anything sneaky like that again. Thing is, when I hit people with that right hand, they don't get back up. I couldn't believe how fast you jumped back up. It done my head in and I couldn't sleep for six weeks thinking someone had beat me. You're my friend and you'll be my friend forever." Lee was a good friend to me and I still miss him today.

I was approached one night at a rave club when a friend suggests I should fight for money. He informs me, "Look, you've beaten every bugger, why not fight for money? You have nothing to lose." I tell him I'd rather just get on with people and not fight. It's different when someone comes looking for you or a fight just breaks out when I'm working. He tells me, "I will put fifty grand up for you to fight Viv Graham, and we can get an empty warehouse and charge twenty pounds a man for them to watch. Do you think you'll beat him?"

"I think I will," I tell him, "I've seen Viv fight and he was out of breath after a few punches. I'm bigger, stronger and a lot fitter."

He goes to see Viv and Viv sends his partner down and he tells us, "Viv doesn't want to know." Now I'd heard all about Viv but never really met him; he did wave to me when I was in prison once but that's all really. His partner told me Viv wanted me to come up for a drink with him some time.

I go for a night out in Newcastle. I'm just wearing my tracksuit and that. The bouncers tell me I can't come in dressed the way I was but once they realise who I was they let us in. I'm sitting with my mate Stephen and a few others and there's this guy next to me, he's going on about how he's a champion boxer and how he fought for England and all that. All night he's bragging and going on and on. He's asks me my name and I tell him Brian.

"Well, what's your second name?" he asks.

"Just Brian, that's all mate" I replied.

"Well you must have a second name," he goes on again.

I turn to one of the guys in our company and tell him, "If this guy wasn't related to Stephen, I'd fucking bash him."

"He's not, in fact I don't even know him," he informs me.

This boxer is still going on in my face so I slap him with the palm of my hand and I knock him out. People around me are shouting how I knocked this guy out just with a slap. I didn't want to do it but I just couldn't take any more off him.

I went to Holme House prison in Stockton first and there were this big lad there from Birmingham and he held the prison record for lifting weights. I think at one time he could full squat about 500lbs. For a crack I went and front-squatted the same weight. Well, the big lad was a bully and he was always taxing stuff off the smaller guys, with this they all hated him. A few years before he had been picking on a mate of mine, so off I go to his flat. It was about three storeys up and I get up there with a friend and I kick his fucking door down. There's nobody in the house so I walk up to the bed, and I can feel it's still warm. That's an old trick I picked up from years of taxing the druggies. I know he's in the flat but I can't find the prick, I'm looking everywhere and there's no sign of him. I stop for a moment and I can hear breathing coming from the settee. The crafty fucker is lying tucked down inside it. I reach in and yank him out and bash the fuck out of him. To give him his due he is quite a strong lad and for a second I have to struggle with him. I get the fucker down and I remember these sunbed tubes in the corner of the room. I grab one and hit him with it. The bloody thing breaks and cuts me open above the eye and blood starts to drip down my face. I lost my fucking head and start to kill the fucker. I'm smashing ornaments, the TV and anything I can find down on his head. My mate Speedy who came with me is shouting, "Bri! Bri! Stop. You're going to kill the fucker." I've lifted him up and I'm going to throw him off the top floor but Speedy talks me out of it, thank God.

Well, we don't see this guy for a few years until I'm in this prison. I had already got the message that he had been training hard and said when I came there he was going to do me. Now he's about 17 stone and, like I said, he's the strongest in the prison and held all the records for lifting. I go out onto the yard at dinnertime and I'm trying to hold my temper when I spot him. I get up to him and left hook him and give him a straight right hand between the eyes, which splits him open. He falls back onto the crowd and once again, to give him his due, he goes to come back at me. I'm right up for it now and I shout, "Come on then!" but he backs off. He gets stitches put into his head then goes and reports me, and the screws come up and tell me, "Bri, we don't want no trouble, will you please come down the block with us?" Anyway, down the block I go. The governor came to see me and tells me I'm not wanted in his jail. I tell him, "Well, I didn't want to come here in the first place!" The governor then gets me sent to Durham Prison. Seems he banned me from his jail.

When I get to the prison, the screws take a look at me. One gets up and tells me, "Here you are lad, you have a coffee and take my seat, I fucking hate that guy you bashed. You'll have any job you want here." One day out on the yard there were two kids and some of the other prisoners were trying to tax them for their gold sovereign rings. I stop this happening and shout to everyone there that from now on there will be no more taxing while I'm in the prison. The screws loved this, they were fighting to get me on their wing. Seems like one prison didn't want me and then another can't get enough of me. Things were going great until the screws noticed that all the top villains in the prison were following me around, they must have thought we were getting too organised so I'm moved out again.

Of all the places to send me, they send me a place called Haverigg, right up in Cumbria. I'm in there a few days when the screw comes and tells me there's a bench press contest going on in the prison gym. The idea was to see how many reps you could get out on the bench press. I think the weight was only 60 kilos or so, the guys had been training for about three months so they were up for it. One guy does about 30 reps, the other a little more. I went up and did about 77 reps and wins this trophy, which I still have today. They thought I must have been a pro lifter and were shouting it was a fix, that I was a ringer. They were devastated but they took it in good heart and it broke the day up a little. In the whole prison I was the only one to not wear the prison jeans, I wore tracksuit bottoms the whole time. I told them to fuck off, I'm not wearing jeans, my legs were too big for them.

I keep out of trouble in this jail and progress through the stages easy, I now have a nice little laundry job. The stage I was at was like a hotel – own room, use of the TV room and could stay up all night and that. I just wanted to do my time easy and not have to hit anyone, I didn't need any more time added onto my sentence. When I first had use of the gym I got some lad to hold the heavy punchbag for me, then I off-loaded some punches. The word got around how hard I could hit, so nobody bothered me and I was free to train on the weights. I always try to get on with people and have fun but there was this one guy, a boxer from Blackburn, he looked in good shape. Mind you, he was taking some gear and looked impressive. The guy was getting a little cheeky, I'm trying to ignore it and not get in trouble. We used to watch this programme every so often, part of the programme was these lads would stand by a pool and some girl would push them in leaving only one standing each week. Well we would take bets on who would be left standing. It got very competitive each week, even to the stage of us all betting Mars bars on the outcome. This boxer was sitting next to me watching the show when he asks me to move along the bench we were all sitting on. I move a little and he edges up more. I move a little more, then I realise the arsehole is stretched out on the bench taking the piss. We start to argue and the daft bastard jumps up at me, so I left hook him. Off they take the prick to the doctor, broken jaw and all.

In this prison, no matter what you do wrong, you're out, so they come to my cell and tell me I'm off to Walton Prison. I told them I wasn't going and they had to make me go. All the screws in the prison turn up to try and get me out; I shout for them to come and try and that I'm not leaving. Well, this one screw comes into my cell and, to give him his due, he explains that I'm going to get more jail if I resist, so off I go again, to Walton Prison this time. Anyway, I turn up at the prison and it's fucking massive. It looks like one of them old gothic-type buildings. It had over 400 screws and holds about 1,700 prisoners. Soon as I turned up, I knew I was going to have trouble there, I just knew it.

Now the screws are tidy with me, and I'm on reception, when this big lad comes in. He was about six foot six and about 17 to 18 stone, big lad but a bully with it. The screws were scared of him because he had taken a copper's eye out with a bottle, so he's doing a ten-stretch for that, but he's out each day back and forth to court for an armed robbery charge. The Scousers there were sick of him because he was getting kids to bring stuff in for him, they would spew the stuff back up and the lads had to clean the mess up. The guys wanted to do him six-handed but that wasn't my scene, so I went to the showers to sort it out. The screws knew this was going to happen and kept well away. He comes out of the shower, wraps a towel around himself and sees me waiting. I tell him he's a wanker and he comes at me. I smash my left into his face and a straight right into his belly. He falls to the floor and shits himself. I couldn't believe it, he was lying there in his own shit.

I said, "Look, you've shit yourself."

"I haven't," he says trying to get up.

I tell the screws that he had fallen in the shower. The lads in the prison played hell with him after that: they got some acorns and put them in a plastic bag and they would wave the bags at him and call him "Shitty". He wasn't long there before he got transferred. So much for him being the big top fighter.

One day all these oranges turned up for the prisoners and, with my mate Steve, we pinched them all. We spend ages crushing them down to make juice. The screw came in and we had cooked steaks and that for ourselves.

"Fucking hell," he said, "it's like bloody *Goodfellas* in here. What about all the prisoners?"

"Fuck them," I tell him. "We have fresh orange juice for a fortnight here."

Having done twelve months, I'm out on home leave. Now, I'm not supposed to be out drinking but you know how it is. I'm in this all-night rave and I'm really enjoying myself, dancing and having a good time. I'm talking to this big lad, an ex-amateur boxer who's had 70 or so fights, a very handy guy. He's got a flat nose and you can tell from a mile away he's a boxer. I've lost a bit of weight inside. I'm down to 18 stone but feeling okay. This flat nose tells me, "You won't be so good now Bri, now you've lost all that weight." It's my first night out so I laugh things off and carry on enjoying myself. I go back to my table and he's talking about fighting and that. "Look, let's not talk about fighting all the time, just enjoy yourself," I tell him. He looks at me and says, "Ah, you're all right, Big Fella." With that, the sneaky fucker smacks me in the face with a Pils bottle. Nearly took my eye out. I went mental and really laced him bad, fractured his skull and broke his jaw. He was in hospital for ten days; the police came and got me. Seems his missus pressed charges but they got dropped because of all the witnesses. A year later I saw him in a club. He said he was sorry so we shook hands and I left the place. No sooner had I left than he started bullying kids. Just don't know what's wrong with some people.

I get out of prison and I'm back up to 20-odd stone and feeling great. I'm out for a night and got my new suit on, just looking to have some fun in this club. All of a sudden this voice says, "Oi! who the fuck are you looking at?" I didn't even know he was talking to me. With that, he tries to head-butt me. I push the guy back and hook him right hard. Well, I hit him a little too hard because I smashed his cheekbone through his nose and into the top of his head. I put a few more into him and all the while my mate Kevin is holding my arm and he's bobbing up and down every time I throw a punch. He's got about twelve lads with him but when I offer them out they all fucked off. Now he goes back to his older brother who was a good boxer.

His brother asks him, "Who the fuck has done that?"

"Big Brian" he answered.

"Oh well, you must have deserved it," he told him. Fair play on the guy I hit, he explained later that he was off it and was in the wrong. The doctor had told him another inch and he would have died. Well, what the doctor told him scared me a bit. I wouldn't have liked that on my hands. It was only the other day that he argued with someone and got killed. He was stabbed about 20 times in the face.

I never, ever go out just to cause trouble, but you know how some people are. I remember one night this big, tall Army guy was chatting to me in a club. "I just come out of the Army, I was in the paratroopers," he tells me. I get him a drink and he informs me how good a boxer he was and that he was a tester for streetfighters like me. He's going on and on about how good he is and how he trains and all. I've got a few charges hanging over me so I want to keep out of trouble. I say to the guy, "Look, let's not talk about fighting all the time, let's have a drink and a good time."

My mate Steve goes and tells the guy, "Ease off or the Big Fella will kill you mate."

"He won't kill me, I'll fight him any time," he shouts out.

Okay then. So I give him a big right hand, then down he goes. The doormen run over and I let them know that it's okay and things are sorted. All the time, the big Army guy is shouting, "I'm sorry, I'm sorry."

Thing is, it don't really matter how big you are, it's how good or how much heart you have that counts. I'm watching some big fucking huge bodybuilder at the bar one night, he's got his top off and he's bumping into everyone. He was being a right pain in the arse, proper bully like. Well he bumps my smaller mate and I shout, "Eh mate, come on. Leave him alone." He tells me to fuck off. I step forward and smash my fist into his face. Down he goes, spark out on the floor. He was out for ages, the doormen struggling to lift the fucker. I must admit he looked good on the floor with all his muscles and his abs and that.

Just because a guy is full of muscle it don't mean he's a good fighter, it means nothing. Once this big bodybuilder was telling people he wanted to fight me. He was one of two brothers both loaded with muscle. I approached him and he even tried to pretend he was someone else. I smash him one and launch all 18 stone of him against the bar. He staggers back off the bar and runs like fuck through the club, knocking everyone over. I catch him and throw him into the corner. He lifts his hands up to cover his face so I smash fuck into his body. While my mates try to talk me out of it the guy runs like Linford Christie out of the club. Of course he tells everybody I tried to stab him and all that shite.

I hate people who use knives. It's just not on, is it? I get a phone call once from some guy who said he had work for me. I go to the guy's house and I'm invited in but it's a set-up, there's about twelve guys with guns, knives, you name it. One puts a gun to my head. I hit the gun away and smack him. Another comes from behind and smashes my head with a baseball bat. They are hitting me with bats, pokers, hammers and all sorts but I won't go down, I just keep fighting back. Out of the kitchen comes a boxer whose jaw I had broke ten days earlier. Seems I put an end to his boxing career. He's carrying a pot-type bread bin, of all things. Now I had just gone over with holes in my head, hammer blows to my legs and stab wounds everywhere. He starts to smash my ribs in with this pot thing. They weren't just going to do me over, these guys wanted me dead. I get one huge blow to the top of my head and the blood is shooting out and hitting the ceiling, I have to hold my hand on it to stop the blood. One big lad smacks me with this big sock full of marbles, it wraps around my head and I thought it was going to pop my eye out. I didn't get knocked out but I did think I was going to die. I was shouting when they left that I would fight them all when I got out.

I'm trying to walk but my legs are full of holes and I'm losing too much blood. The guy next door gets me in his car and drives me to the hospital. Thing is, he takes me to the wrong hospital – he takes me to the maternity hospital, which was no fucking good to me. Well, I get there in the end and tell the doctor that I fell over. They give me over 100 stitches. Now the police were there and I'm thinking they are there for my protection but they go and fucking nick me. Seems they wanted me for a fight I had in a club a few weeks before. They had been told that I went to the club with shotguns and all sorts. I'm in court and I got so many holes in me and I'm in so much pain that I nearly pass out in the dock. Well, I get off with that and some people were charged with the set-up on me. I can't see someone go to jail over me so I explain that it wasn't them, so nobody was charged. From what I gather I was on the news with the attack and in all the papers. The boxer and me have shook hands and his mates said I must have been an alien because I just wouldn't give in, said I wasn't natural.

[Another time] I'd been out all night, and it's the next day in this pub. I'm with my mate Dennis when the guy who killed Lee Duffy walks in. I'm starting to think I've been set up, with me being Lee's mate and all, but he starts to fight with a smaller lad. The other guy's a good ex-pro boxer but he's just too small. The boxer goes down and the other guy is hitting him with a stool. I'm thinking he's going to murder him so I try to stop the fight. With that, he grabs my heavy gold chain and tries to pull me in close. I head-butt him three times and drop him to the floor. At this time of my life I was 22 stone and doing ten-minute rounds on the bag and 20-minute circuits each day so I was fit and big. He gets up and runs at me. I smash him with two body shots and a left hook and down he goes between these two parked cars. I'm shouting to him when he gets up that I'd fight him and his mate together. His mates, two big guys, ran off down the road and left him. Well to give him his due he admitted to friends that I was just to good for him.

I've lots of respect for people who box or train in martial arts. They are sometimes very committed people. I admire their dedication. But one karate guy came one night to try me out, he was a big lad and was a fourth or fifth dan. He came at me throwing all these kicks and punches so I just stuck a couple into him and over he goes, fast asleep. Well, I know I shouldn't have but I took off the guy's shoes and socks and threw them up on a pub roof. When the fucker woke up he had to walk home without them.

Some guy I had previously hit jumped out at me one night as I left a club. I just catch him with a straight right hand and down he goes. As I threw the right hand I somehow moved awkward on my knee and dislocated it. I had to push the whole knee over to get it back in. I jump on the guy and stick some more into him when he shouts, "I've had enough." I though, *thank fuck for that*. The pain in my knee was killing me. When I was fighting, I had pushed one of the doormen there. A few weeks later I went up and said I was sorry to him. I had just bought him a drink and that when he comes up to me and tells me he wants to see me outside. I'm thinking he wants to shake my hand and accept my apologies. He tells me he wants to have a go. I drop my glass and right-hand him into the doorway. I unload some more, then I bite his nose off. His mates come and I threaten them but they don't want to know, they close the doors and go back in.

I got sent down for two-and-a-half years for, believe it or not, dangerous driving. I was driving my Cosworth when the police are on the lookout for me. They thought I had been involved in a shooting. I'm in this 40-minute chase and I'm driving like a rally driver and they can't catch me. The only worry I had was if I run out of petrol. They blocked my car off at all exits so I handbrake my car and slip through two of the cop cars. The copper behind me tries to do the same thing and smashes his bloody car up. I went to the station and admitted my guilt but I told them there was no way I was going to be stopped by armed police – they may have shot me. I was remanded in prison and from what I gather the police had told the screws that I was a very bad lad and should be down the block. This stopped me getting an easy jail so I ended up in Durham Prison, which is a "Cat C" prison.

They remanded me first for six weeks because the bloody judge was on holiday. I was supposed to get a video to watch every three days, which the Home Office entitled me to because I was a remand prisoner. There were these two guys in the gym mouthing off so I battered the pair of them. They went and stole two knives from the kitchen to stab me with. Well, they found the knives and I got the blame so they stopped my videos. I'm shouting like fuck for my video when more and more screws turn up.

I'm shouting to the screws, "Come on then you wankers, if you want to have a go, come on then."

"Look Bri, we don't want any trouble," one of them tells me, and off they go, and I'm locked up again. This was on a Saturday.

Next morning, fucking loads of them turn up with all the riot gear on. I'm up for it so I'm yelling, "Come on, I'll fight the fucking lot of you!" There was this big lad in the front and I thought, *one move from these pricks and he's the first.* I tell him that I am going to punch my fist straight through his facemask and bust him open first. After a while I decide to come out and there's every screw in the place in pairs all the way down to the block. I walk on past them all and enter the block. It was fucking tiny in there, I couldn't even stretch out my arms. The screws demand my shoes so I threw the fuckers at them.

I'm sitting in this tiny fucking cell with compressed cardboard table and chair and I'm devastated, no fucking video and I'm down the block. Now I've always been a well-liked guy and get on with most people. Turns out 500 prisoners do a sit-down protest out in the yard. They said they wouldn't come in unless I was out of the block. They sat out for two days. I could hear all the screws they had recruited from all the other prisons marching past the block dressed like Star Wars stormtroopers. It was hard to believe

I was the cause of it all and how so many people liked me and stood up for me. Eleven of them got onto the gym roof and smashed up the gym. This went on for two to three days. I felt sorry for some of them who got an extra two years for it and will never forget them for it.

I would have liked it if I had never had to fight and would be happy if I never fight again. I really enjoy my training and have a nice home and a good family around me. I just want to get on with people and I never ever hold a grudge.

HENRY FRANCIS

Newark, Nottinghamshire

Born in 1960, Henry Francis is said to be the most dangerous traveller around. Equally deadly with his fists and his head, he has been fighting and beating rivals since the age of 15. He has survived shootings and stabbings and was nicknamed "the Outlaw" by former Gypsy King Bartley Gorman. Is Henry the new King of the Gypsies?

MY FAMILY ARE from Newcastle-upon-Tyne, though for most of my life I have lived at Newark in Nottinghamshire. My dad met my mam in Yorkshire and they stopped down there ever since. My mam was a Middleton and Higginbotham. My grandad, Henry Francis, was a fighter and so were my mam's people. I had a great-uncle called old Tommy Higginbotham and he was a fighter. In war-time he cut his wrist not to fight in the war [many gypsies faked injuries to escape war-time service – JD]. I had three brothers but one of them, Michael, was killed recently in a road accident.

I have just always been able to fight. It's natural in me. I was a young lad when I had my first fight, against Johnny Cash at Worksop. The Cashes are a big name among fighting men in Ireland. I was 15 and he was 18. We had a good fight and I won.

I licked Bob Gaskin [a well-known gypsy fighter from Yorkshire] when I was 17 or 18. I was in a nightclub and his brother Tiny picked on me and picked a fight. I didn't want to fight him but gave him a bad hiding and it caused bad blood. Then I had a fight with Henry and Kevin Gaskin. They came one night with all these bottles and stuff. I put them both in hospital

My dad had a site at Dinnington near Sheffield and someone shot up my dad's caravan. Then a fellow called Young Billy Gaskin and Bob Gaskin had hit my sister. Bob Gaskin went to Newark to fight me. At the time, I couldn't get as many people together as I could get now, whereas there was loads of them. Anyway, as I was going to fight Bob I got stopped by the police. They turned us back around. But we met him afterwards in a scrapyard in Rotherham. The Gaskins used to weigh their scrap in at one yard and we weighed ours in at another. We were passing this yard and saw Gaskin's motor outside. I went into the yard and we had a fight and I hammered him.

I was training to go professional as a boxer at the time and was about to put my application in for a licence on the day that Bob Gaskin sent down from Rotherham Infirmary a warrant for my arrest. The police arrested me and I never did get to apply for my boxing licence. But nothing came of it with the police; I wasn't convicted or anything. I also got locked up over Joe-Boy Gaskin. His wife told a lot of lies about me because she thought Joe-Boy was in danger. And I beat Hardy Gaskin and he is the biggest of them all. I went through all of them.

I was fighting men when I was a boy. I had a good fight when I was 19: Big Ralph Pilkington, at Dinnington. He is not a gypsy but a fighting man. He could lift a car shell onto the back of a truck. He had never lost a fight in his life and I took his reputation off him. But we have always been friends since.

I also had a fight with a good friend of mine at Dinnington. We used to do a lot of training together, jog to the boxing club every night, six miles a night, and train every day. We were the best of friends. One night he had fallen out with another man and was talking about setting fire to his caravan. I said, "You mustn't do that," So he challenged *me* to a fight! My dad was there and he made me look small in front of my dad.

I fought him and gave him a very bad beating. He was in bed for a week. A week after he came out of bed, he knocked on my door, still with a bad face on him. I looked through the window and thought he had come to fight me again. He said, "Henry, I'm very sorry," and shook my hand. We went for a drink and went in two pubs and they wouldn't serve us because he looked so rough, still with the two bad eyes. Then we got drinking and have been the best of friends since.

Me and Simon Docherty [a very influential Irish traveller and former knuckle fighter who runs campsites in England – JD] were the best of friends. Simon was like the Don King of the travellers. He would arrange all the fights. Simon is like myself: he could fall out with somebody but would always make up with them. He was a rough man when he was younger. He took me to London for the first time. I would look after him, a bit like a minder. One day we went in a pub and there were some huge Irishmen in there. One of them was the biggest man I have ever seen. I'm about five foot eight and my best fighting weight was 13 stone, though I'm nearer 16 now.

And Simon, right in front of them, said, "This is Henry Francis from Yorkshire and I'm going to get him a fight for £10,000."

So when Simon went to the toilet, I followed him. "I want a word with you," I said. "What are you trying to do, get me killed?"

He said, "Don't worry about it, they are no problem to you."

I said, "Simey, whatever you do, leave it."

These guys were a bit *too* big but, whatever Simey said, they seemed to be alright with me. We had a drink for a couple of days.

Then we had a fallout because I thought Simey was going to get me in a bit of bother. I didn't know it at the time but the Gaskins caused the trouble for me with Simey. Tiny Gaskin told Simey a lot of lies about me. Anyway I rowed with him one day; that was my fault. And I said, "Fetch any man to me, Simey. I don't care who it is, Ireland or anywhere."

And he fetched a man from Ireland called Ernie McGinley. At about 4am one morning – I hadn't long been back from having a drink and was in the trailer asleep – I heard a knock on the door. Old Simey had come with McGinley and all his cousins, Collinses and so on. McGinley was about 26 and was boxing in the ring at the time. I was 18. Simey gave him £3,500 and a horse to fight me.

He said, "I'm Ernie McGinley, I'm Golden Gloves of Ireland and I want to fight. I have heard a lot about you."

I said. "There's no problem. There's enough of you, but I'll fight you."

McGinley hit me and, as he shook my head, I went straight into him. He could spar up and he was solid. I hit him a good few times and he was like a trunk. He was getting stronger all the time. He fought southpaw against me and he was awkward. Simon Docherty was referee and split us up three times, so I couldn't use the nut – and everybody knows me by my head. They call me the best headbutter in Britain. My mam came out screaming for us to stop. We fought for about 15 minutes. It was a good fight. He boxed well and was fighting southpaw with me. My mam did a lot of screaming and so I gave best to the fight. That was the only time I ever gave best. I was 18 at the time but I never had a mark on me.

McGinley said to me, "This is the first time I have been on British soil. Now I have fought you I want to fight Dan Rooney. The next man is going to be Rooney and then I'm going to build the biggest house in Ireland." McGinley did fight Rooney but it was years later. It was Simey who got them to fight. These days they'd both be in their early fifties. A man called Barney McGinley now referees all the fights and takes ten per cent of the money. They often fight wearing handwraps over there but they wouldn't be allowed in a bareknuckle fight in this country.

The best man I fought was of Polish descent, called Richard Freddie Hancock. He is one of the roughest men in Sheffield and Rotherham. We fought twice. The Polishman was 28 and I was 20. He wouldn't fight me in a car park but always in a toilet, and for five or six minutes he would hit me hard but his wind would go. I beat him but I came off worse. He broke my cheekbone and did some damage to my eye.

There was a lot of fighting men in Newark when I went there. I quietened them all down. The local police at Newark are red hot on me. All the doormen are frightened of me. I have battered a few of them. When I go in a nightclub in Newark you always see a paramedic ambulance outside.

I have been shot twice. My relations, one night we had a fallout and they got frightened of me and the next night five of them came to Newark. I came back from the pub and recognised two of my relations. I was surprised at them coming to fight me but they hadn't, they had come to kill me. One pulled a shotgun out. I said, "Right, if you have got it, use it." He shot me in the shoulder with lead shot. He was aiming for my face but I moved my head out of the way and it shot my shoulder straight off and half of my neck.

The blast was like a burning fire. Then I ran and they shot me in the back. I was only about 24 and just married. I was in hospital but signed myself out. Then I got arrested for assault on somebody, GBH. But they never pinned it on me; all the charges were dropped. I have got 38 pellets in my neck and shoulder and every so often they dig one out.

I also got stabbed by a black man once. That was about four years ago at Nottingham. I was in a black man's club and, as you do, we all took chances and didn't realise we were in big danger. We had to fight our way out. This man whipped out a knife and tried to get me. He stabbed me under the armpit and I have a big scar there; he nearly chopped my arm off. I managed to hit him with my head and get away. We all got out of the club.

I once had a fight with an Irish lad called Par Doran. He took me on the car park. I was all on my own and he was with a gang. He was a lot bigger than me and I was young at the time. I connected a couple of times and knocked him out. All the women took off their high heels and hit me all over the head. That was at Sheffield. They beat me off him.

I fought Jimmy Stockin [a London gypsy fighter who wrote the book *On The Cobbles*] over a game of pitch and toss at the country and western fair at Peterborough. I had been drinking with my brothers-in-law and they are quiet fellows. It was head-and-tails and some men were turning the coins over unfairly. There was a young lad there of 14 and they were bullying him and we weren't happy about it, but this Jimmy Stockin said, "Don't pick on the best because the best won't mess." He had had a lot of fights. The brother-in-law took a swing and Stockin slapped him and then went to slap me. He didn't know who I was until I hit him. But other people there, they knew I would act.

Boxer Tom [another renowned gypsy fighter of the Seventies] said, "Make a ring," and he was the referee. And when I hit Stockin with the first shot, I broke the bone on my left hand, the metacarpal. It was very painful the next morning but I kept hitting him with my left and with my right and did give him a few shots with my head. There was a lot of London men and only three of us and they were all shouting, "Go on Jimmy." The only person shouting for me was an Irish girl, Patrick Docherty's daughter Belsie. She was shouting, "Go on Henry." She was the bravest there because she had the guts to shout up, and I have admired the woman ever since. I hit like Mike Tyson would and I split him. He looked like he had been set about with a pickaxe. I closed his two eyes and broke his cheekbones. It lasted five minutes.

Later Boxer Tom came up to me and said, "Henry, I have known you all my life. He wants to fight you in the morning."

I said, "Tom, he's in no condition to fight me in the morning." But I didn't tell anyone I had a broken hand.

Anyway, the next morning his brother Wally was going to come and fight me. Well, when you are coursing you don't put two dogs on one hare, do you? That night I went back to the caravans and my wife said, "Look, there is a lot of London people here and there is only us. There are too many of them." And it wasn't my woods; not my territory. So I pulled away about 4am because my wife was very worried that we were outnumbered and that there was a crew coming from London with Wally to fight me. I went to Burton Hospital. My hand was broken and had poison growing in it out of his teeth. It took about a year to get right.

Five weeks later was Doncaster Races. I didn't know Jimmy Stockin was going to the races but I wasn't planning to go anyway and also my wife didn't want me to go because I used to gamble a lot and have a good time. Anyway, at the races apparently a man told everyone he had a gun to shoot me. A year after was the country and western at Peterborough again and Stockin was telling my mates what he would do. Someone went on the mic and called me a few names and told the lads he was going to shoot me. He was carrying a twelve-bore sawn-off shotgun under his coat.

There two best men down London way were said to be Stockin and Johnny Love. They had a very long fight against each other.

Well, on Appleby Fair, Henry Arab, who they call "the Dentist" because he has knocked out that many teeth, knocked Love spark out. Johnny Love was always wary of me because he was beat by the Dentist and he knew me and him had had quarrels. Me and Henry Arab were going to have two fights that have been stopped before they started. Old Billy Welch stopped one. Since then we are the best of friends and have great respect for each other. Them that don't respect me are just bad losers. Love owed a relation of mine some money once for a debt and I went to collect it off him in Kentland; that is what they didn't like me for. He was very wary of me.

I also beat Dinny Kelly and Booty Kelly together once at Chesterfield at a funeral. I broke Booty's hand and his nose and Dinny's jaw. Then Booty said, "Will you do us a favour? Will you take us to the hospital?" I took them to Doncaster Royal in the morning in a Morris Marina van. Dinny said, "Look at the state of us. What can we tell our mam? We will have to say we bumped into a lot of football fans and they did this to us." And we laughed about it and were friends.

I have fought Booty Kelly five times and beat him every time. Booty is very short but thickset and muscular and thinks he is a killer. He caused the trouble between me and Bartley Gorman [Henry fought Bartley, the renowned King of the Gypsies, in a pub car park in Nottinghamshire in 1995 after a row at a funeral. The short, brutal fight was broken up by police. Bartley was then 50 and Henry was 33. They never fought again – JD]. I looked up to Bartley and I thought then that I would get Booty if it took me ten years. Then, three weeks after my brother died in a car crash, Booty came to my caravan. It was Christmas Day. I had just come back from the pub and was lying with my little girl in the trailer and was so upset about my brother Michael.

He knocked on the door and said, "Now then, cousin. You are supposed to be after me, are you?" I didn't recognise him because I hadn't seen him since he caused the fight with Bartley. But like

you give corn to chickens, there he was at my door. He had the
bottle to fight me because he'd had a few drinks. We fought right
there in my yard. I absolutely splattered him. If it wasn't for my
sister and wife and son I probably would have killed him.

I have had hundreds of fights. I've fought loads of Welshmen,
including a few Prices. I've also knocked out loads at Cambridge
fair; I can't even remember their names. I'm the only modern
fighter that has been to many fairs: the others don't go because of
the danger. Everywhere I go, I get it done. I'm a one-man band; I
go on my own. I'm known as the Dynamite Kid. I'll fight anybody.

I even had a fight in an aeroplane coming back from South
Africa. The man was six foot five and 30 years old and supposed
to be a killer. He was saying who was no good as a fighter: this
man and this man were "no good". Everybody was no good
except him and his dad. I said, "Stop talking about fighting. The
best thing to do when the aeroplane goes down here is you and me
have a fight. You have got £5,000 on you and I can match it." I
threw an apple at him on the plane (laughs). I also had fights in
Germany while I was working over there.

Terry Welch is a man of six foot four from Newark. He has
been a pal of mine since we were kids. He is about 33 and 16
stone, and trains himself. I was at a funeral only a month ago,
Danny Fisher's funeral at Newark. I had a lot of drink there and
people could see I was very drunk. I fell asleep twice.

Terry's glass was empty. He said, "Whose turn is it?"

I said, "It must be your turn, collier.' Collier means *gorgi*,
someone who isn't a gypsy. I was only having a bit of fun but he
thought he could take me because I was drunk.

He said, "Get outside, you have got me to fight."

I said, "Look Terry, I'm very drunk, I can't stand up. Come in
the morning and bring who you want and I will fight you."

He insisted. I took my coat off and went outside. I fell down
before I went out, but that is how I am. He hit me four or five
times and sobered me up. I went down and got back up. I said,

"You can't knock me out." Then I got to it. I broke his nose and three of his ribs, We fought for seven or eight minutes and his knees were going. His chin was stuck up in the air and I hit it and he spun around and went down hard on the floor and broke his leg. The bone came out of his leg. There was a referee called "The Monkey Billy" and I hit him for being a monkey and broke his nose as well.

Even more recently, my son was fighting a lad in Derby, at the auctions. He is only 14 and was fighting a 16-year-old. I went to the auction, just me and my lad, and there were ten of them, half-bred Gaskins. My lad flogged his lad. Then there was shouting and I cracked this other one. He grabbed me and bit a piece out of my ear and I knocked him out. It took ten men to pull me off him. He said, "Give me a month to get right and I'll fight you." He rang and rang, he must have thought I wasn't going to turn up. "Come with plenty of men because I've got plenty," he said.

It was arranged for Derby again. When we got there, we had 200 men. There was that many people that there was three miles of traffic with me. I didn't realise I had that many friends. And he never came – he chickened out. He rang and said he wasn't coming. He is a half-bred gypsy whose name is not worthy to be mentioned in this book.

Good fighters wouldn't fall out with me because they would rather be my friend. They respect me and I respect them. We would sooner do each other a good turn. I'm very good friends with Ivan and Joe Botton, who are top men. I used to look up to Bartley Gorman and was sad when he died recently. I didn't go to his funeral because I knew there would be certain people there and I would end up fighting, and I didn't want to show disrespect at his funeral. But I want to dedicate this to Bartley.

Fighting is in my blood: God's gift. Everybody has one. I am naturally fit. I can fight all day. I don't hardly train now; I don't need to. When them get tired (fists) I switch to the centre-forward (head). I get second wind as well. Boxing and streetfighting are two different things. A boxer can't fight a streetfighter. I was better out of the ring than in. When I fought people it would sometimes be "all-in" and sometimes not. If it's all-in, you let the rules blow in the wind. When I fought them you never seemed to hear of them again. I quieten them down.

One man I respected as a fighting man got killed at Newcastle: Viv Graham. I knew him for years. He could fight, he could. He was about my match and had the same way of fighting. He was the best man around that part of the country. The other was Lee Duffy and them two was going to fight but it never came off.

But I'm 40 years old now and want to settle down and enjoy my life. I want to keep my title. There are people who say I'm the King of the Gypsies now. They say about me, "He's not to be underestimated."

STEVE "PIGEON" LOTE
Walsall

One of the Midlands' best-known streetfighters, Steve has used his talents on the doors of the most dangerous clubs. A cold, calculating fighter with natural physical strength, he's the last person you would want to come looking for you. It's better to be turned away from the door by Steve than turned over by him. A frightening fact about Steve is that he has never been tested to his limits.

ORIGINALLY I'M FROM Essex and moved down to the Midlands when I was about seven or eight. My mum was like a guardian angel to me as a kid. She kept me out of trouble and drummed it into me to be fair and not a bully. Around here I've always been known by the name "Pigeon". It's a nickname I've had since I was a young lad. I had pigeons as a kid and when I was in school I would sit in class and keep checking the window to see if the birds had come home. I could see my house from the school so I'd sit there on pins waiting for them to return. When they did, I'd look at the teacher and they would let me go home to let the birds into the bird coop and that. I was a very nervous child, a little quiet and could be intimidated by others. I got to a stage where I had to stand up for myself and start fighting back. I think most kids have to confront the same problems and have to make a stand somewhere.

I started to get a name for myself as a fighter. It's not something I wanted to be, I just did what I did to survive and get through life. I think it may be because of my nature that I became known for fighting. I always put 100 per cent into things, always want to prove myself and win. I started bodybuilding and could see guys in the gym who were real big guys. I found that a challenge and trained hard until I became the intermediate Midlands champion. The same with fighting, I just couldn't take second prize, had to win and be better than my opponent. I like a challenge and that's why I used to love working the doors. I had this reputation as a fighter on the doors. I was fighting all the time so I thought I'd better start training to fight, so I started tae kwon do, which kept me fit and fast.

I have had more than my fair share of violence on the door. I've knocked out over 50 guys who have come at me, most with a right hook. I keep my hands low and when they come up to me I make eye contact and throw the right hook. All the time they are making eye contact they can't see my hand come up. I have sometimes been over 20 stone when I was training hard, it does help being that big because they see the size on you and they mostly back down straight away.

I remember once I was working in Reynolds bar and we had about 25 Pakistani guys attack these three white guys. They were giving these three guys a right hiding so I jumped in to stop the fight. In the process I knock out a few of the Pakistani lads. A while later the police turn up and all they want to know was who knocked out the Pakistani lads, they wanted to arrest someone for it. Well nothing happened but I still can't figure out why they didn't arrest some of the larger gang who caused it all. I myself have never been racist but the Pakistanis said they had been beaten up in a racist attack. I would have done the same thing if the odds were the other way around.

You can't work the doors if you can't fight, it's as simple as that. Sometimes when someone wants to fight, you have to put them away. They don't always stay down with one punch, you have to be prepared to go full out on some people. I was watching the doormen of a club I was running on a CCTV monitor, and there was this stocky, well-built guy on the front door playing up. He approaches one of the doormen to fight him. The doorman puts the guy down with a straight right hand but the guy gets up and comes forward. The doorman loses his arse and backs away. Now I ran out and confronted the guy, who turns his attentions to me. With that I bang him one, overpower him and do him over well. As I return to the club all the punters are clapping and cheering me. It seems this guy was a well-known bully and everyone hated him. It was good to know that the punters supported me because it's not always that way.

Over the years I've sorted things out for people in return for cash; after all, I have to live as well. A mate and myself travelled to Rotterdam to sort out this scumbag for a few grand, well for the money that I was offered I would have cut his fingers off. We were led to believe the guy was a lowlife who had caused some big problems. When we got there, we found that the guy had ripped someone off for a few million. Now with someone who has that kind of cash, you know they are going to have some good back-up and some big lads with them. Well, we still want to go ahead with the job but find that the guy who was going to identify him for us was on holiday in Spain. Well, we came for the money and they still paid us for our troubles, which was a good result. Money can get you out of a lot of trouble. You must remember if someone has enough money they can always pay to get their problems fixed. I don't just take any job on. I have to believe that the people I work for are in the right.

When I work the doors I need to work with other doormen who need the money, not guys who just stay back and don't help out. When I take on a club I always take on the responsibility of hiring and firing. If a doorman's out of order then he's history, simple as that. You may also find other doormen out having a drink on their nights off turning up giving it the old "yeah, I'm a head doorman" routine. This involves them telling everyone within earshot just how hard they are, basically boring them all to death. This big doorman from Wolverhampton did this one night and before he could take a punch I belted him out. He decides to take me on with the police. A while later the police drop the charges but it was against this guy's wishes, he wanted to take it all the way. One night I go around to a club that he was at and there he was with two other big doormen. I confront him, then I knock him clean out and he falls backwards, fracturing the back of his head as he fell. The guys with him just froze and let me get on with it. Normally I wouldn't hit someone like him because I had already beat him, but he was the type who made other doormen look bad, so he had to have it.

This big Irish guy turns up one night with a woman who had previously been banned. The guy had the rep of being one of Ireland's hardest men but things like that don't bother me, I just don't care who they are, if I say they don't come in then they don't come in. He starts to perform on the front door and I don't like to make eye contact with them, because if I think they are directing their anger towards me, then I will give it to them. Well, he starts swearing and moves away from the club, still shouting. About half an hour later this big Range Rover reverses up to the club. Now, I knew that the guy had pitch-forked someone a while ago, so I couldn't take him lightly. The gaffer of the club goes out to him to see what his problem was. The guy's out of the Range Rover and he comes at the gaffer with a pickaxe handle. The gaffer jumps back into the club, locking the doors so that I can't get at the guy, who has now decided to smash the club windows instead. I run through the other doors to the club and straight at him. I throw my radio at him, which distracts him long enough for me to put him down. I get on top of him and start to lay into him, smashing lumps into him. The punters are all out cheering me on because they had seen it all. A police car turns up but don't spot us, so I carry on doing the guy. The police drive away and I get up and look down and the guy lying on the pavement all smashed up. He was supposed to be this big Irish hard nut but he didn't look so hard lying at my feet. I had to make sure I did a good job on him, otherwise if I had backed down then everyone would think they could bring a weapon to me and I'd bottle it. If they come to fight me then fight they will, no weapons are going to put me off, they either win or lose. I'm not going to back down.

Some punters will put a glass in you straight away, without even thinking about it, it don't bother them who you are or if you have family and kids. They have no remorse at all. If there's one thing that gets under my skin, it's glassers, I have no time for them whatsoever. I've seen it done so many times and the damage a glass can do is horrendous. A lad got glassed in a club I was running the door at. I search for the lad who had done it and find him. I don't waste time, and drag him outside, all the time beating the shit out of him. My mate is also hitting him so I decide to leave it there because he has had enough. With that, all the other doormen start to kick lumps out of him, they are all on him kicking and punching the guy. I have to pull them all off him before they kill him, I just couldn't let them carry on. It's funny that I felt it was unfair for all the guys to batter him but he himself thought it was fair to use a glass on some poor victim. It's a pity he didn't possess a little of the morals that I hold.

Gangs can cause a lot of trouble when they start to fight. It can be a bit scary for some people but I find I just take out the ringleaders and the rest don't want to know. I was stopping one gang fight one night and this geezer sprays something at my face. I hold my coat in front of me so he can't get to my eyes with this pepper spray or whatever the stuff was. I grab the guy and knock him out and start to beat the fuck out of him. At one stage I smash him against the side of one of the cars that were parked up. We manage to stop the fighting and chase the troublemakers away from the club. Later on, one of the other doormen starts to moan that someone has dented the hell out of the side of his car. I didn't know what to say to him and he put it down to some of the gang that were outside. To this day I still haven't told him that it was me that caused the damage. Maybe I will tell him one day.

One place I worked at was sort of two clubs separated by a passageway. These two big stocky guys enter one night and I could sense they were trouble. These two kick off in the passage and start fighting. The other doormen don't seem to notice this so I run up. I smack the first one and before I could do anything else someone sets off a CS gas canister. I nearly choke to death in there, it was mental. I couldn't breath or see anything. I spot the guy I had hit, bang him one again, then I get out until all the smoke clears. The following week a dead pigeon was left on the front door to scare me, as if that was going to frighten me. Some of these guys have watched too many gangster films.

I've worked over 20 years on the doors and never had any comebacks, I feel that I have always done things the right way and handled things fair. There have only been four times that I can remember getting hit; I guess there has been someone above looking after me. I speak quiet and always respect others, demanding respect for myself along the way. I have never really lost my temper to it's fullest and feel there's a couple of more gears I could move up to if needed. I've taken a while off the doors to start a family with my second wife and to just get some time to ourselves. I may start running doors again in the near future but after 20 years I think I may have a rest for a while.

TYERONE HOUSTON
London and Luton

An awesome streetfighting giant who has punched and kicked his way through some of the country's hardest, most respected fighters. On the way to becoming a professional Thai boxing instructor, Tyrone completely destroyed several bareknuckle champions in all-in battles. Never one to brag about his achievements, he takes each fight in his stride, considering it "just another day at the office".

I WAS BORN in Hackney, east London, and moved to Luton as a young boy of about five years old. I've got a brother and two sisters, in fact, I have family all over the world, from London to America. From as far back as I can remember I have always been training, some sort of physical exercise. My father used to box in the West Indies, his brothers were wrestlers or played American football. They were all big lads. My father and myself must be the lightest weight of the lot of them, I'm only 16 stone compared to some of them who are well over 18 stone. My father had fought bareknuckle fights and did boxing training down at Bethnal Green but with having a family and that, he gave it all up.

My father brought me up to be independent, stand up for myself. I was always a strong child, mentally and physically. I can remember as a child fighting with some other kid in a sandpit and being too strong for him. I was sort of a hyperactive kid, which sometimes got me into trouble. All the games I would love to play were fighting or wrestling games. I guess I got that interest from my father. To calm me down my father would take me on runs first thing in the morning, from the age of six upwards. He always stressed that I must look after my body, stay in a good physical condition. He would say, "If you treat your body right, then it will look after you in years to come."

I started boxing from the age of nine at the Luton Old Boys' Club, which was an Irish club. First day that I walked in there, I was scared stiff. My father took me in and introduced me to a guy called Pat O'Kaye, who was the trainer there. I looked around this big hall with all these boxers skipping, the class hadn't started yet and they were all just warming up. There were fighters of all ages in there, from ten-year-olds right up to 40-year-old men, all mixing in together. Even now, when I walk into a gym I immediately recall that first day, with that leather, sawdust and sweat smell in the air. In every gym there's always someone who helps the trainers, in this gym it was an ex-fighter called Horace. He took me to one side and showed me how to skip, shadow box and things like how to throw my weight correctly when I punch. I'd always had a good punch for a lad but he took the time to improve it. I started going to the gym three nights a week. I think the reason for this was just to get me out of my mother's hair for a while, just to give her a break.

After about three months they started me sparring. I was nervous as hell going into that ring; the adrenalin would start pumping and I'd start to shake. After I'd taken a few shots I'd calm down and start to enjoy it; I was scared until I got hit, then I knew I had nothing to fear. I did alright as a boxer over the next few years, fighting and doing well in the ABA Championships and all. I started to get a little bored with boxing. I was bigger and physically more gifted than some of the kids I was facing, and felt I needed another challenge. I felt I was training harder than the other kids and my confidence had been built right up. I started going around other clubs, from karate to ju-jitsu, looking for something else.

I was always one of the hardest in school. I think it was because I was one of the biggest; it was me that they all expected to fight. If someone wanted to fight then they would try to take me on to look good, but I would always take them on and beat them. My father worked hard and we were all quite well off compared to most families. At school my first real experience of fighting came when some kids from a council estate, kids my mother would call "rough kids", wanted money off me. A few of them chased me through the school corridors. I ran at first but the one in front, Jason, was a good sprinter and he caught me as I was trying to get through some doors. My first reaction was to turn around and smack him one, which I did. I dropped him and when he got up I was shouting to him to have a go. I could see he was still in shock as his mates ran up to us, but he just shook my hand and we all became good friends. Now I was bothering with kids who loved to scrap, and I became like-minded.

I started going to this wing chun kung fu class just to see what the crack was. I must have sat there each training night for about three weeks, just watching them all train. I noticed that the physical training was very hard, with them conditioning their bodies to take blows. This appealed to me and before long I was joining in the class. I found that the boxing that I had learnt didn't help me at all, they had this close-in style and would stop my punches before I had time to move my hands. They were so fast that I just couldn't work out how they could get me down on the floor, they were blocking my punches and using my body weight against me. I started to learn the techniques that they used and progressed up the ranks. There were guys from all types of styles coming to the old scout hut that we trained in just to get some sparring with us.

In Luton at that time we had a lot of different cultures in the same area: there were blacks, Asians, Irish, English, you name it. Now my mate Jason had a fight with this Asian guy who was a supposed to be the hardest kid around for his age. Well, Jason gave him a right beating. They later arranged a rematch for Friday after school. Outside the school on Friday afternoon there was eight of us in all waiting for this Asian guy and his mates to turn up. He turns up with ten of his mates, ready to fight, but around the corner came about 20 to 30 Asian guys to fight us. Now these weren't kids, they were a lot older than us. They were grown men and guys who had left the school about five years earlier, most of them, carrying sticks and weapons. We stood our ground and fought with them. There were so many that I would knock one down and go straight onto the next guy, and get stuck into him. This was the first real time that I could test my boxing and wing chun in a real fight situation.

This one man ran at me with this large piece of wood. I stopped the wood with my left hand, punched him with my right hand, turned him around and did a stamping kick to the side of his leg. I can remember him screaming at the time but was too busy fighting the next guy to check on him. The police came and we ran off before they caught up with us. Some of the older Asian guys got arrested but we were alright. On the way home we all started talking about the fight. Of course, I then found out that the guy with the wood was screaming because I had broke his leg. One of my mates had seen me hit him and saw the guy's leg facing the other way, when he was on the floor screaming in pain. Afterwards I was angry that we had been so stupid to have been set up as we had been. Now the one thing that I felt good about was that I used the techniques I had learned, and they had worked for me.

Along with the wing chun, I started going to tang soo do and became a national champion in it. One day this guy they called Master Ket came to the gym and said he was opening a Thai boxing club up and wanted to test people to see if they were good enough to train under him. He was from Bangkok and owned a Thai restaurant and was going around all the gyms basically poaching people for his club. I started to spar with Master Ket who was only a little guy and didn't look a threat. He was so agile that I couldn't land a good shot on him, and if I did hit him he would simply roll off it. He just kicked my arse and everyone else's in the club as well, he was so fast and well conditioned, just unstoppable.

I started to go to Master Ket's Thai boxing class. There were 30 of us to start with but within a few weeks that had fallen to just five. The class was so very hard that people couldn't keep up with it all. He would walk around with a length of bamboo and strike us on the heels if our feet were in the wrong position. I was being trained to use my shins as a weapon, a lot of people couldn't cope with the pain barrier with that, but I stuck it out. I went on to win some local titles with Master Ket, who eventually went back to Thailand. I myself kept on entering martial art shows and worked my way up to national level.

People started to recognize me as a fighter and, even though I was still young, I started to get a name for myself. Thing was, all I ever wanted to do was to study martial arts and keep fighting. I left school and considered going into the Forces – due to all the time I had devoted to training, I messed up my school exams. I decided to go to college to try and salvage an education. My mother had hopes for me to be a doctor or something important; my father just advised me to make money out of anything that I'm good at. I took work on the doors with a guy called Roger Joseph, he was the local hard nut and he had boxed a bit and was a quick, powerful man. More than anything he was a streetfighter who taught me a lot about realistic fighting for the street.

I was about 17 and very independent. I would sometimes just hop on a train on the Underground and just see where it took me. I got off once in Southall just to visit the market and maybe do some shopping. I was just walking along when this little Asian lad says to me, "You can't walk down here, only Bangladeshis down here." He then proceeded to direct me to where the black community was. I had never faced anything like this before, so I told him to go away and walked off. Later, walking around the market, I noticed a few boys watching me and following me. Down the high street this old Granada car pulls up and it was full of all these guys. They told me that I was for it and they were going to kill me. I walk off trying to find my way out of the area. I don't know where to go, and got completely lost. Up this other road another car came racing towards me, full of more of these guys wanting to sort me out. Now I'm no fool and can see that I'm onto a loser if I stood and fought so I started to run down this road and can hear the cars behind me. I'm met at the other end by this large empty warehouse. I'm trapped up this dead end with the cars getting closer. I notice the windows of the warehouse were broken so I climbed in. I ran through to what seemed to be some sort of industrial estate. I thought I had lost them but they shot around in the car to meet me; others had entered the warehouse and were behind me. I had nowhere to go, I didn't know where I was and couldn't escape them.

The car skids around and one of the doors starts to open. I had to make a move before they got to me. I run up and kick the door, which smashes on one of the guy's legs as he tries to step out. The other doors open and they all have baseball bats, masks on, the full works. These guys wanted to really fuck me up. I'm fighting on instinct, hitting whoever I could. I manage to grab a bat. I clobber one guy with it. I then take a strike to the back of my head from another bat. I'm swinging the bat at anything that moves. I feel two sharp pains in my back where they stabbed me. I didn't know that I had been stabbed, I had so much adrenalin in me that I couldn't feel the pain. I was trying to stay on my feet and not go down. The blows to my head were so many that they sounded like hailstones coming down. I notice a flash of light and put my hand up as a guard; a knife slices into my wrist, taking the bone out as well. My hand felt strange at the time, I was aware something was wrong with it but couldn't tell what. From the large gang around me there was now only a few left, two had run away and I had managed to knock some out. This one guy was on my back hitting me in the ear, I could feel his blows stinging me. I grab this one guy who was attacking me and bear hug him and clamp my teeth onto his nose. We fall to the floor and the guy on my back now starts to stick the boots into me.

We get back to our feet and it's just me and the guy who stabbed my wrist left. Now, I had been trained with a knife and at the time fighting with a knife was my thing. I disarm him as he attacks me. I use his knife to cut his hand and then his leg. I finger jab him in the eyes and grab hold of his hair to pull him down. As I get him down I start to slash his face open, I get on top of him and someone is still hitting me as I'm cutting the guy on the floor. All of a sudden there's the sound of sirens in the air and the police are all around me. I start to calm down and take in the whole situation. There's a few guys scattered unconscious on the floor and the one guy has blood pissing out of him, all over.

This one copper takes me to the hospital with my nose smashed up, teeth missing, stab wounds in my back and the slash to my wrist. The copper takes me to one side and explains my options: "You have two choices, make a complaint and it goes to court, or get cleaned up here and go home. I don't like what's happened, and I don't like the guys who started this fight, they've done things like this before. The only difference this time is they picked on the wrong one. It's up to you, what you want to do?" I think he didn't want some big racial argument or maybe it was because he had to work in the area and didn't want any hassle on his doorstep. Anyway, I get cleaned up and decided not to press charges and all that. I went to my mate's house and stayed the night. I didn't go home until the swelling in my face had calmed down a bit. I never told my mother what really happened, and to this day, she doesn't know the truth.

In Luton we had large gangs of football hooligans like the Hatters, Millwall and West Ham. I got involved with a gang [who follow Luton Town] called MiG (Men in Gear) and we went looking for fights. Some of our clashes involved weapons like Stanley knives or home-made weapons. I used to make weapons of wood with nails sticking out. I must admit I did go through a violent time with the MiGs, and went off the rails a bit. If it wasn't for the martial arts then I could have easily got more involved with the criminal element in Luton.

I started doing more door work on different clubs; now, instead of looking for trouble, I was more intent on stopping it. At the time there were different security firms running the doors and of course each one wanted the others' doors. The Leicester Arms was a pub that myself and my mate Roger were looking after but other security firms wanted it. Now other firms were coming down heavy on the Leicester Arms, there had been petrol bombs thrown and customers were getting beat up when they left the place. Roger wanted to sort it out himself but I took it upon myself to sort it. It was arranged that I fight this guy called Eddie who ran a rival firm. Eddie was a big fucker, about 18 stone and could handle himself. I was getting to be known as one of the top doormen and felt that by fighting Eddie, I would be well and truly recognized as such. I just felt I wanted a challenge, something to test myself out, I suppose. This was going to be a bareknuckle fight but really I couldn't lose. You see, because Eddie was so tough, if I lost to him it was only what people expected, and I'd get respected for taking him on. If I won then I'd be known as the guy who beat him, and get more work in the long run.

We met up in this car park, I brought a few friends and so did Eddie. It was going to be a straightforward bareknuckle fight but he insisted that it be "all-in"; if it went to the ground, then so be it. I agreed and his friends and mine let us get on with it. The fight lasted about 15 minutes. Sometimes we would trade punches, other times friends pulled us apart, off the floor. I found my agility really helped me, also I was younger and fitter. He was catching me with some good shots. One actually bust my cheekbone up; I heard the crack as he broke it but ignored it at the time. I smash my elbow into his face as we sort of grapple each other, standing up. I spot my opportunity and pull his shirt over his head. One good, clean left hook and the job was finished. Eddie was out on the floor and his mates start to piss themselves laughing, I remember one saying, "Eddie's going to be pissed off with that one. That's taking the piss." When he awoke he shook my hand and that was that. Guess he was a fair guy that way.

I had lost more teeth again and the side of my face was right up. My mate told me to go to the hospital because I looked like the Elephant Man. The hospital told me my cheekbone was fucked so they had to sort it for me. A lot of guys then wanted to test me out. I'd have to fight guys who came to challenge me when I was on the door or just walking through town. Things were starting to get a bit on top now that word was getting around about me.

I was on the door of a London club with my mate Marcus, who was ex-Army and could have a fight. We were working through an agency covering for some of the club's doormen who were off work. This club was getting lots of trouble with vanloads of guys coming there when we were working and attacking the customers in the club. There were two other doormen on that night, we had just met them and they seemed good lads. They helped us get a few out at first but when they saw that some of them were tooled up, off they ran, leaving Marcus and myself to try and sort it. We stood our ground but both of us took a bit of a bashing. We didn't lose and put a few out in the process, just kept on fighting until the police came and most of them fucked off. It was a hard old battle but I was getting more experienced and it was just part of the job.

Word got back to Lenny McLean, the famous unlicensed and bareknuckle fighter, who came down to see us. He explained that he was in charge of the nightclub door and admired us for the courage we had shown. I didn't really know much about Lenny but everyone else was sort of in awe of him. He offered me the head doorman's job at the SW1 Club and that way he was paying me direct, not through an agency. I looked on Lenny as sort of a big brother type; he'd offer advice, laugh along with us and treated everyone with respect. Now I had heard about this guy called "The Guv'nor" who was this larger than life character and a fighting legend. Through Marcus and others I found out that Lenny was the Guv'nor. Marcus knew all the stories about him and I slowly began to find out just how important Lenny was.

There was this big gypsy guy, Stephen, who worked the door of the Jazz Café, he was massive, probably the biggest man I ever fought. How this happened was through Lenny who, as most people know, was involved in the bareknuckle game. Lenny was going to sort out a fight between Stephen and another guy called Peters who Lenny knew was a good ex-boxer who could have gone all the way. I said to Lenny that I wanted to do it, I could use the cash and, as I have never been knocked out, I really thought there was nothing to fear, just a hiding, that's all. I was strapped for cash at the time and there was ten grand on offer, win or lose, so I had to go for it to pay my bills, and of course I was looking to test myself.

The fight took place in the NCP car park in Luton Street, by

Leicester Square. Lenny's boys were in charge of the car park security, so that seemed an ideal place. At about 12.30 at night they arranged on the bottom floor a space for the fight. When we turned up there was in excess of 100 people there, business-men and all sorts. Stephen had his shirt off and looked absolutely massive. Now it does scare you at first when you see someone that big but remember I was always fighting bigger guys than me when I was a boxer. I was used to being lighter than my opponent but also I was fitter and faster, with a good chin. There was a lot of hype and scare talk about Stephen, things like how he had broken someone's back and was one of the top gypsy fighters. He was in his late twenties so was still a fit and sharp fighter.

The fight started and we exchanged blows. His punching power shocked me and he caught me with a few shots that sent me down. I got up thinking that I shouldn't fight his fight because he was too strong. I ran around him and he turned and ran straight at me. I sidestepped him and jumped up onto him, wrapping my legs around him and tying him up. I clamped my arm around the back of his head and pressed my thumb into the nerve on his neck to put him out. All the time he was trying to resist going out but I kept holding him as we fell to the floor. People were trying to pull me off but I wouldn't leave go, no way. Eventually he went out. He was so strong that it took a lot of effort but he was out for a while. The whole fight took just 48 seconds. A lot of people were shocked that it wasn't a long fight and there was a bit of a riot but things got sorted out. I really wanted to win for myself and Lenny; of course, the £10,000 helped.

Lenny was happy that I won, even though he, like everyone else, wanted to see a longer fight. He told me, "Ten out of ten mate, I've never seen a bareknuckle fight over so quickly. How you got past his punches and did that I'll never know. Show me that kung fu shit." I showed him where the nerve was and how to do it and, laughing, he said, "Keep that bloody thing away from my neck." I always liked Lenny and miss him now he's gone.

Every year in Luton at the end of summer, the travellers would set up camp and come around touting for fighters, for barefist fighting. This one year I watched big Dan Rooney [a renowned Irish knuckle champion] fight three guys one after another on some industrial ground. They put the winnings in a bag and it was well up to £5,000. This guy was shouting, "Dan will fight anybody, anybody at all. You there, black boy, do you want to have a go?" I thought, *fuck it, I'll have a go.*

Dan was a big fighter and I had fought some strong guys in my time but Dan was something else. He had these huge hands, no kid, Lenny had big hands but these were something else. I'm not a small boy but at one stage I dodged a punch and Dan caught me in the chest and his fist felt massive. I threw everything at Dan, punches, high kicks, I used everything I had learned over the years. He was just so bloody strong. At one stage I threw a kick that caught him at the side of his neck, which he caught. He clamped just one hand on my leg and pulled me off balance. Thinking he had both hands on me, I couldn't understand where the punches were coming from. Then it dawned on me that he was so big and strong that he was holding me with one hand. I was upside down and he was hitting me everywhere, in my face, stomach and even in the nuts. That's how strong he was; I was over 15 stone and he held me like that. I managed to get away and threw some combinations of kicks and punches. Then I tried to foot-sweep him down. He threw a big right hand and I stepped in, hitting him with my elbow in the mouth. I pulled my elbow back and there were two of the biggest teeth I had ever seen sticking out of my elbow; I pulled them out and I never realized human teeth were that big. They were wedged into my elbow, right in and I'm still scarred from them. As Dan went down he smashed his head on the floor. I stepped in as he was trying to get up and stuck some kicks into him. The gypsies went berserk and it all went up. They were playing fuck, grabbing for the money. I jumped on the bag and stuffed loads down my trousers before it kicked off with the gypsies and guys from Luton.

About two to three weeks later I met up with Dan in a pub and we shared a few drinks together. We talked about my father who had fought Dan years before in a good bareknuckle fight. He told me that he wouldn't have paid me the cash, anyway, win or lose. He asked my how much I got away with and I told him just under £3000, and he laughed it off.

Things were getting a bit rough for me in London. There was this big dealer who had this reputation of being a hard man, gangster type. He was crammed full of steroids and looked impressive but it still only took me two punches to put him down. Now he and his friends wanted to put an end to me. I was getting some trouble from it. Once I was driving along with the girlfriend down the M25, when I notice this Transit van was cutting people up. I just put it down to road rage and that. What I didn't know was that the van was trying to get in front of my car while we were waiting in heavy traffic by road works. The van pulls in front of my car and its back doors burst open. Four guys jump out and start to smash fuck out of the car, while I have to stay in the car to protect my girlfriend. Basically I can't do a thing but watch them smash it up and shout that my days were numbered. I started to pull back on the door work now, I was only working smaller places.

I was on the door in a club in Dunstable when I hear this car pulling up. There sticking out of the window was a shotgun pointing straight at me. My mate Tony saw what I saw and pushes me into the club, closing the door as well. The shotgun blasts the window of the club in and as they drove away they fire another shot that puts in a shop window as well. Another time I was knocking on a mate's door when again I can hear a car driving fast behind me. I think it was the way the car accelerated that alerted me at first. I bang on the door and get in just as they fire a shot into the brickwork of the house.

My missus was on to me about getting out of the game. I had her to think of, and so we moved to Wales. I'd been coming back and forwards to Wales for years, and I love the place, the people are friendly and the pace is so easy going. I work the doors and run my own martial art clubs in various Welsh towns. I have trained the instructors up and they handle things for me when I'm not there. It's hard getting around all the clubs each week but I manage it and hope to branch out a bit more.

JOHN "LAMBY" HATFIELD

Leicestershire

Life on the road was tough in the Forties and Fifties, and John Hatfield learned to look after himself from a young age. Some of his earliest memories are of fighting for his family's honour. Fellow travellers, local hard men or nightclub bouncers, it made no difference, they all went the same way – down.

I HAVE ALWAYS been a travelling man. I was actually born in a caravan and lived most of my early life travelling. My mother was a proper gypsy but my father wasn't. They had 15 children, with only seven surviving. We had a hard life but we all mixed in and got through it all. We would travel around picking strawberries, potatoes, beet and any other work we would find on the farms. It was hard times for our parents, but we kids didn't see it like that, we were travelling the countryside in horse-drawn caravans and loving every minute of it. We didn't have any schooling and had to work from an early age to survive. It's the only life we knew.

We would make new friends every time we set up camp, only to get up some mornings to find they had moved on and we would meet up again at some later date. All the money us kids earned went straight into the pot for the whole family. Sometimes we would stay somewhere for a few months, other times we would only stay a few days, never knowing from one day to the next where we were going to end up.

I'm 66 years old now but can still remember like it was yesterday being a small, 14-year-old travelling lad. We had set up camp not far from here. We often travelled around with the Gaskin family, who are a big travelling family. We all grew up together and go back a long way. There was this older boy at the camp who was a good fighter, he was from the Shackle family. He was about 17 and had beaten all the other gypsy lads. In fact he had beaten one of my older brothers and three of my cousins. Well, it turns out everyone thought I was too young and small to be fighting, so nobody thought about me fighting him. One day my father and his good friend John Gaskin came back to the camp with all the men, they had been out to a pub and were in good spirits. Someone shouted to John that the Shackle's lad had beaten all the other boys and was the best fighter.

John said to the Shackle's boy, "So, you beat all these lads then?" and he points around to all the boys around the camp.

"Yes, I did," said the boy.

144

John looks at him and holds out two large apples, "You fight Lamby here, who's only a baby, and the winner gets these two apples."

He looks at me and asks me, "Lamby, will you fight him?"

"Well, he's a big lad, but yes, I will fight him." I answered.

John shouts at us, "Get at it then!" and we both launch ourselves at one another. We were punching and kicking for about half an hour and I was the winner. It felt really good to beat the boy and of course the apples tasted good. John turned to the Shackles and said, "Lamby's beaten the best lad, so now he's the best lad on the road, the best boy here." That was my first real fight, and you could say I had a bareknuckle fight for just two apples.

Now my dad was a good man, but he drank a lot of beer and him and my mother would have a few arguments along the way. I remember saying to him once, "Dad, when I'm sixteen I'm going to give you a good hiding." I couldn't do it then because I was too young and he would have flogged me with a horsewhip. Just before I turned 16, mother and father had this big row. He came home one night drunk and started to argue with my mother. He grabbed her, hit her once and pulled his hand back to hit her again. I jump forward and held onto his arm. I lifted him up, clean off the floor. I pull back my right hand and shout, "No!" to him. Before I could throw a punch, my mother got between us. "Lamby, son, how can you hit your own father?" she shouts to me. I look at my mother and I realised that she loved him and I couldn't hit him in front of her. He meant the world to her.

I knew I had to leave home, so I pack all my stuff, two shirts and two pairs of trousers and left. From that day on my father never laid a finger on my mother; all us boys were now grown up and wouldn't stand for it. My dad had been brought up hard and I guess this was the reason he was the way he was. As a boy he had fought in the First World War: he once told us that he had watched kids of 14 and 15 die by his side fighting. It was a terrible thing for a young man to witness and it reflected on the type of man he was. Whenever the police came to move us on, my dad would shout, "I've shot better fuckers than you in the war!" to them.

I left home, and travelled around in my van looking for whatever work I could find. I must be honest here and tell you that I would go around stealing copper, lead, brass and any other metal that I could weigh-in to the scrap man. I never stole anything big or directly off anyone, never broke in someone's house or anything like that. Sometimes I would steal the copper back from the scrap man's yard and then sell it back to him a few days later but that's all. I was sleeping in my van at night, then out working all day long. I liked Leicester town and settled here, in fact my family did as well.

I never had any real mates before, due to the fact that I never settled down in one place long enough. Here I was a young lad in Leicester, and now I had loads of friends. Most of them were villains, but they were my friends and we stuck together. I was a little shy and new to having so many people around me. I had spent my early life in the fields and woodland areas. Every Saturday night we would go into town to the dances and that. There would always be fights going on. I would just stand in the background, weighing the situations up. If a few of my friends started to beat one guy up then I would help the guy against them. My friends sometimes didn't like that but there was no way I could stand for it, it wasn't called for. One of the guys was sort of a leader in the gang that I went around in. He would brag to me about how he would have just beaten someone up, but he always had others around him to help when he did it. He was bigger than me and was very fast with his head in a fight. Once he knocked two guys out just with his head. He could really have a scrap.

One night he decides to have a go at me. Everyone said he was so fast. Well, he was the fastest man I ever put away. What he didn't know was that I was fast with everything, hands, head, elbows or my feet. He came at me and I head-butted him twice. As he fell, I left-hooked him, which kept him down.

Now I was known as the hardest fighter, just because I had beaten him. Everyone thought not to mess with me because I wouldn't take it. I was out one night with my girlfriend Colleen, who I later married. We were sat at this table in the White Swan pub. Well, Colleen was a tall girl of about six foot; she stood out a little, being so tall compared to me. On the next table there were four sailors. They kept clocking my missus, so I asked her, "What's up with them, are you looking at them?"

"No I'm not," she answered. "You go and tell them."

Well, me being the jealous type, I jumped up and landed in the middle of their table. Well, we started to fight and I beat the four of them on my own. The word got around about the fight and people were amazed that I had beaten them all.

When all the bareknuckle fighters would be fighting up at Doncaster [during St Leger race week, a big gypsy gathering], they would be told that they may be fighting men but there's a little man in Leicester who fights sometimes up to ten times a week, not once every couple of months. People couldn't understand how I could beat men who were well over six feet tall with hands as big as shovels, but I did.

There was this one nightclub bouncer, a big guy who everyone was scared of. He had a reputation of being a big fighting man. I'm out with my mates one night and I spot him in this boozer with his friends. This big guy had crossed me years ago, and I wanted to settle it with him.

I shout over to him, "You're supposed to be the best heavy-weight in Leicester, maybe you are but how about me and you getting outside in the back yard?"

"I'd kill you if we went outside," he shouts back.

"Well," I said, "Stop your mouth, let's go out and see what we can do."

He shouts to his mate, "You go outside with this man. I can eat him for my breakfast."

I look over and his mate is about six foot six with great big hands, I'm thinking, *how the hell am I going to tackle you?* I shout over, "Yeah, that will do, let's go outside." I couldn't back down, that's one thing I wouldn't do with any man.

We get outside and it's been snowing. The whole backyard is covered in snow. I turn to face the big guy, he runs at me and he's gone to kick me. He slips on the snow and ice and comes crashing down on the hard ground. I look at him and within seconds I'm on top of him. I absolutely destroy him; there's no way I was letting a guy as big as him back off the floor. I walk back in the pub, I'd only been outside for a few minutes. The whole pub is shocked to see me in one piece.

"Right then," I shout to the big bouncer, "your henchman is outside, and I don't think he will be back for quite sometime. Let's me and you go out now."

"Come on now Lamby. Let's have a drink. Let me get you a drink."

There was another little mate there with me who shouted out, "You got a reputation as a bouncer but you're not worth a Woodbine." We never did get to go outside and I just left it like that really.

Back in the old rock 'n' roll days I was always getting into one fight or another; there was always someone wanting to have a go. I was out drinking with this mate of mine, he wasn't a fighter but was a big lad. At the bar this guy wanted to go outside with him, my friend didn't want to and was made to look a fool. I told him, "Look, go outside with him, the worst that can happen is that you get a hiding. At least go outside with the man." Out he goes, a short while later he comes back with just a bloody nose. He lost the fight but at least he was brave enough to go outside. As we were standing by the bar, I move along closer to the guy who had fought my mate and his friends. One of his mates, a real big lad says, "Well, at least you've got the guts to go outside." Now I know he was having a dig at me so I tell him, "What do you mean? I hope you don't mean me, because I don't give two hoots about you." As I said it, I can see him bringing his hand back to backhand me. I duck his hand, jump off the floor and head-butt him, which splits him open. There's blood everywhere. We take it outside into the market place. They tell me he was a good fighter but every time he comes at me I knock him down. He was so big and strong he just kept getting back up. I shout to him, "Stay down or I'll finish you." He gets up and I hit him again and as he goes down I kick him and he's beat.

As you know, I liked to weigh-in a bit of scrap now and again. I pull into the scrapyard and there standing with the gaffer and his mates was the guy I had fought a few days before.

"Do you think you can do the same thing to me now, when I'm not drunk?" he shouted to me.

I tell him, "I got to admit, you were drunk. But I can do things a lot better when I'm sober as well."

We arrange to go out into the countryside to fight. He follows my car with his lorry and off we go. I park my car in my dad's yard and the lorry pulls up behind it. There's an old lane at the back of the yard which leads to a few fields and that. Off we walk down the lane. We get to this field and we start to fight. It's an all-in fight and he's having a go. He's a big powerful lad but I'm a bit fast for him so his big haymaker punches can't land on me. I step back off him and kick him straight in the knackers and down he goes. Remember, there are no rules in streetfighting. You must do what you can to win.

I get back to where my old dad is standing smoking his pipe. "How did you do boy?" he asks me.

"I think he will stop by and tell you on the way out, dad," I answer and drive away.

Sure enough, on the way out he stops by. My dad asks him how things went. "To tell you the truth Joe, whenever I threw a punch he weren't there, and before he moved he would hit me with everything." Well I'm glad he took it all in good faith and we became good friends from that day on.

A load of us travellers go up to Cambridge Fair. I'm stood there with my friends watching the boxing in the boxing booth. My mate says to me, "Lamby, would you fight that man in the ring?" and he points to one of the booth fighters.

"Yes I would, if I had to I would," I answer. I didn't want to fight any man, but if I had too then I would fight. My friend keeps going on about me fighting the boxer and to be honest I could have used the £5 they were offering. When they ask, "Is there anyone in the crowd who wants to fight in the ring?" my hand goes in the air. Next fight in the ring is me against this ex-pro boxer.

First round, and he gets me down quick. I jump up and keep out of his way until I can work him out. He's a bit clever at the boxing job so I had to try and figure out how to beat him. All the travellers were watching the fight and I could hear a few saying that the boxer would kill me in this round. Bell's gone, my plan was to throw a few haymakers then get in and smash him up in close, not box him just fight him. I come straight at him and throw this haymaker which hits him off his feet and out for the count. I don't know how I did it but I beat him. The gaffer on the booth arranges for me to fight him again at six o'clock. I turn up to be told that the boxer hasn't turned up, he won't fight me again. Well I ended up with the £5 winnings and gave everybody something to talk about.

I've always been a fair bloke, never wanted to fight but sometimes I just had to. When it came to fighting I've always had a big heart, I'm only a small guy so it's my heart that's got me through all the fights I've had. Like my dad, I got married and had kids, but I never took my hands to any of them. I got divorced, which was my own fault entirely, I take full blame for that. I remember once when my boy was 16, the same age that if you remember I challenged my father. I was going through a bad patch in my marriage and was in an argument with my wife of the time. My son jumped up and said he wanted to fight me. Now I wouldn't hit him for the world. I told him, "Son, I'm going out into the garden, if you want to fight me then I'll be out there. Just remember that when you come out, be prepared to fight your dad." I waited in the garden, but he didn't show. I'm glad because there's no way I could fight my own boy. Anyway, I get back in the house and ask him what he was waiting for. He says, "I'm not ready for you yet." My boy's a grown man now and I still tease him about that day and how he wanted to fight me and wouldn't come outside.

These days I don't travel around so much, I buy and sell cars to get by. My family all live near and if ever I need them they are here for me.

BILLY PREECE

Maesteg, South Wales

Hardened by life, a streetfighter, boxer, martial artist and doorman – there's nothing this guy hasn't seen. Undaunted by any situation, his pleasant nature masks a natural fighting man who has had to battle for everything he has. He has always been a friend of the underdog, and his sense of humour can make you forget how harrowing his story is.

I WAS BORN one of ten. I've always lived here in Maesteg, in fact I was born in one of these three cottages that I now live in. Life was hard for my family. We had no electricity and the only water we had was from the stream that runs not far from here. I can remember us all having to take turns fetching water up from the stream in buckets. Of course, my mother wasn't working, she had her hands full looking after us lot. My father was a collier so he wasn't always around. It wasn't the fact that things were hard for us that made me start fighting, it started with the local kids and the kids at school. Because there were ten of us, we had to wear hand-me-downs and the kids would tease us. Now I suppose I could have turned the other cheek but even from an early age that was something I just couldn't do. At Christmas I'd walk past other kids' houses and see all the presents and decorations, things our family never had. I was never jealous of them but there was no way I was going to stand for them teasing me about it all.

With me fighting the other kids, I started to get a name for myself. Whatever school I went to, they knew me as a fighter. Other fighters would want to have a crack at me. I'd fight them and beat them but would never be happy of the fact that I'd hurt them. Sometimes I couldn't get to sleep at night worrying about the damage I had inflicted on someone. Thing is, when I started, I wouldn't stop until I finished it. I have always been known as a fighter but I'm also a soft-hearted bugger as well. I never wanted to be a fighter; it was the way that life was that changed me. When bigger lads from town would come up here, they would chase my friends away but I would always stand firm. Don't know if it was pride or courage that made me fight them, but fight them I would.

Sometimes we would have to go and get sacks of coke for the fire. We had to climb up the ash tips to get it all. The sacks would be filled up and we would take turns to carry it all. I can remember when it used to rain and I'd be carrying the heavy sacks with all the dirt running down my back, down the crack of my arse to my feet. My father would sometimes wait for us in the Royal Oak pub and if we hadn't filled the sacks up enough, he would give us a belt.

My father was a very intelligent man – no common sense, mind you, or he wouldn't have had ten kids when things were so hard. He always kept diaries. I still have them here today with all the details of our everyday life wrote down. I never saw eye to eye with him; in fact, if one of my brothers did something wrong then he would batter me because he couldn't catch them. Nothing I did could ever make him happy, he was always coming down hard on me. He was a well-respected, proud man who could do anything he turned his hands to. He stood about six foot two and was a handsome man who all the other miners looked up to. Even though he came down hard on me, I sort of respected him and tried everything I could to please him. But he still came down hard on me. He would think nothing about breaking a brush handle over my head. Once my mother came running out of the house convinced that he had finally killed me. "Ivor," she would shout, "you're going to kill that boy one day."

The coal train would travel through a tunnel not far from the house and my father, brothers and myself would steal the coal off it before it went through the tunnel. I would run alongside the train and jump on the wagons which had the bigger lumps on. I would then throw them off before the train disappeared into the tunnel. I had to be as fast as I could, throwing the lumps of coal off. I remember being too slow once and having to go through the tunnel. It was a nightmare for a 13-year-old kid, as I was at the time. The steam train was high up, so all the hot steam was beating down on me. I have never been in a place that was so totally black in my life, couldn't see a thing. I was still throwing the coal off when I raised this one big lump and as I threw it my hands caught the steel sides of the train. Every finger had the skin torn off, my hands were bleeding and the coal dust was all in the cuts. I still had to throw the coal off because my father would have gone mad if I didn't. The train stopped at the end of the tunnel and I jumped off and hid from the guardsman in the alcoves. When the train left we had to collect all the coal, I had to do this with my hands all busted open. Now this was all done at night time, so you can imagine how hard it was. We would get all the sacks onto a push bike and be back and forth all night. The way we got the coal was a very frightening experience for me. On one occasion I threw off enough coal to last a few weeks, so I wouldn't have to do it again for a while. Thing was that we had to pick up every lump of coal, so that nobody would know what we had been up to all night. We finished at about three in the morning, only to have my father beat me around the head for getting too much. Just couldn't win, could I.

Once, I had just thrown the coal off and was hanging off the sides waiting to drop off before the tunnel. All of a sudden the guardsman appears and, before I could leave go, he stamps down on my face. I fall off into the snow. I never did find out who he was but if I had, I would have battered him. How could someone do such a thing to a youngster? I just can't comprehend it.

I never knew why my old man was the way he was. Maybe it was because I was the oldest or because my other brother was his favourite. My father was also a good mechanic and always allowed my brother to go in his garage and use his tools. If I set foot in there to get maybe a spanner to fix my bike, he would scream at me, "What do you want? You don't know how to use a spanner, now get out." But the love that my father never gave me, my mother more than made up for.

It was through my father that I had my first real fight. I was about ten years old and had to travel through the forestry near here to get to a farmhouse to buy fresh milk. I had been arguing with this lad who lived near and he whacked me over the head with a bottle. I still have a small bald patch on my head from it. I get back in the house crying my eyes out, with blood pouring down the back of my neck. I thought I'd get a bit of sympathy off my father, but he whacked me across the face, grabbed me by the back of the neck, dragging me out of the house and threw me into the field by the forest. "You fucking wait for that boy to come past here," he shouted to me. I was more afraid of my old man than the boy who had hit me, so I waited for the boy to show up. I beat the boy, because of fear of my old man more than anything else.

When I was about 17, I got into a fight with one of my brothers in front of our house. He tried to stab me with a screwdriver. I blocked it with my forearm but the screwdriver went right into my arm. I was still fighting him with this screwdriver dangling in my arm. The fight progressed against a barbed wire fence, which ripped into my shoulders. He stepped back and kicked me straight in the knackers. For some reason – I don't know why, maybe shock – I went completely blind for about ten minutes. I managed to sit down in this old chair in the garden and the pain from my injuries was making my whole body shake. I couldn't see and thought I was blind for life. I was covered in blood but slowly, like a fog clearing, my eyesight came back. I look at my brother and I pick up this hatchet, which was near me. "Right, that's the way you want to play it, is it?" I scream at him. With that he races off before I can get to him.

I leave school not long after and get a job in the Forestry, doing all sorts of work, right across the board from planting trees to cutting them down. I loved the job; it was just my thing. The only downside was that, no matter where in the forests I had to go, one mile or eight, I'd have to walk all the way, in all sorts of weather. My wages at the time were £3 15s a week, which was all right but I'd just been caught drinking under age in the Royal Oak. I was fined £5.

My father said, "Right, that will teach you, now my fine for you is that you now pay five pounds lodge."

"But dad," I argued, "my wage doesn't cover that."

"Well," he said, "up that forestry you can get paid for doing piece-work, so that's what you must do." Piece-work was like a bonus, with you getting paid by how much extra work you did, and that's what I had to do.

The Forestry had just planted loads of young trees and I was now being paid to trap rabbits; seems the rabbits would nibble the tops off the little saplings. This was great because I could now sell the rabbits to local families to make up my money. There was a forester there called Danny who I used to go hunting with, he was the only one who had a licence to shoot deer. He once took aim at a deer he spotted, leant across his Land Rover and got the deer in his telescopic sights. He fired away, but the sights were on the deer and the barrel was pointing at the wing of his Land Rover. He put a bullet hole straight through the wing. He was teased for ages about that one, we all played hell with him. I used to enjoy my days with Danny and learnt a lot from him.

It wasn't long after my stint with the Forestry that I met a girl who later on I married. She was married at the time and her husband was in prison. Well, things came to a head when he came out of prison and she returned to him for a short while. I was out drinking in town one night when he caught up with me. He was a big lad of about six foot two. He had his mate with him who was a pro boxer, which didn't help me much. He takes a swing at me and we get into a fight very quickly.

"I only want to talk, that's all," he shouts.

"Well, that's a funny way to talk," I answer him. We agree to go down some back alley, to "talk it out".

His mate shouts out, "Just put a fucker on him and let's go." I can hear him coming up behind me and I get a tap on my shoulder. Next thing I remember, I'm walking from the alley up through the main town. I was disorientated and so I sat on the window ledge of an Indian restaurant. Two policemen turn up. "Who done this to you boy?" they ask me. Slowly I start to get myself together and start to work out what had happened. The guys in the alley had done me over; the boxer must have hit me when I turned around. My whole face was smashed up, I was in a terrible state, both my eyes were closing and my mouth was cut to shreds. People couldn't recognize who I was, they had done me over that bad.

A short while later, I get my mate and we go into town. He takes one end of town and me the other. "We will search every pub. If you see them, you know my route, just come and get me," I tell him. We searched for a few nights but he wasn't out drinking. Then one night I catch up with him in this pub. We get outside and I must admit this was the first time that I really wanted to kill someone. We start to fight and I'm destroying him. I get him down between two parked cars and start to batter him. Same thing happened again, the boxer sneaks up behind me but this time my mate was there to stop that. The police turn up and restrain me from doing any more damage to him. While I'm being held, he runs up and throws a punch that goes whizzing past my face. It was the only decent punch that he had thrown in the whole fight and he only did that when my hands were being held down. I talked my way out of things with the police and jumped on the bus home, before I'm charged. I'm sitting on the bus covered in blood, not my blood but his. I ask the driver to stop on the way for me to be sick. He lets me and I eventually get home. A tiredness I had never known comes over me. I had put so much into beating him that I was mentally and physically exhausted. It must have been the release of so much anger that made me so very tired.

Anyway, I get back with my ex-girlfriend and we get married. It wasn't the best of marriages but we spent twelve years together and had two boys, Ivor and Carl, before we split up. She already had two kids, Gareth and Anne, who I brought up and consider as my own.

I was now working on the door of the Four Sevens Country Club. By this time I had got myself a nice Jaguar car and was doing alright. I must say that temptation got the better of me and I started to see various girls. My wife would get up in the mornings before me and search the car. If she found one hair that wasn't mine then there would be hell to pay. It was a stormy marriage to say the least, but I take full blame for the break-up.

To supplement my earnings, I started selling firewood. I'd pinch the wood from the Forestry and sell it door to door. Well, a couple of young girls would hang around and I started to see Mary, who I later married. Now Mary was a lot younger than me and also I was still married at the time. I came home from work one day and there was all my food laid out on the table. I sat down and ate my dinner. My first wife turned to me and said, "Right, you've had your food, I know what you've been up to, your bags are packed, now get out." I left the house with my young boy Carl crying his eyes out, he kept crying to my wife to take me back. That really choked me up to see him like that but there was nothing I could do. I had split up with my wife before but this time I just knew it was for good.

My whole family and Mary's family turned against us. The fact that I was a lot older and married caused a lot of problems for us. I now found myself homeless, so I moved into an abandoned stone cabin in the forest. The building had no windows or doors and the only bed I had was an old thick piece of foam. I was doing stonework at the time and didn't have far to walk to work. Each morning, first thing, I would wash in the stream before getting to work. I never thought water could be so cold, it was like an electric shock hitting me. Mary would walk from her house each day all the way over the mountain to where I was working, just to bring me some food. I would work my heart out on the stonework, getting there hours before anyone else and leaving after everyone had gone home. The only food I was having was the food that Mary brought me. I needed the money so it had to be done. I'd get back to the stone cabin absolutely shattered, really worn out. The only company I'd have was the sheep that strayed up there, but of course Mary was a lot prettier than them, so they were of no use to me!

Things were very hard for Mary and me, but we got through it all. I can remember days when we had no money and I would go poaching to make ends meet. Mary would have to stand watch for me when I caught fish or even drove the car for me when I shot deer. Thing was, we would sell the deer for about £35, and that was good money back then. When you are desperate, you'll do whatever you can, and we did everything until there was enough money for the house that we have today. It was an old wreck of a house at first, with only goats living in it. There was four inches of goat shit in every room of the house. It looked terrible but we felt we could do something with it. We worked our fingers to the bone to get it the way it is today, and looking at it I'm glad we did. My ex-wife found someone else and moved away. With that happening, my two boys came and lived with me and Mary.

I was still working the doors to get the extra cash in. Most of the time I'd be on my own, with no back-up at all. I can remember throwing a few guys out one night and there was this big coloured lad there who I thought was with the troublemakers. Turns out he wasn't. We get talking and he tells me, "Tell you what, if you can sort it for me to start a karate club here, I'll come down on weekends and help you with the door." I have a word with the manager and it's sorted. Now I start to train in karate and also I have back-up on the door. From that first conversation I had about a karate club, I went on to get heavily involved in the sport. I and most of my family took it up and haven't looked back since. There are loads of stories I could tell you about the competitions we have entered over the years, but that would fill about ten books.

I've had some memorable times on the door. I can remember once a gypsy lad arguing with a barmaid at the club. He was ten pence short for a pint and was giving the girl a lot of aggro. I get involved, and explain that I was working on the door and weren't just sticking my nose in. "Oh," he says, "you're the tough guy are you?" and throws a punch, which I slip. At once I hook him and down he goes. Now, I didn't know that he had others with him. I was grabbed from behind and this big fat guy punches me in the face full force. I could feel my nose break and with that I was released and slid to the floor. I get back up and in front of me is one of the guy's friends, a tall lad with greased back hair. I wade into him and put him away. I turn and put another away. I look for the big guy who took the sly punch at me. I catch him in the club's foyer. I throw a beautiful hook that catches him on the side of his head. I launched him into the air and onto a table. He was stone cold unconscious before he landed. I get on top of him and start to plough my best shots into his face. With each punch, his face distorts with the impact. It was like hitting dead meat. I didn't hold back on him because he was out, and he looked a right state.

There was one of the gang waiting in the car park for me, hands on hips, shouting for me. I ran up and put him straight away, didn't mess with him, just laid him out. One of them was hiding behind this rose bush and every time I came at him, he ran around the other side of the bush. It was like ring-a-round-a-rosie. I keep going around and around until I'm out of breath. My nose is busted over my face with blood pouring out of it, my hands are smashed up and my thumb is broken. I'm back at the door to shake the last one about a bit. A good friend of mine says, "Leave it there Billy, we've done them all." There was a mate on the door who used to collect the money in. "What do you mean?" he states, "Nobody's done anything except Billy. He did the load of them on his own."

Some people at the end of the night in a club will just drink up and go home, but there's always one or two who just want to be awkward. This one guy in the club was trouble from the start, bumping into people, and just out and out looking for it. He was a professional boxer at the time and was in tidy shape, he looked the part. I told my mate on the door with me that when it kicks off, that he was to be left for me. It's the end of the night and I'm walking around the club asking people to please drink up. I get to the boxer's table, I ask them to drink up and the boxer tells me to

162

fuck off. "Come on lads, just please drink up," I ask again. He gets up and takes a swing at me. He missed me and I get stuck into him. I beat him bad, real bad and it's only what the man deserved. I couldn't take a chance with him so I let him have it.

Later his friends are cleaning him up in the toilets when he says to me, "You are dead."

I answered back, "Yes, you can come back and try your luck any other night you want."

He tells me, "I'm going to fetch my brother here to sort you out." I couldn't believe it, he was supposed to be this big tough boxer and here he was threatening me with his brother.

I've had knives thrust at me on many occasions on the door, people have also tried to glass me. One guy I had banned for fighting came back to the club after his ban was up. Halfway through the night, he wants to have a go at me. "I could beat you," he informs me, so outside into the car park we go. What I didn't know was he had hid a pint glass behind a car wheel. He had planned to get me outside and cut me open. He picks up the glass and waves it around. "Come on then, you gutless bastard, go for it," I scream at him. He lunges forward and I sidestep him, knocking the glass from his hand at the same time. He realises that he has no weapon, and in the few seconds that he's stopped to think about his actions, I'm on him. Anyway, I do the business with him and I also ban him for two years.

Not long after, I'm at the club and I realise that somebody has let him into the club with three of his mates. I approach the owner, Clem, about it. He informs me, "Thing is Billy, it's been quiet in here of late, and we need the money." Well, I let the owner have it his own way, but later on the trouble starts. The guy I banned comes up to me and again he wants to have a go outside. Out we go. It was a dark, winter's night and freezing out in the car park. He pulls out this huge Bowie knife. I can still remember the way it shone in the moonlight. Anyway, same thing as before: sidestep, disarm and then batter him. I take the Bowie knife into Clem and ask him to call the police, because the next person he tries to stab just might not be so lucky. He says, "No, we shouldn't do that Billy, bad publicity. I tell you what, you keep the knife." As if that was going to make me feel better. Can you believe that?

This one night, things had been particularly bad, I had been in a few hard fights and my hands were cut open. The skin was hanging off my knuckles from punching. I was in the kitchen washing them and I was worn out and breathing heavy from all the fighting. The owner comes in.

"Are you alright Billy?"

"Nah, my hands are killing me," I answer.

He looks at my cut open, smashed up hands and informs me, "I've got something to make you feel better."

I'm thinking a brandy or something. He comes back five minutes later, and puts a bloody can of tomato soup in my hand.

"What's this?" I ask.

"You get that down you Billy, do you a world of good it will," he replies.

I didn't know whether to laugh or cry. A can of tomato soup of all things, what the hell good was that going to do for me?

A coachload came to the club one night. I had this one guy marked out as a troublemaker straight from the start. Sure enough, trouble starts and he started it. I give it to the one I was watching and after a while we manage to get them all out of the club. Around the back of the club was a place where we kept all the empty bottles. Next thing, there's crates of bottles coming through the windows. Glass was everywhere. My two mates realise that one of the gang is still in the club, and they grab him. They lift him up and hold the poor bastard in front of the windows as the gang was still throwing. He was screaming his head off. The gang tries to kick in the locked doors of the club, so a few of us pick up these draining rods with brass attachments on as we exit the club via the basement. We come around behind the gang, who were very surprised to see us, to say the least. I throw my stick away and get onto the first guy, I have him by the hair and I'm punching hell out of him. My brother Jimmy for some reason thought I was on the worst end of it. He brings his stick down on the guy's head but it lands on my hand, paralysing my hand for the whole night. He shouts, "Sorry about that Billy," as I'm stood there nursing my swollen hand. The gang gets back on their coach. First thing that went in were the headlights, then every window on the coach. The driver couldn't go anywhere, the coach was totally wrecked. Most of the gang needed the hospital and I must admit things got a bit scary that night.

I used my car to roadblock a street once. A friend had been beaten up by a gang and we knew which way they were travelling. I cut the street off with my Jaguar and they turn up in a minibus. There was a few of us in my car and we jump out and pile into them. I'm giving this rough bastard a right tuning when this streetfighter I knew grabs me. "Look, it's got nothing to do with you, you're not involved," I shout. With that he launches himself at me. This guy later on in life becomes like a brother to me and I love him to bits, but back then we fought for about 15 minutes. There was hardly any grappling, just both punching each other, and really going for it. Let me tell you, he was a hard man, strong puncher with a heavy muscular frame. I put him down but up he jumps. He was in such a temper that he was almost crying with rage. There's blood all over his face and he still comes at me. I put him down again and again but still he comes forward. My brother Jimmy shouts, "You'll have to put him out somehow Bill." I knock him down one more time and as he falls to his knees I grab his mop of curly hair. I slam his face into the kerb. I had to slam it down about three times before he went out. To this day I regret having done it. I just wish I could turn the clock back on that one.

I spot two guys going into the same cubicle of the toilets one night. I look underneath the cubicle and I can see one has his trousers down to his ankles. The pair of them were shagging. I couldn't believe it. I just crept out of there. No way was I going to break them up, no way. *Carry on boys, I'm out of here*, I thought.

On the subject of naked men, we had this live group playing once and right by the stage this guy was dancing bollocks-naked. I start to grapple with him and the fight goes to the floor. All the time that I'm grappling with him, the singer is still singing. I smash him around a bit and we got him out of the club. Everyone was laughing and shouting things like, "I didn't know you were gay, Billy."

This headcase is giving me some trouble in the club, so we go outside to sort it one night. All the time he's calling me on, he's backing away from me. Closer I get, the further away he moves, until he actually ran away. Well, I don't know how he got back in the club, but back in he gets. I hear girls screaming inside and there's the buzzer going off. I leave the foyer and get to the dance floor where the screams came from. There he was, stripped to the half, with this bloody big butcher's knife. This big 20-stone bouncer is backing off and he tells me, "Billy, he's got a knife." But I don't care about that. It was my job to get him out, come what may. I sweep his legs, take his arm and disarm him. For good measure I snap the blade, in case he picks it back up. I manage to get him to the front door and throw him out. I'm a bit thirsty after all this so I go up to the bar and ask the barmaid for an orange juice. "No," she tells me. Now, I can't figure out what's wrong with her, so I ask her. "I'll tell you why," she says, "I didn't have a decent kitchen knife here, and you go and bloody well snap that one." And I just laughed my head off with her over that one.

I've had a problem with some farmers from up the road for the last 20 years now. I was taking my son Carl out in my van once when the farmer sees me and drives his tractor down the lane straight at my van. At the last possible moment, my son sticks his head up and the farmer puts the brakes on, trying to scare us. I jump out of the van and pull the farmer down from the tractor. I hold his head against the tractor's wheel and start to pound it. His brother runs down the lane at me and I throw a cracking left hook which takes care of him. The father of these farmers comes down and smashes me over the head with his walking stick a few times. I hit him once and he flew across the road and lands on his arse. The police turn up and it's not looking good for me because the farmers are all bashed up, with teeth missing and black eyes. They wanted to press charges but after I showed the police the walking stick that was broken over my head, there was no charges pressed.

Over the years a few things had happened with these farmers. One tried to pitchfork my brother. He also told my wife, who was heavily pregnant at the time, about how he was going to shoot me in the stomach so she could hear me screaming. Well, this one day, my daughter Kelly was only about seven years old and Mary and myself were taking her into town. There's a gate up the road and the one farmer was standing there having just closed the gate. I ask him to open it but he gives me this sickly smirk, so I get out of the car to do it myself. With that, he opens his long wax jacket to pull out this small, red-handled fireman's hatchet. He lashes out at my face. "Come on then!" I shout. Now, he hesitated for a second, which gave me time to raise my hand and catch the handle in mid-flight. I step in and knee him in the balls. The older farmer turns up and tries to pull a large stone from the wall to smash my skull in, but couldn't get it out. My daughter was screaming all the time. My wife gets out of the car and comes over to me as the other farmer gets on top of me and starts attacking me. Mary pulls him off me and grabs the hatchet by the blade. It was so sharp that it leaves a five-inch gash in her hand. Kelly runs back to my house screaming, hysterical, to my mother and sister. She told them the farmers were trying to kill me. Well, I get back home covered in blood, their blood mind you, not mine.

The police turn up and arrest me, I know it's hard to believe but they do. Seems one of the farmers got knocked out by me and his face was damaged badly. To tell you the truth, as I knocked him out, I saw his eyes roll back in his head as he fell. I didn't hit him any more, so it looks like I caught him with a good one. They charged me with GBH, even though they tried to kill me. From what I gather, his mouth needed ten stitches, his face ten, and his teeth were smashed in. The solicitor phoned me and we both agreed that I should be bound over by the police to keep the peace. I agreed to this just so my little girl and wife didn't have to give evidence. One condition that I insisted on was that the farmer was bound over as well. I couldn't understand it all, how could the police charge me? They even took his hatchet back to him, delivered in the police car of all things. If I hadn't have taken it off him it would have been in my head.

Another fight broke out once in a field nearby with me and the farmer's sons. They both pulled knives out, so I swept them down and bashed them up. The older farmer saw what happened and rushed to the farmhouse to come out with his two shotguns. I thought it was best to fuck off at that point, because I felt he would use them.

One thing I would like to tell you is that you are never too old to accomplish things. We had a team challenge with our karate team and I had to take ten women and ten men up to Bradford as our squad. The event took place in a hotel. I was fighting top of the bill, and it was just gone midnight on my 45th birthday when I was to jump in the ring to fight. I mention this not because of the fight but because of my age at the time. You see, if you have heart you can do most anything you desire. Never be put off by our age, just go for it. What's the worst that can happen?

This big, 18-stone prop-forward came to the club one night with two of his friends. I let his friends in without paying but asked him for the money. "Why should I pay?" he asks. "Well," I tell him, "the other night when myself and Mary came to your club, even though I had been told I could get in free, you insisted I pay. So now you have to pay." He didn't like it, but he paid and went inside. For the next few hours he sat inside staring at me. People were coming up to me telling me that he was going to kill me and I should watch out.

I walk over to his table and I ask him, "What's your problem then? Everyone says you want to kill me. Well there's no time like the present so let's go outside. But remember there's nobody to blow the whistle outside."

"Come on then lads, let's sort this one out," he tells his mates. They in turn inform him that he was on his own with this one.

He gets up and has changed his tune; he now insists that he wants to see the manager, so off we go to the manager. After he tells his lies to the manager, the manager asks me if everything he had been told was true. "It's the biggest load of bullshit I have ever heard," I inform him. With that, the big prop makes a mistake in grabbing me by my suit to butt me. As soon as this happened, I push his hand aside and start to punch him up against the wall. I'm giving him hell and he eventually slides down the wall onto the floor, unconscious. He's making these gargling noises, which some people often do when they are knocked out. I lean over him and give him my best shots. His nose completely spreads over his face as it breaks.

After about ten minutes, he comes round to find his face smothered in plasters from our first aid kit. "You've had it Preece, you've had it now," he shouts to me.

I answer back, "You know where I live, knock my door anytime."

"I don't mean it like that," he says, "I'm going to report you to the social, for working down here." I lose the little bit of respect that I have for them when they say stuff like that.

I was working the door of the Four Sevens Club about 27 years ago. If I remember correctly it was a Saturday night and it was pelting down with rain, a real pig of a night. I'm getting a bit of mouth off these two guys. I throw one out and his mate follows, after us. I'm in the car park sorting these two guys out on my own, getting absolutely soaking wet as well. Inside the club a good friend of mine called Shawn is looking for me.

"Where's Billy?" he asked one of the lads inside the club.

"He's outside, fighting two guys in the car park," someone answered.

"Well, what the fuck are all you lot doing sitting down? You should be giving him a hand," he shouts.

Now Shawn isn't a mug and can do the business when he wants to. Out he storms in his fancy white suit and brand new shoes. I had just foot-swept one of the guys to the floor and was wading into the other when the first one starts to get up off the floor. Shawn ploughs straight into him and his fight soon goes to the ground. They are grappling with each other in the stinking puddles of the car park. Shawn's suit is now completely black and soaking wet. He gets a few good shots into the guy and, as he gets up from the floor, he sticks the boot in a few times. I put my one away and the fight comes to an end. We both go back in the club to get cleaned up, using towels from the kitchen to dry ourselves off.

Shawn looks down at his feet and shouts, "Right, I'm going to kill that twat I left in the car park."

"What's the matter now" I ask.

"Look," he says, "his fucking teeth have scuffed all my new shoes."

With that, we all just burst out laughing. It was a funny end to a serious situation. I'm glad Shawn jumped in, it shows just how good a friend he is, and of course he did make us all laugh.

The tallest guy I ever fought must have been about six foot five and was on leave from the Army. He was sitting with his mates when I get told that he had just stolen a few bottles of orange juice from the bar. I walk over and as he gets up I ask him to return the drinks. Of course, he informs me that he hadn't taken them. I ask him one more time. He then gives me abuse and pokes me in the chest. I told him not to do it again, but then he tries to poke me once more. I throw this beautiful left-hook, right-hand combination which sends him spark out. He lands on this big oval table full of drinks; he was lying there covered in all the drink. I knew soon as I connected that he was out, it's that certain feel to a punch that lets me know I've connected right. If you go to the gym, you see the big guys pounding away at the bag, just throwing these big haymakers that, in reality, don't do much damage. It's the quick, sharp, snapping punches that your opponent doesn't see that puts them all away.

I've spent years training in gyms with karate, boxing or just lifting weights. I sometimes expect the kids I train to be as committed as I am, but I shouldn't really. It gives me such a good feeling to get these kids training, they are all like a big family to me and I look after each one still. I never award belts to them until I feel they earn it. It's a big achievement getting a black belt, so they must work hard to get it. You should see some of their faces when they get their new belt or win a competition, it makes it all worth while for me. Money isn't the most important thing in my life, it's my family and the respect of others that matters to me.

Due to the upbringing that I've had, I could have turned out a bully. I've known others who have had their lives turn out that way. I myself decided to be a fair person, not look for fights or cause trouble. I think that is why I have so many good friends and get on so well with others. Just because I had a hard life doesn't mean I have to make life hard for others. My wife and kids have never wanted for anything. There's nothing I wouldn't do for them. My wife Mary has always been by my side and I owe everything to her. She has given me 25 years of faithful love and of course our beautiful daughter Kelly. There's not a day that goes past when I don't think of how much I love them. You see, even though I have always been known as a fighter, I'm a soft-hearted bugger as well. If I made friends with someone now, I would be their mate for life. I'd rather have 1,000 friends than one enemy. I've had so many fights that I haven't mentioned here, each time I've fought with cold hard aggression but I still would rather be known as a nice guy than a fighter.

GREG HALL

Manchester

Greg Hall (right) receives his blue belt in Brazilian jiu-jitsu from the legendary Royce Gracie

It takes a certain kind of character to survive for more than a decade as a professional doorman in the gang-haunted clubs of central Manchester. Greg Hall draws his spirit from an unhappy childhood and from the martial arts that gave his life direction and meaning. No-one is more knowledgeable about realistic combat techniques.

YOU SHOW ME a tough guy and I'll show you someone who was bullied as a child. When you have had that awful feeling as a child, you never want it to come back again. I was born in Crumpsall, north Manchester, in 1970, and had a rough childhood. My mam and dad had a lot of trouble with each other. It gave me an inferiority complex and I was bullied a lot at school. It affected my self-worth and the bullies could see that weakness.

I had a circle of friends in this park where we used to go and they weren't so rough, but you could go outside the area and there were rivalries. Crumpsall would fight Blackley or Cheetham Hill. Wherever you went, you got, "Where are you from?" It was like asking what football team you supported and you had to fight your way out. I wasn't a sportsman at all: I used to forget my PE kit on purpose and stand on the line watching the others play football. But from being a young boy I used to ask my dad to take me boxing. I wanted to go when I was seven but my dad wouldn't let me.

Brian Robinson and Dave Massey used to teach at Boniface's gym. I finally went when I was 14. It was the wrong night and they were doing morris dancing! The lady said, "Come back tomorrow night." So I returned the next night. I felt a bit intimidated on the way there. I didn't know what to expect. Brian Robinson was the pro trainer and Dave Massey was the amateur trainer. Dave said he had beaten Dave "Boy" Green [former double world title challenger] as a boxer. In my mind, I took to it straight away, because I knew I was forging a good, strong will, but physically I was just a skinny, gangly kid. They were all from Salford and when I sparred they tried to punch me up. The gloves were really old and blue and came up to your elbow.

I have always had an addictive personality and I just got into it. I kept seeing Pat Barrett [Manchester-born former British and European Light-welterweight Champion] in the local *Express*, so I went to the Collyhurst and Moston gym, where he trained, and enjoyed it. They were a bit better trainers there. When you see somebody who is the business, you suddenly realise what is a bad teacher. They were showing us the proper body mechanics. I had quite a few fights there, then went to the gym in Moss Side run by Phil Martin. When I first went in it was all Moss Side guys, mostly black, and from the minute I went in it was intimidating. Phil Martin used to have the heating turned up to 100 degrees and the fitness was really intense. It was really good for your mind: your brain wanted to blow up but you had to keep going. There were some champions at Martin's: Frank Grant, Ensley Bingham, Maurice Core, Carl Thompson, Stevie Walker, Ossie Maddix. I started doing Thai boxing for a couple of years as well, when I was about 15, with Master Toddy. He had been over in England a while and was "the man" at the time: him, Master Sken, Master Toddy and Master Woody. They were all the top men. I would train every day and still do. I had loads of energy: I was hyperactive. My son has got the same thing and he is nine.

Outside the gyms, I was part of this crowd of young kids who weren't tough, but I met a couple of guys and went down the wrong track. I minded this guy who was drug-dealing, and he used to rob cars. I would make sure that if anyone came while he was taking a car, I would do them. The drugs were lucrative. We used to go to this nightclub and he sometimes paid me up to £200 a night and sometimes he was so off his face, he didn't even deal anything. It was Es and acid and all that stuff.

There was a lot of big rival teams [of young gangsters] at the time. We never got caught by them but you were always worried that various teams might find out. It was only me and him, and so we usually avoided the clubs. I didn't know too much, I was just a young boy thinking I was a tough guy. There were some people, the top Manchester hard men, who I never saw but I heard the names. There were stories about them: some probably true, some blown out of proportion. A lot of my pals have gone to jail or got shot or got caught up with dickheads.

I started dealing myself. One day I was sat in my flat in Blackley with my dealing partner and my girlfriend at the time. In the daytime this guy had come to the door and asked, "Have you got any draw?" I said, "No, we have finished." He started looking around the house. The door of the flat was wired up and strengthened but had a cut-out switch so it wouldn't kill anyone. A lot of the dealers did the same: you would get wrought iron and fix it into the floor with scaffolding and put a plug into the wall and put the positive to one strip and the negative to another and the minute you can see there is trouble you can activate it. In the flat door was also a spyhole. There was a blind spot and I had a mirror to cover that. It was to protect against "taxers".

At night this guy came back. My pal opened the door and the guy had a pump-action shotgun. My pal went to hit him but was knocked over by another guy. I heard the door go boom and all the hairs on my neck stood up. I had this big sword but before I got close enough this black guy had the gun in my face and said, "Fucking get down on the floor." I kept trying to go for it again but he had the gun on my girlfriend. It was January 2 and he said, "Get down there and kiss that Christmas tree."

He got away with nothing because me and my mate blagged it. We didn't live at the flat and made sure we kept the place bare. We opened all the cupboards and showed them there was nothing there. We knew who they were and went looking for them straight away. After they left the house, there was a carload outside and I ran towards it and they drove off. The anger overcame the fear: I was just thinking, *what shall I do?* Martial arts training helped me control the fear.

I stayed at Master Toddy's about six years and became fully qualified in Thai boxing and tae kwon do and got my belts. But I was just doing martial arts, not really thinking about it. Then I met a man called Steve Powell. He had been a doorman himself and he opened me up to karate and then jeet kune do and then my martial arts just exploded. It had all come home to me when I was in a pub one day with a pal, wearing my imaginary black belt, when it went berserk. These guys were hitting each other with chairs and bottles and I thought, *how can I deal with that?* Powell dealt with reality stuff.

I started working on the doors when I was 21, in Manchester city centre. I was at a gym in Salford and they needed spare doormen and asked if I could cover and I stayed there for six years. Most of my fights were there. It was a hotel, the Britannia, near Piccadilly bus station, with a club called Saturdays, a bar and another club. It was for hotel patrons and there was a dress code. When I got there, I thought we had a good team and they blocked most of the undesirables.

You could get into the club from different areas, so you would block them on one door and they would get in the other. It was rammed out every time. I think it was 2,000 capacity, mainly soul music. Because of the trouble around it, some clubs have it in their licence now that they can't have soul music. When I first got on the door I was green about how it worked. I thought we were one team and they were another and it was us against them. I soon found out it wasn't like that. There would be 15 doormen on at the weekend but only three during the week and if they came back during the week, you had had it. The manager was weak as well.

The two worst types of doormen I have worked with are the guy who talks a good fight and couldn't fight sleep, and the guy who stands there with his chest out looking at himself, with his head up his own arse, not aware of anything going on. We started getting quite a few of the first type and when it kicked they were shaking like jelly.

I was on the door once with this guy and these two known faces came to the door. I said, "No trainers or tracksuits." One tried to grab my larynx and I knocked his arm away. So the guy said, "Are we fighting now, or what?" The 19-stone doorman next to me was visibly shaking. I said to the lad, "How can I fight you? Look at the state of this cunt." Meaning my supposed back-up. And I let them in.

177

Another night, I was stood on the door and had had a run-in with this guy from a certain team the night before. I didn't know he was from this team and he had mouthed off and was about to hit me so I said, "What's up with you?" and while he was thinking about it, I knocked him out with a right hook to the jaw. The one he doesn't see is the one that gets him. The next night, it was near Christmas, and they came with tickets for Christmas. I was taking these tickets on the front door, which they had paid £35 for. This guy came back and pushed my arm and said, "I have fucking got something for you round the corner." I pulled my arm away and said, "You have got fuck all round the corner for me, dickhead." The next minute, they all came out of the woodwork, seven of them, and started going for it. I had to fight my bollocks off to get back to the door. The reason I got there was because the sleeve of my suit came off with three of them holding onto it. When I got back to the door, the other doorman, who was from the same part of the city as this firm, said, "That's what happens when you fuck with guys from our 'hood." I thought, *thanks very much, you bastard.*

Steve Powell was a doorman in the town for ten or twelve years so I knew that what he was telling me, he had done. It wasn't theory. He was the most frightening guy I had seen up to that point. He had this delivery system, the double-hip. Basically, you use the rotation of your hip to create a whiplash effect in your upper body and can generate enormous power for punches, elbows, whatever, without having to wind up your shot. And they were doing it from no guard, just however they were stood, and still generating massive power. The pioneer of it was a Japanese guy called Shigeru Kimura. He had a physics degree and put diodes on people to work out the most effective body mechanics. There are 13 different pointers to the double-hip delivery system. One story told about Kimura was that he was in America and a guy pulled a gun on him and he has done the double-hip and the guy just moved his head a fraction and Kimura's punch ripped his ear clean off.

178

I was doing tae kwon do, thinking I can do a high spinning kick like Jean Claude Van Damme and knock people out, but then found that I was standing in a four-foot doorway with not enough room to spin a cat. Whereas Steve Powell was doing massive punches from a stationary start. And he was blending everything himself, all different styles of martial arts. The system that he taught me is still my basis in martial arts but I have added lots to it, from grappling, jeet kune do, Filipino arts, Brazilian jiu-jitsu, vale tudo and so on.

I remember when Ultimate Fighting first became big in the United States, where they match different martial artists against each other in competition. Me and some of my pals had already been doing something similar and called it "hard core". We used to pad up and fight: boxer versus kicker, karate versus wrestler, do scenario work simulating knife attacks. We tried to make it as realistic and possible and put surprises in, so one guy would hide a knife in his trousers, then go to ground with a grappler and be in the worse position but then suddenly pull out the knife. The grappler wouldn't know about it and would have to try to deal with it straight away. There is no best martial art. It is what is best at the time. Usually it is not the best art that wins anyway but the guy behind it.

If you go one-on-one, size does make a difference. A big guy can absorb the blows, put pressure on you because of their bulk and also put more mental pressure on you because they are bigger and more intimidating. Anyone who tells you otherwise is full of shit. But fights don't usually happen on a simple one-to-one basis. Usually nobody knows when it is going to go off, and then it is down to who is quickest to the gun, with the most power. My style on the door is, I always try to talk to the guy. But usually you can tell if it is no use. In the film *The Good, The Bad and The Ugly*, there is a scene where the bad guy, Tuco, is in the bath and a man comes in with a gun to shoot him. The guy goes into a big spiel about how he is going to kill him, then Tuco calmly pulls the trigger of the gun he is hiding beneath the bathwater and blows the guy away. Then he says out loud, "My friend, when it is time to shoot, shoot. Don't talk." It's who is quicker to the gun.

Then there are the big groups you have to deal with, rugby players, stag nights, whatever. When things turn nasty, what you want to avoid is them all kicking off and smashing the place up. You always get a ringleader, so the idea is to isolate him without causing all the others to kick off. What I learned to do was to go up to him and just say some gibberish into his ear. With the thumping music, the club packed full of people, he would think he had misheard you and would go, "What?"

I'd say exactly the same nonsense and, again, he'd say, "What?"

Then I would shout into his ear, "Come out into the hallway mate, and then I can tell you. It's too loud in here."

Then I would walk out and he would follow, curious to know what I had to say. His mates might see us but because I wasn't dragging him out or looking confrontational, they would think nothing of it. Once in the hallway, we would jump him and sling him out. Then we would go up to his mates one by one and say, "There's someone outside wants to have a word with you." When they came out to the door, we'd just push them out into the street and slam it shut behind them.

My worst opponent was this guy who always used to pop up. He was just a big fat beer fighter but he couldn't half give it and take it. He has tried to bite my ear off, my nose off, he pulled my eye out of its socket once, he has glassed me. I have knocked him out every time but each time, for the first 30 seconds it has been like fighting Tyson.

The first time I came across him, I was on the door and there was this absolute babe who used to come in the club called Angela. Well, her sister came to the door and said, "If you can meet Angela at about quarter to two, she will take you home tonight." I wasn't supposed to finish on the door until 2am but I swerved off early, as any man would. I met Angela and we were sitting on a wall: me, Angela, her sister and her sister's boyfriend. Anyway, this guy started flashing his arse in the street. Her sister said something to him and he came over and hit her.

I used to run a pub called the Cheshire Cheese in Manchester, by the old *Daily Express* building, and I knew this guy from in there. I intervened and he grabbed hold of me and wouldn't let go of my coat. BANG, I front-kicked him. Then his mates came out of the woodwork. Two of them were easy. I had bought a bottle of champagne for my big night with Angela and gave it to her sister's boyfriend to hold. As it was kicking off, he held the bottle like a baby, then threw it and one of our attackers grabbed it and smashed it to use as a weapon.

I end up on the floor with the guy who had started it all, rolling around. It was a bad situation. It was dark, late at night, I was knackered from fighting, I was tense anyway because of looking forward to going out with this girl, and I was down on the deck. Anyway, I got this guy in what is called a closed guard: me lying on my back but with my legs wrapped around his waist to control him. I was going for a choke and his finger came into my eye. He was also trying to bite me and his mate with the broken bottle was trying to hit me. Well, you can train in grappling for as long as you like but nothing is going to prepare you for a situation like that.

Just as his mate went to stick the bottle in my head, I moved the guy on top of me into the way and he got bottled. Then I bridged and threw him off. I got hold of the guy with the bottle and we were both locked on to each other, panting. Things had got out of hand now so I said to him, "Look, you and I both know a certain guy." I mentioned this guy's name. Let's just say he is a very well-respected person in Manchester. "Drop the bottle now and we'll have it one-to-one, otherwise I will come through your door at four o'clock one morning and kill you." He knew I wasn't bluffing because he knew that I was a friend of the guy I had just mentioned. So he dropped the bottle. That's real weapons defence for you, not the moves you see in books. Anyway, then I finished it.

181

The funniest thing that happened to me on the doors was a bit rude, but I'll tell you. I was at the entrance to this nightclub, talking to the doormen, and this bird came up and said, "Listen, if I give you a blowjob, will you let me in for free?" I said, "Okay." So we walked down the road to a dark spot and she gave me a blowjob. I zipped up my pants and, as I walked away, I looked back over my shoulder and said, "Missus, I don't work there, it's free to get in anyway, and it shuts in half an hour." She chased me up the road, hitting me with her handbag!

I was the landlord and tenant of the Cheshire Cheese when the Manchester Bomb went off in the summer of 1996. It was my best day ever for trade because mine was the closest pub to the town centre that was still open. All the other pubs were either damaged or evacuated. It was a rough pub when I first took over. We used to get a lot of lads from Ancoats and also a lot of gypsies from nearby campsites. The gypsies used to love smashing things up: when it kicked off they would smash the optics, the windows, the tables and chairs, everything. They just liked wrecking things. We used to be running around trying to put things away before they smashed them. Occasionally you'd get some heavies in. One guy came once trying to demand protection money. I collared him and said, "I'm the protection in here mate." He didn't come back.

Manchester has a particular problem with people being "connected". It has got a lot better because most of the "heads" have now moved out of town. Now it is the CCTV and the police you have to watch out for. There were clubs closing down because of one or other rival door teams, managers being terrified, landlords being leaned on. I have never been connected to any of the teams. I'm a firm believer in karma: what goes around, comes around. If you punch someone on the nose, sooner or later you will get that back. If you are nice to someone, same thing. But righteous anger, when you or those close to you are threatened for no reason, is justified. I have done "house visits" but I never did it unless it was personal. I have had a few run-ins with the law but you wipe the camera, get your story straight and get rent-a-witness and you are straight. But you can't have a piss in Manchester town centre these days without a camera being on you.

The first time I saw a guy knocked out on the door it was a shock and the first time I got the threat of getting shot I nearly pissed myself. But one of the other doorman said, "Don't worry mate, we get 'shot' every night here. You hear it all the time." I just got used to it. You get desensitised. I used to wear a vest sometimes, when I thought it would be rocking: usually stab-proof. If it is a gun you are usually fucked anyway because they will stick it right in your face.

I have had guns pulled on me a few times. One time this guy came up. I had had a really bad fallout with my girlfriend. I was really upset and I didn't give a fuck about anything. This black guy came up with his team and stuck a gun in my face. I said, "I've fallen out with my girlfriend and the pain I have got in my heart, if you pull the trigger you will be giving me a release. And if you don't pull the trigger, you're going to look bad in front of all your mates. So it's up to you."

And this guy looks at his mates and said, "This crazy white man, he doesn't give a fuck. He's got bad woman trouble."

And all his mates start saying, "Man, I can relate to that," and, "Oh, don't tell me about that, I know where he's coming from." And they ended up sympathising with me. But I got a bad rep for a while with the other doormen around that period because I was a loose cannon.

I have done the door ten years. I am a professional doorman. I have been shot at, slashed, hit with bats, had someone try to kidnap me, had house visits, pub visits. Most doormen are show. Only a couple have impressed me. You won't get many who will go one on one who aren't connected with teams or aren't violence men. But there was one guy: he used to wear steel toe-capped boots and he would kick them in the shin and when they bent over with the pain he would just boot them full in the face. End of story. I must have seen him do it 50 times and it never failed. I still do the doors nearly every night but my goal would be to get a full-time martial arts academy, teaching reality-based techniques.

Martial arts have changed my life. If you know you can handle yourself it makes such a difference. If you go to the pictures and the guy behind is kicking the back of your chair, you know you can tell him to stop. It gives you that personal confidence. Even just going in a restaurant and sending back your meal if it is not right. You read of all these road rages, anger displacement, people getting ulcers and having heart attacks from stress and tension. Well, if you train martial arts you just go to the gym, punch the bag and get it all out. Simple. I would recommend it to anyone: there would be a lot less violence. I think all girls should learn some self-defence and I think it should be mandatory in schools to combat bullying.

Rick Young is the best martial artist I have trained with. He is a full jeet kune do instructor under Dan Inosanto, who trained with Bruce Lee. He is the most frightening I have seen. He is also the nicest guy you will meet, but with a lot of these guys, when they tell you a story they start to relive it and you can see in their eyes that they are the business. They have what war veterans call the "1,000-yard stare". I have trained with top guys like Erik Paulsen [former shootfighting champion from America] and Royce Gracie [legendary Brazilian jiu-jitsu exponent and winner of three Ultimate Fighting Championships]. Royce was a gentleman. When we trained, he was talking to some other guy while at the same time tapping me out for fun. He gave me my blue belt, at a gym in Manchester. I have trained with Dan Inosanto in America and I have instructorships under Ricky Faye and Larry Hartsell. I have also been to America in summer camps, training. Some people *do* martial arts. I am a martial artist.

Greg Hall teaches his own reality-based martial arts system, called G-Tek, at gyms in north Manchester. He is also working on a book about his experiences as a doorman.

DARREN PULLMAN

Swansea

Life dealt him a bad hand, and the boxing gym became Darren's reason for existing. His harsh upbringing provided him with survival instincts second to none and the ability to turn from being a gentleman to a cold-blooded killer in nanoseconds. Although still young, he has packed in more action than men three times his age, leaving him with more stories to tell than many a war veteran.

LOOKING OVER MY life, I can't say that my childhood was a good one. In fact some people would call it a nightmare. My father, who I don't really know a lot about, was a drinker, and my mother had a lot of mental health problems. Due to my mother's condition, she was always getting into trouble and, of course, the trouble sometimes followed her back home. I can remember being three years old and getting mauled by an Alsatian dog, quite serious in fact. I had bite marks all over my face and body. The same week as I was getting over the attack by the dog, the back door of the house was smashed in; it completely flew across the room and a few men rushed in and battered my mother senseless. It was a frightening thing for a small, defenceless child to witness. It was also one of the first malicious things I encountered.

There were times when she just wanted to take her own life. She herself had a bad childhood and it affected her. There were times when every window of the house was put through. On other occasions we found out she had tried to kill herself. It was a traumatic childhood; I don't know how I managed to keep things together over the years.

Maybe the one thing that kept me from going down the wrong road was the introduction of the boxing gym in my life. I went to the gym with friends and would sit and watch the older kids training. I was too young to train but I'd sit and take in the whole atmosphere. The coaches would look after the young boxers, really taking an interest in them. It may sound crazy but as a youngster, with all the problems I had at home, I found the gym to be the place that I related to as home. It was the only place I could relax and be at ease. And when the coaches started to train me, they were the only people who were taking an interest in my life at the time. If I'm ever feeling down or have a problem, then I always return back to the gym. It's the only place where I really fit in.

It could be that, because I didn't have anyone to stand up for me, the bullies found me an easy target. They would always be in gangs – it's funny how they work like that, never on their own, always in a gang. I took some terrible hidings. They would get me on the way to school, in school and on the way home. I had all these things going on at home and to make matters worse the bullies took me to be their victim.

I thought things would change when my mum met this Army guy. He moved us to England for about two years. We moved frequently around England, so I was always the new boy, and of course, I had a Welsh accent, which made me stand out to the school bullies. In Southampton during the Falklands War, we had an area on the Army barracks that was cornered off, a sort of play area which was inside a large protective metal cage, the whole idea being to protect the kids from any bomb attacks if they did occur. The bigger kids were battering me each and every day. The teachers must have known what was going on but they didn't lift a finger in my defence. It got the point where I offered to fight the biggest bully in the cage. I thought if I could beat him it would stop all the trouble I was getting.

I waited by the cage for him to turn up and he did, bringing all his mates with him. It felt very lonely there on my own but I had to put an end to it all; even if I got beat, I just had to fight him. We entered the cage, both taking a corner each. They slammed the metal door behind us and all took their places, looking through the mesh at us. We ran straight at each other and started to grapple. I was taking a beating by this bully but I threw out a right-hand, left-hook and both connected. The punches took the fight out of him. I could see it in his eyes. He just wanted out of the fight but I just kept punching him to the floor. I pinned him down and all the hidings, all the trouble I had at home, everything that was bothering me came to my mind and I let him have it. His friends tried to pull me off him, so I got up and started to beat on them. I just exploded and anyone who was in range got hit.

A short while later, we got moved back home to Wales, and by this time I had picked up a bit of an English accent, so the school bullies thought I was once again a victim because I stood out a little. This time I got it into my head that if I was going to fight all the time, then I was going to learn how to fight properly. I joined the Gwent ABC gym and took up boxing a little more seriously. First night back in the gym, I was put in the ring to spar. This was the first time for me. I got hit by a big right hand at one stage but threw one straight back and he went straight to the floor, shocked and dazed. There was no more sparring for that lad, so they put me in with a champion boxer who took me around and showed me a few moves.

At home my mother had got up and left, so there was just me and my step-father, who I didn't really know that well and who had no interest in my upbringing. After all, he was only a couple of years older than me and had no kids of his own, so I can't really blame him for not being there for me. I was getting expelled from school, thrown out of classes, but started spending more time in the boxing gym. I started to get more discipline in my life. You must see boxing was giving me something to focus my energy on, an escape from the family, and provided me with a way to prove myself. That may sound stupid to you but I just needed a way to prove to myself and show others that I could do something worthwhile with myself.

I trained every chance I got. Nothing could stop me from going to the gym. My friends were leading normal lives but me, I was sleeping on the floors of their houses. I even used to sleep in the abandoned cars in the quarry nearby. It didn't bother me what was happening to me outside the gym; in fact, it might have made me a better fighter. It wasn't long before I started competing in boxing matches, winning various titles along the way. I loved it when the opponent would come straight at me, never wanted to just jab and move, always I looked for the in-close fight. I was never put down or counted out no matter what blows I took. If they caught me with a good punch then I'd come straight back at them, often knocking them out.

I started to train in pro gyms, which I found to be harder but were just what I wanted. Sometimes when I went out to a nightclub I ended up fighting but now I was fighting stronger, bigger guys. It didn't matter to me who they were, if they wanted to fight then I'd give it to them. After all, that's what I was training for. I was learning martial arts to give me an edge when a streetfight would go to the ground. I knew how to box but I was also learning how to grapple and kick as well. The bouncers were okay at first but when I started putting people away they started to treat me different. I could sense some fancied their chances. Don't get me wrong, some were tidy and still are. It was just that I was a young kid knocking out some good-named streetfighters. I started to get into fights with the bouncers as well as the local "hard men". I was sometimes fighting three to four times a night, three nights a week. There were loads out there who wanted to fight and I just couldn't back down to them. If someone got bullied then I'd fight the bully. I was constantly fighting bigger and bigger guys. I was getting arrested all the time; men I had beat in fair fights took me on with the police. They were happy to cause the fight but when I ended it they complained and I got pulled in.

One of the fights that got me recognised as a streetfighter started in a local club. I had just laid out this guy when this big fucker started to have a go. The bouncers broke it up and politely asked me to leave and I left the club. I waited outside for the guy I had been fighting. It was still early so I had to wait four or five hours for him to leave the club. I had asked the bouncers to get him out but they were friends of his and let him stay in the club. They told me to go away in case he battered me when he came out. I sat outside in the car park by his car, waiting to settle the score. When the club emptied, I saw him in the crowd. I couldn't miss him: he was about six foot two, a well-built guy who was a debt collector for local drug dealers. It didn't matter who he was, or how big he was, the point was that the fight wasn't over until one of us was beat. I sometimes just can't leave things lie; there has to be a decision one way or another.

I shout over to the fucker, "How about settling the score now?" We both entered the multi-storey car park, me on my own and him with all the bouncers and loads of customers. We started to fight each other, both of us hell-bent on winning. He used some throws that brought me down hard, winding me. We fought for nearly an hour, both worn out with the battle. His size and strength was wearing me down; being drunk didn't help me much either. He was tired as well but still had the upper hand. He was beating me to the punch, his long reach gave him an advantage. He started showboating to his friends, trying to humiliate me, pushing me down and laughing to his mates. I grabbed his legs and brought him crashing down. With the little strength I had left, I started to beat into him. The fight was gone out of him – he never thought I could turn the fight around and his confidence was shot. I just smashed my fists into his face, and wrapping my legs under his stopped him getting me off him. He managed to bite a little chunk of my ear away so I started putting my elbow into his face as well, splitting him open. He screamed that he had had enough but I just beat the hell into him. He was biting and trying to gouge my eyes out. My hand was broken and my shoulder was dislocated. I was aware of the injuries but it wasn't till later that I felt the pain. I got up and walked away from him. He was a beaten man and had lost the respect of his friends.

From there, the fights just went crazy. Every time I went out I was getting into some right old scraps. I had beaten a known face, so others thought they would have a go. Bouncers would wait until I was drunk before they would make a move, mostly with their mates as backup, but I still beat them. All the known faces around town couldn't believe that, for a guy of five foot ten, I was putting the big six-footers away.

About this time I started to play rugby. I'd always loved the game, so now I wanted to play. Our team was always getting into fights. If we thought we were going to lose, then the team would start a fight to get the game abandoned. I remember one game where I had just put some guy down with a straight right hand. Most of the team came at me, so I dug my studs in and started smashing anyone who came near. A good few of them came straight at me, so a couple of my team-mates helped out. I was fighting with loads of them but they couldn't put me away. They were big guys and I was catching loads of punches as well. I was getting punches to the side of my head and heavy kicks to my body, scar tissue was opening up in my mouth so I was spitting out blood. They were all around me trying to get me down, and I was kicked so many times in the back that I almost went down. Maybe if I had gone down the fight would have been over but I wouldn't fall and still kept fighting. Eventually the fight stopped but my back just didn't feel right.

I was then told by the hospital that I had a few hairline fractures in my vertebrae. I just shrugged it off and kept playing in rugby matches. Every time I played I must have been doing more damage to my back, I was so used to having injuries that I just tried to ignore the problems. My hands would start to twitch on their own, and so would my leg. Also I was starting to get numb feelings in my hands. Seems I had caused some nerve damage and these were the early effects that I was experiencing. One morning I got up with pain all down my spine. I strapped my body up and went out to play rugby. All through the game I felt strange and when I had the ball I just couldn't run with it. It felt like I was carrying the whole team on my back. I got home and collapsed in the house. I couldn't feel my legs, so an ambulance was called to take me to the hospital.

I was told to stay in bed for a year but after three months I had a guts full. The only way I could get around was in a wheelchair. Most of the time I couldn't feel my legs but now and again I'd get some feelings, so I knew the back was knitting back slowly. Now you would think that I'd be out of trouble in a wheelchair, but some of the guys I had beaten up wanted revenge. Others just wanted to be known as the one that beat me. I had a friend who wheeled me around and he would get battered and then I'd be next. It was impossible to defend myself, I just took the beatings and hoped one day to get them back.

Slowly my back got better and before long I was up and about. I went looking for all the guys who took a liberty when I was wheelchair-bound. Every one of them was paid back in full; I slowly got around to them all. I'd find out where they worked or where they drank and have a straightener with each one. Some wanted to fight but most tried to talk their way out of it, but I still did them anyway.

Now all my energy and fitness was back. The boxing was going well but I was still mixing it on the street. The police again were pulling me in but the charges for fighting were getting more serious. Prison was unavoidable. I was arrested and sent down for a while. Inside I just tried to get my head down and do my time. Thing is with prison, you'd get guys bragging how they had shot, knifed, slashed or bottled somebody. These were the so-called prison hard men and I was beating two or three of them up at the same time. They were trying to be the big gangster but that didn't wash with me. I'd come out of my cell to face a few of them and most of the time it would take me just a couple of punches to put them all away. Some of these guys were in for up to 15 years, they were known tool merchants who would stab you to death, and here's me putting them away with one punch. These guys had been living off their reputations for years but it didn't bother me, I'd been in the ring with British champions, sometimes world champions. Why should I worry about them? They didn't bother me, in fact I wanted them to try it on. They were just big-mouthed bullies who nobody ever stood up to, just the type I liked. They may have been big guys in their own area but I was still taking them out with clean shots. The other prisoners got to respect me. If they wanted to do someone in, they would come and ask me first. I would tell them, do what you have to do, if it's beating someone up or cutting them. Just don't try it with me or I would bring it down on their heads tenfold.

Out of prison I still had my pro licence. At this stage I hadn't fought as a professional but I was back training for it. In the daytime I'd work in the scrapyards or labouring, at night I was in the gym sweating it out. Everyone was telling me that I was wasting my time streetfighting, I should put it to work in the ring. My first pro fight was set for three months time. I had something to go for now so I was working out every chance I got. I even travelled to Bristol to train at a top gym, same gym some of the best in the world trained at. It was great. I was mixing with the best fighters and learning off them all. Every time I sparred with a top pro I'd learn a little more. For the first time I could find my life coming together. The only problem was that I was still streetfighting and the police were always on my case. They had warrants out for me and were pulling me in for them. I even got pulled in when I was leaving to do an exhibition for ex-world champ Steve Robinson. I know I should have just kept out of trouble but I just can't walk away from it like others could.

Each time I got close to the day of the fight, I'd get a phone call saying the other guy had pulled out. I started back training in a local gym. Most of the other fighters had all left for different gyms and most of the time it was just myself training. At one stage the roof blew off, and I would train with the snow coming down. I got the call to fight a seasoned fighter for my first pro fight. I had one week to get ready for it. It didn't matter that the guy had a good few fights, I just wanted to get it on, so I took it.

Talk about being cursed: my uncle died the week before the fight, I split up with my long-term girlfriend and then my cousin died the day of the fight. I just couldn't get an even break, but I still fought. The fight was hard but I felt I had won it; they called it a draw but everyone I spoke to said I should have won it. A short while after the fight, I went to the hospital for a check-up on my shoulder. Turns out I'd been fighting with a broken right collarbone and hairline fractures in my wrists. They operated on me and took away a part of my collarbone. Looks like all the streetfights had caused some damage after all.

When I was healthy again, I returned to the gym but now everyone had left, there was just me training. The gym was falling apart. I was finding it harder to train. How could I punch bags that were soaking wet? A few times I got to travel to other gyms to spar with the likes of Nicky Piper [world-ranked boxer from Cardiff] but things weren't the same any more. I dislocated my other shoulder, broke my hands again and had a bad strain on my Achilles heel. I tried to fight on as a pro but injuries were making it very hard for me. Seemed the more I wanted it, the harder it got for me. I didn't get my pro licence renewed and stopped training for pro fights. I was learning different martial art techniques and just training to keep fit and for fighting on the streets.

The biggest problem I had was when I was out clubbing. With all the fights I had been in, the club owners saw me as a liability. They wanted me out of their clubs and also some of the bouncers would take it on themselves to try and get me out. One guy working the door was a known bully who thought he was a top fighter. He started on me downstairs in a club and I knocked him spark out. I just carried on upstairs to the bar and forgot about him. On the way out all the door staff are there waiting for me. In front of the whole club, I do all the doormen. They found it easy to get a drunken man out but they couldn't move me. I smash up about seven of them before I left.

About a week later, I get a message to come to the club. I do this only to find they've got new doormen from other towns. They tell me I'm banned and they had this big new bouncer to back up the ban. I knew he was there to fight me so I asked him where he wanted it. The club had an area out back which couldn't be seen from the street so that's where we all go.

I look up at this guy that they have paid to fight me, he's about six foot three and must be weighing over 20 stone. He was a giant of a man. The other doormen stayed around the sides of this courtyard just waiting to see me beaten. Thing was, this guy was paid to come and fight me, he had no hatred for me. He just wanted the cash and thought the fight would be easy. Now me, on the other hand, wanted to smash fuck out of him. I wasn't being paid loads of cash to fight, I was fighting to survive and hated every inch of him.

He sprinted straight at me. I braced myself for the impact. He throws a right hand over the top but was too open. I throw the same right hand, which connects first. My hand crunches into his face, it literally sunk into his face. My hand breaks on impact but his whole face is now smashed up. He crumples up on the floor. I jump on top of him. I use my good hand to inflict more damage to his face. I hold him down and elbow strike him until I'm covered all over in his blood. His cheekbones and his eye socket were just smashed in. I jump off him and start on the bouncers; they had all been standing there shocked. This just wasn't what they had planned. I have so much adrenalin pumping now that I start knocking the bouncers out. I leave the ones that didn't back off lying on the floor. I could have just left the club but I thought *fuck it* and went up to the bar for a drink, just to wind them up.

About a week later I'm back at the club, upstairs by the bar just having a few drinks with friends. It had been a good night and I'm just laughing and chatting to people I know. All of a sudden, someone's rushed me and grabbed me around the waist. It's a takedown that shootfighters use. I'm trying to regain my balance but I'm grappled through the fire exit. This judo guy has got his grip on me. He's trying to get a full mount on top of me but as we land on the floor I spin him so I'm on top. His legs are wrapped around me and he has got my arm locked. He's trying to break my arm. I have to admit he knew his stuff; even though I was on top, he still was in the better position. Suddenly he releases his hold. My arm is free so I start to smash him with my elbows and my head. I started to go too far on him, so a few friends pulled me off him. With that, I'm straight down the stairs to confront the doormen who got the judo guy in to fight me. As I'm running down the stairs the doormen are on their way up, each one I knock out on my way down. I would have done the whole door that night but a few ran away. I chased them outside to be confronted by the police. There were going to be charges against me but they got dropped in the end.

After that scrap, the fights become more organised, with club managers getting bigger and harder fighters in to try and sort me out. I made sure they all had my phone number. I wanted them to know how to get hold of me. I wasn't going to hide from them. Every so often the phone would ring and they would ask me to come to a certain club. The phone numbers were always withheld. I would turn up to meet their new hard man. A few would ask to fight for money but I'd tell them if they are true fighters they would fight just to win, no money involved. I just wanted to see what they were made of.

If I leave a club early then I need to watch my back as I walk home. If someone can't beat me on their own then they tend to come back with friends. This don't bother me, it just means that I have to fight harder and meaner. I got followed one night, three guys who I had fought followed me out of a club to jump me. I hear them coming up from behind. I turn to confront the first two with a left-hook, right-hand, one punch for each of them. The third was a huge steroid-head, he didn't bother that I had put his mates to sleep, he just came towards me. Seems I had been fighting with him earlier and it had got broken up. I could see by his attitude and the scars on his face that he was a fighter. His chin was up high as he ran at me. His full weight and my straight right hand on his chin put him out. Strange thing was that he was still on his feet but out cold. He must have been trying to fight it. His eyes were closed, chin was down and his arms were at his sides. He just stood like that, I jumped up and threw a few more punches that put him away.

The fights have taken a toll on my hands. They were always getting broken. Now, instead of taking a while to beat a guy, I try to get it over as fast as I can. Before, I would just go straight at them, but now I leave them come towards me when possible. This way I can strike using their bodyweight against them. I also use my elbows more when I'm in close. I never bite a man until he does it to me. When this happens, I just don't stop and have torn loads of flesh off fighters. If it's a nose or an ear, if I get a grip on it then off the bugger comes.

I fought another judo guy who thought he was clever biting me. We were grappling each other and both using different armlocks and holds on one another. We were both rolling around on the top floor of a multi-storey car park and he managed to dislocate my arm, I actually heard the arm pop out of the shoulder when he did it. After a while he tries to bite my ear off but I tear it away in time. He just tore the tip off. He was clamped tightly around me so I just kept beating his head on the concrete until I broke free. With that I bite off his whole ear and part of his nose. I just tore them off and spat them out. I just kept biting and punching until he passed out, then the fight was won. Like I always say, if that's the game they want to play then I will play it, but I can be a lot dirtier than them.

Over the years I have had so many bones broken that I have lost count. I've been stabbed, slashed, bottled and jumped by gangs. I never go to the hospital unless it's my hands because I need to look after them. I was Stanley-knifed across the forehead once by some prick who looked like a regular clubber. You know, I didn't even see that one coming. Even though he did that, I still went on to smash him up. A friend has even Superglued my head when I got bottled. The cut just wouldn't close so he had to glue it for me. He was actually being sick while he did it. It turned septic and I developed blood poisoning after it. These days I keep my back to the wall when I go out so that I can see who comes at me.

I have done some things that I'm not proud of, but I do believe that if I hadn't sorted the bullies out then it could be some poor little kid getting battered by them instead. The so-called hard men who have come after me just don't care who they beat up to get their name.

These days, when I walk into a club the owners just call the Old Bill to get me out. Now the big steroid-heads can throw the 16-year-old kids around and I'm not around to stop them. A few guys I've hit have ended up in comas. Now, I'm not happy with that, especially as one didn't come out of his right in the head. He still can't walk or talk tidy. It hurts me to think about sometimes. I wouldn't wish something like that on them, but they wouldn't care if I was wired up to a heart monitor or lying battered in some alleyway. I've never been punched down or knocked out. I've been grappled to the floor, even held above one fighter's head and brought crashing down onto the pavement, but even then I didn't go out.

I know that if I carry on this way it's only a matter of time before something more serious happens to me, so I've decided to change my whole life around. I've made a few contacts in the unlicensed boxing game and feel that's the best way for me to get this all out of my system. I've started to train hard again and I'm once again travelling to different gyms. There's a Merthyr gym called the Slaughterhouse, it's a rough old gym and they have offered me their facilities. Trainers have agreed to train me and the phone rings all the time with guys who want to come to the gym with me.

I get asked if I'm ever scared stepping into a ring or an alleyway with an opponent. Well, as a kid I came home to see my mother cutting her arms open with a razor blade, so anything else I face in life don't seem so bad.

SHAWN COOPER

Kingswinford, West Midlands

Shawn has given many cause to remember his name. To have him at your side in any confrontation would have more than an equalizing effect, whatever the odds. A tactical fighter who has taken boxing onto the streets and has combined finesse with brutality in awesome measure.

I WAS BORN in 1968 and spent my childhood living on the Priory Estate in Dudley in the West Midlands. My mother brought me and my two sisters up by herself – my father had left us when I was about one year old. The fact that I didn't have a father around didn't bother me; where I lived everyone near us was like part of the family. One of those places where you could leave your door open knowing the neighbours would watch your house when you were out. It was a rough area in those days but nobody would steal off their own kind, it was sort of like steal off the rich and bring it home.

I was a cheeky little fucker as a kid, always getting into trouble on the estate. A gym opened up nearby and a friend took me there. I can remember how it felt the first day I walked in there, the atmosphere was electric with all the kids training, and the smell of the leather and the sweat hit me as soon as I walked in. They put these big sparring gloves on me, they were huge and full of horse hair. I did about ten rounds of sparring and thought it was great, I was only a youngster at the time so the whole buzz of the gym had this dramatic effect on me.

I was getting into more trouble on the estate as I was growing up. The kids in the different areas were forming various gangs, from skinheads to Mods. Whatever area we would pass through, there would be a different gang. Of the group of lads I went around with, I was the smallest one, so I felt I had to prove myself a little bit more. I remember once myself and my good mate Lenny Hawthorn needed to earn some extra money so we had the idea of getting scrap metal to sell to the scrapyard. We noticed that all the houses in our area had this copper overflow pipe coming out of the houses from the kitchen sinks. We had this great idea to cut off all the pipes at night and weigh them in. The whole plan went well; only being kids, we didn't realise that people would notice that our houses were the only ones which still had an overflow pipe. So we got caught for that one. I know that wasn't a really serious thing to do but it was only a matter of time before I got involved in other things.

I think I was lucky that a mate took me back to the gym, where I was eventually told that I had talent and should stick to it. Within twelve months I was fighting in the ABA Schoolboy Championships and was travelling all over the country. There were many times when I would fight two or three times a night. I didn't really find that as hard as it seems because I was winning and was always hungry for the next fight. I couldn't wait for the next opponent and then the next one after that, I just wanted to get in the ring and fight. I had 96 amateur fights and only lost nine. I also boxed for England and fought over the world. I was twice on Henry Cooper's *Golden Belt* which was shown on Channel Four.

I lost interest in the amateurs when I lost to Robert McCracken [future British Light-middleweight Champion] in the ABA Championships. I had fought three times that night before I fought him, it was his first fight of the night but I still felt I had beaten him and deserved to win. I then decided it was time to turn professional. I fought for promoters like Barry Hearn and Pat Cowdell and I jumped from one promoter to the next, because they were always offering better deals. I was being trained by the likes of Dean Powell, who at one time was voted the best trainer in England. I had 18 professional fights and won them all. After my 18th fight, I was training for fights that would get cancelled the day before, I'd then train for a few months and the next fight would be off as well. I had phone bills and everything to pay, so of course I wasn't happy with that. What also didn't help was the fact that I was working full-time to make ends meet as well as being a pro boxer. I would get up at four in the morning, run to West Brom then back to Dudley. There was a block of flats which had nine floors and I'd run up and down them five times. I'd get home, wash, change and clock-in for work by half past seven.

I worked as an upholsterer and had to make about 30 suites a day. From Monday to Friday I was training at half past four, so as you can see I was putting my body through too much. If I hadn't had to work as well, then I strongly believe that I could have been an even better fighter. I had done so well as an amateur that I felt there was a lot of pressure for me to do even better as a pro. I could cope with the pressure but having to work as well wore me down a bit. I just upped and packed the professional game in.

I started working the club doors and found at once how much hassle it could be. Some guys would think that if they beat me, being a boxer, they would then gain other people's respect. I would always speak tidy to them and let them keep arguing with me, I wouldn't lose my rag, so they would get more confident. I'd wait until everyone could see what was happening and then I'd let them have it. That way people knew that I was a nice guy who when pushed could do the business.

There was this local guy who had just come out of prison for killing his wife by shooting her in the head with a shotgun, then he turned on his wife's lover and blew the guy's foot off. He had just done a 15-year stretch for this and was only out for five weeks when he has a go at me. I had just driven my van down the street and was passing the kids out to go to their grandmother's. He pulls up behind my van and jumps out. As he comes towards me, I can see in his eyes that there's something wrong. He's a schizophrenic and has this mad look on his face, he just wants to have a go at me, for some reason. I put him straight down on his arse and make the mistake of turning my back on him. He gets hold of his baseball bat and puts it over the back of my head, splitting me right open and scarring me for life. All I could see for a while out of the one eye was a white light. I thought he had knocked my eye out and was lucky that I hadn't been knocked down to the ground. I turned on him and put some time into him. I shattered his jaw in four places and punctured his lung.

Once, a few of us were doing security on this club in the country when this large gang of rugby players turns up. They start to take the piss in the club and want to have go at one of the other doormen. He was a black guy and he was taking some serious racial abuse off them. We try to calm the situation down a bit but they were having none of it. In the end we had to confront them outside. There were four of us and about 15 of these big rugby lads. It all turned into a big free-for-all fight. It was a good job that we were all game lads or we could have been in some serious trouble. I remember one of the rugby guys ripping this big wooden post out of the ground and, as my mate came running in, he takes it full belt over his head. In the end we get the better of them all. It was a bit stupid of them really. I myself am not racist one bit and can't see the point of it.

Some of the clubs that I got called to work at had loads of trouble in them. Along with Lenny we got known as guys who could sort out the troublemakers. Lenny's always been by my side since we were kids. I know I can rely on him, he's my right hand man, just like a brother to me. We got a call to take on this one club which was having some terrible trouble from some travellers, one big family in particular. This was a hard job for us to take on. We knew if we didn't then we would lose respect from other clubs, and also the punters. Over a period of just a few weeks we had sorted the club out. We were getting into fights on the door and knocking them out, having one-to-ones in the car park and beating them all along the way. Now these travellers were game for a fight, they had so much front and really wanted to have a go. It got to a point where they would want to have another go when we were in town with our families, sometimes pointing shooters at us. We had to sit down and work out some kind of game plan. We decided to take the trouble to the campsite, confront them at their own homes. Make them feel intimidated and vulnerable. The threats they were putting out, to burn our houses down and to burn the club down, made us take a stand and if it went all the way then so be it.

We fill up four Range Rovers with some very handy guys and

we all drive down to the campsite. Now Lenny loves dogs and on the way he brakes hard because there's this little dog in the road. The other drivers all brake and swerve to avoid a crash, Lenny nearly killed us all before we even got to the camp. We got to the camp and confronted the troublemakers. After a few of them got weighed in, they pulled a gun on us. They said they were going to kill us but what they didn't know was that one of the guys with us was a proper hit man. Our guy pulled his gun out and put it in the traveller's face, he puts the barrel in the guy's mouth and pushes him down onto the floor. This guy was well prepared to kill the traveller. It was a strange feeling to find out that one of your mates was willing to do something like that just for us. One of the other lads with us kept shouting, "Go on, pull the trigger, blow him away, go on do it." I really felt he was going to do it.

When all this was going on, the police had turned up, and when they saw what was happening they just froze and didn't interfere. More police turn up so we decide to make off. We all just disperse. Most of the police follow Lenny, who now starts to throw tools out the window as they chase him. They block off the road, so Lenny eventually pulls over. The police search the car. They found a sack in the car full of machetes, butterfly knives, divers' knives and other weapons. Lenny gets locked up and to get out he explains that when it all came on top with the gypsies he decided to make a run for it. The gypsies saw the police and must have dumped the weapons in the car. The reason he didn't stop for the police was because he was so terrified. This worked and they released Lenny.

Three days later, the police came for me and pulled me in. I denied being there and started talking rubbish about my dog and all the fights I had as a boxer. They thought I was off my head and let me out. All the time this was going on, the travellers were telling everyone how they had done us over. They had told other gypsy families that they had put us in hospital. When we came back to the club people knew they had been lying, and we became known as guys who could get the job done.

We started to get more clubs to run due to the trouble we were sorting in other clubs. Sometimes I would be working the door, other times I would be like undercover, in clubber's clothes, dancing and walking around the club. I would be on the lookout for the dealers or the guys who were up for trouble. This one night a big lad was out to cause trouble with his mates, they were messing around with the girls in the club, who didn't like it. I have a word with him and later he and his mates start trouble. The other security guys sort his entourage out and leave him for me. Off comes his shirt and he's got this big boxing glove tattooed on his chest. We must have fought for 20 minutes solid. Every time I hit him down he got back up and came back for more. I got more of a buzz from this than anything else. Most guys I fought just lasted one, maybe two punches but he was up for the fight, big time. He was in a terrible mess, covered in blood and all. It was a cold night and every time he was knocked out one of the lads would turn the hosepipe on him. This would wake him up for me to give it to him again. Eventually we threw him out through the main gates up the club. I went back to my car drenched in blood, thinking I had been cut, but it was all his blood, not mine.

Rave parties were big back then and we were security for some of the biggest raves. They became so popular that punters from all the cities were coming to them, but of course so were all the major crews. This one night we got told that this major firm was coming to take over. They had been around the other raves, taxing the door, taking all the money and that. I was on the main entrance and was on edge all night waiting for them to turn up. Just when I thought they weren't coming, this car drives up and these four big skinhead-type geezers get out. They had come for our gate but I had to stand my ground. The biggest one confronts me first. He had this large torch with him and smashes me with it. I counter with a hook that breaks his jaw, the full weight of him coming forward and my hook does the trick. I completely wreck his face, putting him in a really bad way with his head swelling up from the hiding. The lads all come out and we do them all over and smash up their car as well. I know I went overboard with him but these were very dangerous people and they wouldn't have thought twice about doing me in. Years later, I met up with the big guy who I first hit and we shared a few drinks together and laughed it all off.

This one lad was a known knifeman who had cut loads up and wouldn't worry about knifing you. He had taxed a lot of people over the years and had taken over loads of nightclub doors. I think he was a bit jealous of our success and wanted our doors. He came down to confront us but of course he had his blade with him. He was talking to Lenny and didn't notice me sitting on this Harley Davison wearing sunglasses. He was the type of guy that if you fought him you would have to take it all the way. He's the kind of guy who would turn up at your house armed. This time he had picked the wrong time and place to try his luck. Lenny was arguing with him and hits him, now Lenny wobbled him but thought this was not the right place to end it. Lenny turns to walk away and the guy starts to pull his blade out. I just didn't have time to think about it, had to put him away as fast as I could, which I did. For about two weeks he was out looking for me with a shooter but that died down. He sort of changed after that fight, he don't bully no more and seems a changed man. In situations like that, you have to use everything from boxing to streetfighting and explode fast and hard.

I can only ever remember losing one streetfight and that was when I was a young kid. I still see the guy these days and we laugh about it, I don't bear grudges at all. It's bullies that get to me, if I see someone trying it on with a smaller guy then I'll make it my business to confront them. Over the years I've found that kids respect me and listen to what I have to say, this comes with training with them in the gyms all these years. I love children and I feel I can help youngsters, maybe guide them in some way. I've started working with the social services and I'm going on a course to help kids who are in the homes, with no parents to look after them. I want to be an independent visitor and feel the life I have led has given me the experience to help kids. I'd rather kids didn't follow some of the mistakes I have made and if I can guide them, maybe give them the confidence they need, then there's hope for them in this dog-eat-dog world.

DECCA SIMPKIN

Derby

A no-frills fighter who has beaten the odds no end of times. On their own or mob-handed, it makes no difference to Decca. From unlicensed boxing bouts to nightclub brawls, he has often remained the last man standing. You would rather have Decca inside your tent pissing out than outside pissing in.

I WAS BORN in Derbyshire in 1953. I come from a big mining family: my dad and both grandads worked down the mines. When I was young there was something like twelve pits around here but now there's not one left. My great-uncle was a champion barefist fighter in the days when barges would come down the canals trading with each town. His name was Jack Carter, and he would get off the barge in different towns fighting for money. Must have been a hard way of life.

I had a good childhood, doing the things that all young lads did. One of my fondest memories as a child was playing in a place called Dead Dane's Valley. It was the place where, back in history, the Saxons slaughtered the Danes. As young lads we would get dustbin lids and sticks, make up two sides – either you were a Saxon or a Dane – and we would re-enact the battles. I always enjoyed this game, nobody got hurt and we would have a great time.

People ask me why I became a fighter. Well, I put it down to the fact that I have all this energy all the time and get a little short-tempered if I can't release it. I was always fighting in the playground as a young lad. One day I knocked this kid out and he said that it wasn't a fair fight. The teachers knew we were going to fight no matter what, so they organised it in the gym for us. The headmaster even charged the kids a few bob to watch it. It was supposed to have been a sort of wrestling match but I went mad and smashed him up, breaking his nose and all. They couldn't stop his nose bleeding for about a day and his eyes were all black and that. I loved the sound of the crowd when we were fighting and later after the fight they were all coming up to me saying, "You're the best, you're the hardest." I thought to myself, *this is alright this is, I like this.*

In my teens, I became obsessed with running. I would love to run but as I got bigger I found it was getting harder and harder to run as good as when I was lighter. I started knocking guys out and fighting all the time, so I found the best place for me was the boxing gym. I boxed as an amateur and also started boxing at unlicensed shows for about £50 a time. I was training one day in the gym with the Bodell brothers when Jack Bodell [former British Heavyweight Champion] said there was this unlicensed show where we could fight gypsies for money. I thought, *right, I'm having some of that*, and off we all go in the big van to Uttoxeter. I get to the venue and I go to my dressing room to get a little sleep. Some people can't do this but I just relax and off I go.

I'm fast asleep when this gypsy that I'm going to fight comes in and wakes me up. "Tell you what Decca," he starts to tell me, "let's agree to split the money between us no matter who wins, half each like."

I put him straight when I say to him, "Fuck off, I want all the money, I'm going to batter you."

He looks shocked and says, "Oh, you are, are you?"

"Yes I am, now get lost so I can get some sleep," I growl back at him and go back to sleep as the gypsy goes away. I've always been greedy, me.

The fight starts well and by the third round I'm well ahead, I start to give the gypsy a right battering so he spins around and turns his back to me. I just carry on beating the shit out of his back, I thought, *fuck him*, and kept punching. There were three judges on the panel and they all stood up and shouted, "Disqualified!" All my crew, and there were quite a few of us, jumped up and threatened to wreck the place if that happened. Well they agreed to let me win. I think if I was on my own I would have got turned over by them all. The unlicensed game can be a hard one but if you've trained tidy and have your wits about you it can be okay.

I started working the doors when I was about 19, so that's almost 30 years of being a doorman. I went up to this club for work called the 76 Club. It was quite a rough club at the time. The manager told me there was no work available so I said, "Fuck it then," and walked out. The head bouncer, Colin, said, "That big geezer looks like he can look after himself. You had better get him back. Looks like we have trouble in here tonight." They got me back and the manager said, "Look you'll be on five pound a night, but see that big geezer by the bar? He's been causing us trouble. If you knock him out I'll put you on seven pound a night." Now that was good money in them days. I was right up for the job, so he had no chance. Up to the bar I march and give the big troublemaker a clip and drag him out by his ear. That was my first introduction to bouncing and I took to it like a duck to water, I just loved it.

When you work the doors, sometimes in a fight you can hit a person a little too hard. You can never work out how much another man can take for certain. This happened to me once, in I think it was 1976, at the 76 Club. I'm having a quiet night when I notice this big Army guy beating some smaller guy up. I walk over to them and stop the fight but the Army guy wants it with me. I throw a straight right hand and launch him off his feet. Down he goes with his nose broke and all his front teeth smashed out. I swear I only hit the prick once, but the next day the police arrest me. "Decca," the sergeant informs me, "We have you for assault, but if the guy don't wake up you're on for murder." Turns out this guy hadn't regained consciousness, just my luck. Well, after two days he decides to wake up, about time as well. He told them he was in the wrong and wouldn't press charges, which was fair of him. Just goes to show you that your whole life and somebody else's can be changed with just one punch.

I've had some good boxing trainers in my time that really knew what they were doing. I was fighting down at the Bath House in London and one of my trainers, Les Bodell, was with me. I was fighting this big, fat guy called Smith. It got to the eighth round and I was battering lumps out of him. Les came to my corner to rub me down and that. Without warning, he dropped down dead as a doornail. I can remember us driving down to the venue and he complained that he had pins and needles in his hands, "My bloody hands are tingling Decca, what the hell can that be?" he complained to me. I told him, "You want to see a doctor about that shit, it could be bad," and now there he was down on the floor dead with a heart attack.

I shout to the promoter, "My trainer's bloody dead, look, he's gone blue."

The promoter says, "Carry on fighting, you don't get paid if you don't fight."

With that, Jack Bodell had to get in my corner and I had to fight on as they carried him on a board and put him in the back room. I couldn't believe it. I fought on and knocked Smith out in the tenth round. How the hell I did that, I shall never know. He was my trainer and a good mate, he was a good lad Les as well. I don't know if he was dead going into the back room, after all I'm no doctor, but when they pulled him out after the fight he bloody well was.

I had a professional fight in Norway once where I was a bit worried about the referee being biased. Well I had nothing to worry about, they didn't mind us, it was the Germans that they hated. I was fighting this big six foot six lad and I was ahead by the sixth round. A big right hand knocks the guy down. He gets back up and I come rushing in like a steam engine looking to finish him off. With that he butts me straight on my nose, blood everywhere and my nose was swollen right up. I still manage to beat him and I was expecting the judges to be on his side but, like I said, they were very fair.

After a while I felt like a change, so I went up to a club called The Regency in Swadlincote. I walked in and asked for a job. The job was going fine until one day I threw out this Scottish lad, he was from a big family who were well known around here. The next day I get up and the club had been petrol bombed, the whole place went up in smoke. Bloody hell, I was out of work for six months. My good mate Izzy worked a club called the Rock House. They were getting some trouble from a group of bikers, and Izzy said, "Right, I'll get my mate Decca and some friends to sort things out," so I'm back in work again. The bikers were called the Road Tramps; this was in the days before they amalgamated with the Hells Angels. Well, we battered fuck out of them and the club was under control again. Thing was with the bikers, once I beat one of their hardest they kept bringing harder and harder guys to fight me. I just kept beating them up so I sort of gained their respect over the years.

Some bikers wanted to buy one of the clubs that I worked at. With me off the door, they could put pressure on the owners to get the place cheaper. They sent three guys round to sort me out. These guys spent the night at the club and got themselves a few drinks for Dutch courage. I'm sitting in my chair when they walk down the stairs to exit the club. "Could we have a word with you Decca?" the biggest biker says to me. Now I don't know these guys but they knew my name. I felt these guys were trouble, I could sense the nervous tension in the air. The other lads working on the door shout over to see if I was okay. I told them I was and approached the three guys. They started talking about bike rallies and gangs that I may have known. It was all idle talk just to catch me unawares.

"Never mind the bullshit, tell me what you really want," I scream at them. With that, the biggest starts to pull out this huge knife; I just catch a glimpse of it as the light catches it. Without thinking, I hit the bastard. Before the knife is out, he's on the floor, out cold and twitching in his sleep. The other two don't want to fight and run off down the road. I look down the taxi rank outside and there are about 50 taxi drivers and customers, who are all clapping their hands. I'm feeling great now, right in my element. The prick with the knife wakes up and starts to go for his knife again. I inform him that if he does I will kick him to a pulp. He decides against it and fucks off. If he had pulled that knife out then it would have been a licence for me to do what I want, and he knew that. I was pretty lenient anyway. Most people would have kicked his head in.

When I get someone who pulls a knife out on me, I never worry about what may happen. I hold no fear for that person, neither do I have any anger or compassion, just pure cold aggression. I work by moving up gears on each person who I fight: somebody who needs a clip I go to first gear, but someone who pulls a knife I go straight to fourth gear and want to completely destroy that person. All this shouting stuff just gets in the way, I just get straight in and smash them to bits as fast as I can. There are certain types of people who know they can't fight me barefist so that's when they come with weapons. I've had knives in my back, I've been hit by axes and knuckledusters in my head. These people are not real fighters and I have no respect for them at all. Show me a man who can fight with his fists face to face: these are the only fighters I respect. For somebody to want to use an axe on me just tells me how scared they are of me and in a way it's a form of flattery.

The culture of some of the bike gangs is such that they tend to carry weapons like guns, axes, knives and anything they can use on someone. This gang came up to the club one night looking to fight with a rival bike gang who weren't in on that night. They had come into the club in two groups and met up inside. I had my eye on them most of the night. After a while they start to smash the place up. They smash a window and attempt to steal the till with all the takings in it. I run up and before I can grab them I hear a few coming at me from behind. I spin around as a meat cleaver smashes into the side of my head, ripping me open. I duck another blow and the cleaver takes off the very tip of my head, like a knife cutting the top off an egg.

I get to the pool table and grab hold of a cue and go absolutely berserk. I'm right up for it now. These guys wanted me dead so nothing's going to stop me now, I was in fourth gear. I battered the cleaver man with the pool cue, I just splattered him all over the place, and at one time I thought I had killed the arsehole. My mate working with me gets a knife right through his thigh, he was screaming in pain. Another mate called Harley gets three huge stab wounds down his head, he was a bald bugger like me so you can still see the scars. They really beat the crap out of him; I felt really sorry for him later. There were about 15 of these dickheads still trying to kill us. Three police officers turn up, take one look at the fight and fuck off down the road. There were two of us against all these bikers and the police decide to run away to get help, bloody great.

I'm using the pool cue to put a few away. I shout to my mate Izzy, "For God's sake, wipe the blood out of my eyes, I can't see nowt."

"Decca," he shouts, "there's no blood in your eyes mate, its flowing down the sides, you've fucked your eyesight up."

I thought, *the fuckers have blinded me.* After a minute or so my eyesight comes back, thank God for that. I start to beat the rest of them up. At the end there were three ambulances full of these bikers all broken up and covered in blood. Then the police decide to turn up like Star Wars stormtroopers, all in riot gear, and there's no one left fighting, they are either in hospital or home in bed by the time the police had come. The police asked if I wanted to press charges and all that shit, I tell them, "Nah, it's okay, I just fell over, that's all. I never saw any fighting." Funny thing was that all the bikers, customers and staff that got hurt said the same thing. The police wanted to know how we run a club with blind bar staff, customers and doormen.

Some people get the wrong impression of me and think that I'm going to be violent all the time and that I'm going to be unapproachable but that's completely wrong. I'm a bit loud sometimes when I'm having fun and that, but aren't we all? Once when I was working the doors in Spain, I took the night off. I don't drink much but on that night I had a few. I got to the club I was working at and after a while decided to get up on the stage with the strippers. This stripper shouts to the other doorman, a big lad called Malcolm, to get me off the stage. He takes one look at me then runs out of the club and down the street never to be seen again. Well for God's sake! He was in charge that night and all he had to do was ask me to get down, I'm a reasonable guy and I respect another doorman's authority.

One club I worked at I had this armchair set up by the entrance just for me. When I wanted five minutes to myself, I would sit there with my coffee. One thing about me and coffee is I don't like to be disturbed when I'm having a cup. This one night, three Irish navvies came in. They were big lads, all brothers I think. They walked straight past the girl collecting money. They had no intention of paying. I watched them come in and carried on drinking my coffee. When I was finished, I got up and said to the girl, "Right, now I'll sort them all out." I've worked the doors for so many years now that I can smell trouble before it starts and I knew these guys were trouble.

I walk up to them all and I shout to the biggest one, "Oi, boy! You haven't paid." With that, he turns around, real fast like, and throws a right hand. Soon as I see it come I tuck my chin down and he busts his hand on my forehead. I get the big one down on the counter and no sooner had I done this than his brothers grab both my shoulders. Now I was on my own and they were big guys so I have to go up a gear. I pick up a Newcastle Brown bottle and smash it down on him, splitting his eye open. Blood squirts over the mirror and the counter. I turn to his brothers, who are now legging it down the street. I pick him off the floor and stick three more into him. I drag him to the exit and smash his head into the wall for good measure. Once I throw him into the street, his brave brothers turn up and take him away. Now, once I beat a man, the fight's over and I bear no grudges against them. I'm not the type to sit around all day seeking to beat them again, it's sometimes just business and not personal. I just want to get on with my life and I'm happy for them to get on with theirs. A few weeks after I had beaten the biggest brother, he stood in front of a train and waited for it to hit him, which it did at about 100 miles an hour. So that was the end of him.

Drug dealers try to take control of most clubs. I just won't let them control any that I work at. One night one of my sons, James, was working the front door when these crack dealers came in, right rough-looking guys they were. This big bastard pushes my boy and says, "Out of the way, I'm packing here." With that he opens up his coat to show a sawn-off shotgun inside. Now my sons don't mess around, they are big lads who know how to fight. James butts him straight on the nose and the guy staggers back but doesn't fall. The guy shouts out, "I'm on angel dust, now you are for it." With that, he calls his mates to smash the place up. Turns out they had come to the club to get the till, with about £7,000 in it.

There were loads of them in the club by now and they all jumped on James, kicking the shit out of him. He was on the floor being kicked by loads of them. I was sitting down relaxing at the time when the manager comes up and says, "Decca, they are kicking your boy to bits." My heart starts beating like hell and I run to where James had been standing. As I'm running to this crowd beating on James, this big wave of bottles and glasses came flying toward me. Well I must have timed it right because I went under all of the glass. Now my other boy Luke and my mate Stan "The Man" get hit by all the glass because they were just behind me. I jumped into the gang and start punching them out. I can't see James and the gang start to jump on me so I disappear amongst them onto the floor. They are hitting my head with brass knuckle-dusters and anything else they can get their hands on. Luke picks up a fire extinguisher and throws it at the pile of arseholes on top of me. At that moment, I fight my way to my feet and the extinguisher hits me on the top of my head. It put a big dent in the extinguisher and my bloody head. I fall back down, dazed.

I stagger back to my feet and we all start to beat them up. James is now on top of the Rastafarian and is plucking out the guy's dreadlocks like he was plucking a chicken. He shouts over to me, "Look Dad, I've scalped this one!" James had already had a real bad kicking but when they jumped on me they left him alone; he had got back up and dived straight back into the fight. Well, we beat the shite out of the lot of them. It could have been a lot worse than it was. The next night we are all back in work all black and blue, I have lumps and bumps all over my head from the knuckle-dusters and of course that fire extinguisher. I put it down to an occupational hazard, all part of the job, another day at the bloody office.

A good few years ago I built my own house, right big place it was with six bedrooms, two bathrooms and everyone lived there: my sons, their girlfriends and some mates would stay over as well. It was set in a nice part of the countryside; the neighbours were pricks but I loved the place. One of my sons fell out with someone and the police called around, to search the house. There were about eleven coppers searching. I didn't have anything to worry about and just sat back and let them carry on. One of the coppers picks up a loose patio slab and finds someone's stash of drugs. Anyway, they arrest me and lock me up. Now the stuff weren't mine but because I knew who they belonged too, I took the blame.

When I was being arrested, they asked would I like to say something. I told them, "Yes, please. Don't hit me again copper." Which they didn't find funny. My solicitor told me I was looking at three years. Of course, this started to worry me. I just sat in my cell meditating and trying to work out how to get out of the mess I was in. I had to go to Crown Court and asked for some books from the library and some of my old boxing posters and photos for evidence. I showed the court the books, which stated that sportsmen used the drugs to lose weight, also my boxing posters and some photos of me knocking the boxer Neville Meade out. The judge seemed to be a boxing fan and said it was a shame that I had resorted to using the stuff to lose weight. I couldn't believe my luck when he gave me a £200 fine. The coppers were pig sick; they all looked gutted.

You don't get anything in this world if you let people walk all over you. My parents have never been the sort to complain about things, but me, I'll argue all day if I'm in the right. A few years ago I went to the hospital with my mum and my sister, who, believe it or not, is a Sunday school teacher. My mum needed a hip replacement and we took her to see a consultant. The consultant told us that she could have a replacement in maybe two years. I start to swear and shout at the consultant that my mum could be dead within two years. He leaves the room and comes back a few minutes later. "She can have the replacement in two days time," he now tells me. So I may be a bit loud but it's the only way you can get things done sometimes. I sometimes wonder how many other people are out there waiting for an operation when, if they had stood up for themselves, it could have just taken a few days to sort out.

I train every day of the week, it's the only way I can get rid of all my energy. Our week starts with Monday, we lift weights in the morning and work on the heavy bag at night. Tuesday starts with a run for a few miles then later we go to Birmingham to spar a few rounds and some pad work. This is repeated throughout the week, we train hard every day and all push ourselves to the limits. When I've worked out I find I'm a more relaxed person. If I was in a prison cell with no training, I know I'd end up killing my cell mate. I've just got to have some sort of physical outlet; the doctor once told me that when I was knocked off my motorbike.

That was a mad day, that was. I was driving down the road on my bike minding my own business when this van full of Pakistanis hit me. I flew through the air right over the top of this van and landed on my head, all 19 stone of me down on my head. Witnesses who saw this all happen thought I were dead, to them it looked like I snapped my neck. I awoke to find loads of people around me. I said, "Right, what's cracking off?" With that, my arm started flapping as if it had a life of its own. "That will be the shock," someone told me. "Where's my fucking bike?" I asked. The ambulancemen told me not to move because they thought I had broken my neck. They explained that if I had tried to move, I could have severed my nerves and paralysed myself. I thought, *right oh, I'm not moving*, and they put a collar around my neck and all that shit.

This all happened just down the road from the club where I worked. The police went to the club and asked if I worked there. Stan told them I didn't because he didn't know about the accident and thought the police were after me. He even said he didn't know me. The copper said, "Yes you do, look, he's lying down there on the pavement." Stan sees me on the floor and starts going for the Pakistanis, thinking they had killed me. By now everyone is out looking, lots had scanners in their houses so they had heard it. Seems like everyone knew about it before I even got to the hospital. When I get to the hospital, apart from them having to glue some cuts on my head and a few bruises, there wasn't any real damage, thank God.

Now I couldn't train tidy for a while so I was getting a bit short-tempered and that. So the fuckers send me on behaviour therapy/anger management course. I thought, *bugger that*, and even though my knee was playing up, I used a pushbike each day to get rid of the aggression. I was only using my one leg to work the thing; I must have looked mental riding on it. The worst part of all this was the fact that the Pakistanis had run over and destroyed my bike.

The thing with being in such a high-profile job is that people think they can make friends with you and then take liberties. They may try to impress their girlfriends or boost their own self-esteem by giving people the impression that they are big mates of mine, they may even say or do something that only my close friends could get away with. Well, over the years I have learnt to keep these people at a distance, I don't need any weak-willed person trying to cut branches off my tree. I treat people the way I expect them to treat me, and if they want to be rough then I can change gear and be rough as well.

221

If there is one thing that life has taught me, that is, don't plan for anything. Things have a habit of going up in the air, so I never plan too far ahead. I don't think I want to go on fighting when I'm past 50 but who knows what may happen? There are some bareknuckle fighters who go on fighting until they are 60. It don't really matter if it's unlicensed boxing or bareknuckle fighting, when I get to a venue I feel it's where I should be. I just love the whole atmosphere at the fights, there's nothing like the fire in my belly that I get when I'm in the ring facing an opponent.

NIGEL SULLIVAN
Merthyr Tydfil

Nigel is adept at reading people and within seconds he will have their measure. A gentleman first and foremost, he has another side ready for those who deserve it. With a sixth sense for impending trouble, he can react to any situation that's thrown at him.

I WAS BORN in South Wales in 1957. I was never a big kid but I could hold my own in a fight even back then. How I started with martial arts was through my mother. She worked on the line in Hoover's factory and, through the sports and social, some office staff could use the canteen area for badminton at night. There were two guys, Alan Thomas and Dai Davies, who wanted to start a little judo club up. Turns out they were stopped because of the badminton; some of the women there weren't happy and started a petition up – well, you know what women can be like. Before long they had the hall but, of course, there wasn't enough people going to justify the class. One night my mother came home and said, "Right, you're off to judo." I had no idea I was going, it came as a complete shock. Off I go and just didn't know what to expect, that was the first time I saw a black belt. I remember saying to the guy there, "Excuse me sir, but is that a real black belt?"

I was petrified going there the first time. The thing that scared me the most was seeing so many kids I didn't know. I didn't know them or how they would react to me coming to the club. After a while some of the kids would drop out and we would be left with just the ones who really wanted to learn. Of course, I had made friends with them all by then so I was having a great time.

I started going to different clubs and learning different styles. I even went to boxing and trained at that for a while as well. I never lost a fight as a kid, what with boxing, judo, and all, it made me pretty fit and able to fight quite well. The only fight I can ever remember losing was when I was about 34 and I was drunk, to say the least. I was going through a divorce at the time and went out and got absolutely hammered. I was standing by the bar when the bouncer said, "It's going to kick off in here now, give us a hand will you?" Me, like a fool, said yes. Thing is, he was getting paid for it and when it came to the fight, the git dropped me in it, I went outside with the two troublemakers and he stayed inside. I could barely walk, I was so drunk. Anyway, before the fight even

224

started I trip and break an ankle, just my luck as usual. I manage to put the first one away but I couldn't handle the second one in my drunken state. I got battered and I mean battered well. It serves me right. Being in that state, I couldn't even see him.

Back when I was ten, maybe eleven, I met this guy called Emrys Jones who wrote a book called *The Secret Fear*. It absolutely captivated me. He would train the adults in jiu-jitsu, this was back in the days when it was considered too dangerous to teach to kids. Now I was doing judo at the time but when I saw the sneaky punches and the gouging I knew jiu-jitsu was for me. I just had to find out all I could and I've been seeking knowledge ever since. When I started in jiu-jitsu I was training the same time as this big, 18-stone feller. I was only nine-and-a-half stone but we still had some right old wars. I wouldn't back down with him. He was so heavy that when I used to take him down onto my knee it would tremble under his weight. The fights we had were right battles but we became friends through it all in the end.

I was in a judo competition once and my dad drove me all the way up to Crystal Palace. I'd been training for months for this competition and was all keyed up for it. My first fight was at three o'clock. I was ready for it and, of course, my dad was watching, so it made it more important for me. I got on the mat at three o'clock, bowed and was down straight away. I had lost in a matter of seconds. Within minutes, we were back in the car going home. My dad wasn't happy at all, he didn't talk to me all the way back to Wales. You could have cut the atmosphere in the car with a knife.

I then trained privately under a guy called John Warfield, whose brother used to be the bodyguard for Eartha Kitt and Johnny Mathis. He was something else. When he was 18, he had an operation on his stomach and had a pipe put in, but carried on fighting until he was 70-odd, which goes to show you what type of guy he was. John trained me well in the fighting arts but he also trained me to be humble as well. You see, at that time of my life I would fight anyone and wouldn't care who I took on. It was through him that I learned to respect people more and try to walk away from trouble, unless of course things had gone too far. He had the strongest fingers that I had ever come across: once he grabbed you, there was no getting away. In jiu-jitsu it's common to have some get knocked out, and when I was training under John I would regularly be choked out. Even this week one of my own black belts was choked unconscious by me. It just happens, it's all part of learning to fight.

I was in this local pub once and this big rugby guy was there, he was about 18 stone and I was just ten stone at the time. Well, the pub was chock-a-block at the time. I was just standing there with my brother having a pint. He barged passed and bumped into me, tipping my pint over my brother. I look up and he just gives me this look, so before I knew it I had thrown a punch and he's on the floor out cold. The guy wanted it and I reacted before he could, so he brought it on himself. I could tell by his body language what he wanted. I guess that just comes from years of training.

In martial arts, we are trained not to go looking for trouble. I myself am always fair with people but sometimes even I have no option but to strike first. For instance, I was on holiday with my family and we were having a great time at this holiday camp. My boy was only about five years old at the time and was playing in this soft toy area. Believe it or not, the area had a bouncer who was always throwing his weight around. Now, these were really little kids so you can imagine what type of guy he was. I was talking to this guy in a wheelchair, both of us having a quiet pint, when up comes the missus with the little one crying in her arms. Turns out this bully bouncer had pushed over my son. When she complained, he gave her a right mouthful.

"Don't worry," I said, "I'll go and have a chat with him." I didn't show her but I was going up to plant him. I have no time for his sort. I went up and told him he was out of order and did him in seconds: I bust up his nose, ribs and knee before he could move. He just lay there on the floor in agony. Well, up comes security, ranting and raving, so I did him as well. This other guy comes up the balcony and BANG, he has it as well. By then I was off it and there was no stopping me.

I left there but the police told me they understood the problem but I should apologise. Well, I thought they were being fair so up I went. This was 20 minutes later and he was still there waiting for the ambulance. I tell him I'm sorry but he had hit my boy and that wasn't on. Well, his mother happened to be there and she was a good sort, she turned to me and said, " Don't worry, its all part of his apprenticeship," which I thought was really funny at the time. Seems his dad was a right handful and the bouncer was following him that way.

I got into training with an ex-SAS combat officer and that led to me doing a couple of bodyguarding jobs with my mate Jim. There was one job we did for a famous diamond dealer; his father was a renowned Impressionist artist. He done this one display, which was full of his son's diamonds, about £250,000 in all. Well, we stayed up there for a while looking after the diamonds. We had to keep checking the display and watching out for trouble. The diamond guy had his mate with him and he was a right prick. Jim hated him, he really hated his guts. Well, we were there keeping our eyes peeled, I had a dagger concealed on me and, of course, Jim was carrying as well: even though it was "lady this" and "lord that", we still couldn't be sure somebody wouldn't try something.

After the show, the dealer's girlfriend had taken the car so we had to walk. We thought it was better not to look suspicious so we put the diamonds in an Asda carrier bag. I walked all the way through London with all these diamonds in this carrier bag. No trouble at all. Got back to his house and got the diamonds into his safe. He had hired us both for the weekend and he wanted to go for a drink. A few drinks later and he was gobbing off about us being his bodyguards. Jim and myself weren't drinking and we were getting some strange looks from the crowd in the club. We decide to get them out and walk home with them. No sooner had we started walking when the prick starts on Jim. The dealer's girlfriend was now with us. "What would you do, let's say, if I grabbed her tits, Jim?" he says, pointing to the dealer's girl. With that, Jim steps forward quick as a flash and head-butts the prick, and he's lying there spark out on the pavement. I look down at him and I'm thinking, *bloody great, there goes our wages*, and it's up to me to carry the dick all the way back to the dealer's house. We still got paid a thousand each, which I was more than happy with.

The next time we worked for the dealer was up in Yorkshire, in this big private school which was run by monks. It was an antiques and diamond fair and we were hired for three to four days and we were bored stiff. There was this six foot-odd ex-SAS guy, seems he was a big boxer and was on to me all week to show him jiu-jitsu. He wouldn't bloody leave me alone about it. Now he was a big nasty bastard and one day when the place was cleared out we went in to gym. "Come on, show me in the ring," he shouts. There we were, sparred up to each other, he moves toward me and bang, I hit him straight in the balls and down he goes to his knees. I step closer, grab him and choke him out. I can still remember Jim standing over him slapping his face to bring him around and saying, "I told yah, I fucking told yah."

Back when I was about 19, my brother took me to get chips at the bottom of town. This guy calls me outside and says, "Hey Butt, get me some chips."

"Get your own chips, Butt," I tell him.

With that, him and his buddy approach me and before I knew it he had stuck the head on me, catching me off guard. I'm sitting on the pavement and as I get up the two of them run off. I tried over the course of the next few weeks to find out who they were but to no avail. Thing is, I still remembered what they looked like. I'm driving down the road one day a few years later and spot this guy thumbing a lift. I stop and he gets in. We are driving for a while, chatting away, when I realise he was one of the ones from the fish shop. I stop the car, get out and lift the bonnet up. I'm standing there, pretending to look inside, when he gets out.

"What's the matter, Butt?" he asks.

"Come and look at this," I reply.

With that, he sticks his head under the bonnet. Soon as he does, I give him the finest hammering of his life. I battered the fuck out of him and left him on the side of the road where he fell. It must have been another seven years later when I spot the other one. I call him over and just clip him. Seems drugs were doing more damage to his body than I could do.

I strongly believe that we should all have goals in life: my goal these days is to get my sixth dan and make my club bigger and better. The club is expanding each day with different techniques being taught, things like footwork, groundwork, throwing, sticking and grappling. I make my black belts evade, come in and use all these options. Fighting's a passion for me and I still look for different styles and love everything about it all.

BILLY CRIBB

England/USA

Billy Cribb (left) with former Kray henchman Tony Lambrianou

Known as the "Tarmac Warrior" due to his "have-fists-will-travel" attitude, Billy earned his living the hard way, on both sides of the Atlantic, making his name on the Extreme Fighting circuit in the US, and challenging men of all shapes and sizes in the UK.

I WAS BORN to a Romany family in 1949. My mother was from a Jewish background. Mum's grandmother was what was known as "granny-raised" within the gypsy community. My father was Romany. The Nazis would have had a nice crack at me during World War Two, wouldn't they? I would have been dissected and gassed by now. My family travelled until I was about 14 years old, picking fruit or hops, sometimes working the seafront on the Isle of Wight selling toys to the tourists. Not many people went abroad in them days. In the winter months, we would turn to a more local-based means of earning, since we travelled only from April until October.

The family came initially from Cumbria and our family lineage is Taylor, Stewart, Gray, Dunn, and McCann. There were also Lees, way back four generations since. My own family moved gradually south, eventually settling on our own land in Northamptonshire during the mid-Sixties. Many of the Taylors, however, moved in to south and east London. Horses were always our greatest love, well mine and dad's anyway. We would always have a good stallion or two to put to service and would have mares *puvved* all over Northamptonshire, Leicestershire and Cambridge where friends and family would keep an eye on them. *Puvving the gry* we call it, which is *poggardi jib* (English-speaking Romani language) for grazing the horse.

There were many other things we did for *wonga* (money) of course, like tarmac-laying to industrial estates and driveways, carpet-selling on the knocker or in office blocks, selling gold and jewellery round the building sites. We just did what we could to make a living. Our women often went *dukkering*, which is telling fortunes, and did quite well. The family would always pool its income at the end of the day – my brothers, sisters, mum and dad. It was a bit like that programme on TV, *Bread*. No one objected. I learned to read and write properly when I was about 24 and have been hungry to learn ever since. I trained to become qualified in counselling whilst living in the USA but between the fight scene and my current way of living I had a good and long career in comedy entertainment. I still write comedy for radio and television.

The first real fight I ever saw was a great gypsy man called Hughie Burton, I am pleased and honoured to say. It was a fight on the hills of Appleby [in Cumbria, the scene of a big annual horse fair] at around 5.30am, dew-laden grass and the smell of excitement in the air. I guess I was about six then. Mum wasn't too happy about it but my Granny Taylor talked her into letting me go with my dad and his brothers. It was an awesome sight and although it didn't last very long, it stayed in my mind as a mass battle. I guess that's a kid's-eye view of things. I will never forget that day and I am sure that any man you speak to who saw him fight will say the same. Burton's fights were always considered classics.

My own first actual fight was when I was 14 years old. My father was challenged by a young lad of 17 or 18, but he felt he couldn't fight the boy as he would humiliate him by knocking the granny out of him, so he came up with what he thought was a great compromise: "Fight my boy and beat him and I will fight you tomorrow." That got dad out of it all nicely but landed me firmly in the shit, as I was never really an aggressive boy. I knew how to hold my hands up of course but I was better at talking than fighting. Now I had to defend the family honour and myself in my first-ever real fight. I was under a lot of pressure but fortunately won the day. The boy made so many silly mistakes, the main one being trying to put the nut on me. First of all, the fight was to be a straightener and I was annoyed that he sneaked in a dirty play, and second, it's stupid to try and put the nut on a man six inches smaller than you. I just stepped aside as he toppled forward and lifted him up the side of the head with a right-hander. I sparked him good.

I have never felt such exhilaration. As I approached the fight area, I began to feel a stranger inside me, an aggressor within me that I had never known. I was sort of frightened but not of my man, just of failure in the family's eyes. I seemed to go deaf all during the fight as I concentrated on my job, but as I realised I had sparked the man, the sounds of cheers and shouts brought me in to a new life. I was not looking back and that had been my wakening to a destiny. My heart was pounding. Grandad, dad and the brothers were lifting me high and patting my back. I was covered in claret and felt fantastic. Dad and grandad threw me into an old water trough to clean me up and I just lay there laughing, with claret floating around me in the water. Straight after the fight though, I was over the moon. No one could ever take that moment away from me, it was mine for life. I ached like hell the next day though.

Being so small, I had to learn a lot of little tricks, especially if I thought I was in for a long haul. One trick that always fared me well was to work the opponent's arms. If you punch someone in the arms long enough, they can't lift them. Sometimes I couldn't just go steaming in so it was work low, then work up and underneath. I guess it depended on whom I was fighting. This is where psychology, technique and structure were to play a big part in my life.

I began working full-time at around eleven years old, as most gypsy kids do, and although I could hardly read or write, driving a car or working a *mark* (punter) was no problem. I was always on the lookout for good earners. Often, though, this took me on the wrong side of the law. I had the gift of the gab and started working some traditional cons when I was older such as the "over-order" scam. My brother and myself would drive to the carpet mills in Worcester and buy some cheap end-of-line carpet for a few pence a square metre. Then, dressed in a convincing workman's boiler suit, we'd pull up at an office block or even stop people in the street and show them a swatch made from the carpet. The patter that followed would involve a tall tale about having just completed a contract to fit out some smart offices but having over-ordered the amount of carpet. We would be in really

234

big trouble with their employer if they returned with the excess. The carpet, we assured our target, was worth £20 a metre but we were "willing" to let them have it for "only" £2.50 a metre. The office girls would fall for it every time.

When the various scams came to an abrupt end with the imprisonment of my young brother and cousin, I turned to the occupation of road tarmaccing. I went to work with other family members on a contract resurfacing the A1 road, the *drom* to nowhere, my uncles called it, *drom* meaning road. Working on a road like the A1 seemed a never-ending project. At a roadside cafe one lunchtime, as we tucked into our fry-ups, a group of truckers started making remarks about "fucking pikeys". My gypsy honour was offended so I waded in. A tear-up began; there was claret everywhere, with sauce bottles being used as bludgeons. It also became my showcase for an opportunity to make big money as a fighter. A highly-respected fighter happened to witness the brawl and was impressed enough to introduce me to a fight manager called Benny Harris.

Benny's plan was to take me onto a new circuit based around the network of motorway service stations and A-road cafes up and down the country. My first fight as the "Tarmac Warrior" was on a patch of concrete in a desolate corner of the Blue Boar service station, off the M1 near Northampton. It was where I knocked out a trucker who called himself "Tattoo". This sparking was convincingly executed with a good right hook. That night, back in our trailer, my manager flung a fat wad of notes on my bed. My first fight had netted me £500. I was hooked, eagerly embracing my new career as a professional bareknuckle fighter. Although still leading a nomadic way of life, I had unwittingly now left the gypsy culture behind. I travelled the English motorway network in search of contests arranged by my manager, who paid all the expenses in return for half the purse and all the lucrative side bets, a share of which I could also expect.

We'd take on all comers. It might be someone who thought he

could fight and they'd see the size of me and say, "Yeah, I'll have it." There were no rounds or anything, you'd just fight till you couldn't get up, and you'd had enough. If you gave best you'd just say something like "You've fucking done, me mate." And that was it. There were enough wins though and as the Tarmac Warrior I built up a good reputation until one day I found myself in a lay-by off the M62 near Manchester. A ring was formed from steel posts taken from a roadside working. Some rope was strung up and I was matched against "Midnight", a black Brummie who did martial arts. Now martial arts were pretty unheard of at this time and I didn't know what to expect. He did cop me with a few nice roundhouses, though I stuck to him like glue. But before either man could get the upper hand, the *gavvers* (the police) stumbled on the scene and all hell broke loose. By the time everyone had fled, one of them *gavvers* had been speared with a metal stake and another had received horrific facial injuries. Benny, my manager, had been taken away before and did time so he didn't want to go down again, for sure. I was wrapped up with him because he was my manager, my brain. He was my living and I was his, so when he said run, I ran and we drove off down that road like a bat out of hell. I didn't know where we was going and I didn't much care, weren't my job to think.

Benny came up with a great idea. Since we were making ourselves scarce, we could find a living fighting on the cross-Channel ferries. In the winter months, with few tourists and "normal" people about, the dank cargo decks in the bowels of the ferries became barefist arenas. This sea-going variation paid very low rent, with fight purses as low as £40. Benny would put out the challenge to the lorry drivers on board. One of them will have a go, once they're pissed. Things gradually improved, with purses often part-paid with goodies rifled from the truckers' loads. Once we got two sheep from a French freezer truck as part of a bet. We had beer, wine, bloody all sorts of stuff that we had to sell afterwards to turn into hard cash. International fights with

Germans, Dutch and French drivers drew good crowds, £1,000 paydays and the odd battering. I had my head pulled down on one of those bars that hold the Continental trailers together and my mouth was in bits, but you don't feel it until afterwards. I lost my front teeth that way.

Fighting became my life. I just couldn't get enough. I was working in the Canary Islands when some expatriate gangsters invited me to a bareknuckle fight night. I sort of got carried away when watching the fights: in the excitement of the evening, I jumped into the ring and ripped off my shirt. "I'll fight any man for a monkey," I said. An American stood up and shouted, "I'll make that a grand, winner takes all." Now that was serious money at that time.

A man climbed in through the ropes, a fellow bouncer who happened to be psychotic – and my greatest mate on the island. He was a Geordie called "Makka". We had done a bit of sparring together but it was always in sort of earnest fun, as men do. I thought we were just going to go at it for a while, a bit more than usual, serious but not too damaging. What I didn't realise however was that my pal had a cocaine habit that left him in a lot of debt. He needed that money bad. We moved around for a minute or so. Crack! The first blood went to Makka. He caught me on the forehead. Then I put together a nice combination, throwing him backwards. Makka came back with a flurry of poorly-aimed punches. He was angry and wasn't thinking. His blows went nowhere, while I remained calm and focused. I countered and caught him with a nice blow to the nose and the claret washed over his face. Makka came towards me. I was ready to sidestep him but he anticipated my move and brought his knee up into my left side. I went down. He had cracked a rib and punctured a lung. I was fighting on fifty per cent breathing capacity and pure adrenalin.

As I got up, he came down with the nut. I stumbled backward and ripped off some of the tape covering my knuckles. I moved round the ring backwards as I fumbled trying to tie the rag around my head to stop some of the blood. I just wanted to re-direct the flow from my eyes so that I could see properly. The blood was everywhere and the screams from our pals were deafening. Makka lurched forward and sunk his teeth into my shoulder, causing a searing pain to go down my arm. I grabbed his head and pulled it into my face, taking off the tip of his nose. I don't know why, I just couldn't reach anything else. We rose to our feet and were still fighting. We had gone beyond pain. Sheer determination and hatred was driving us now. I cupped my right hand and lifted it smartly under his nose – what was left of it anyway. That filled his eyes with tears and caused temporary blindness. He brought both his hands over his face in agony. I gave one more hit to the body, a straight-fingered blow under the ribs as hard as I could. He spun in agony, not knowing whether to hold his face or clutch his body. That was it. I came up with the left and across with the right and he hit the ground, out cold.

It was following this fight – and after leaving hospital – that the Yank that upped the purse hit me with a proposition to go to America to fight. Now, any young man with only his self to keep would jump at the chance of going to the States. This was like a lottery win to me and I jumped at the chance.

I fought in three distinct arenas in the USA. First of all, I fought in Florida, down at the Keys. The Florida scene was very laid back and proper. I then travelled up to New York City, where it was much more organised and controlled. This was my first brush with real violence, I suppose. I was fighting in a syndicate-controlled circuit where you did what you were told unless you wanted to feel severe pain. I was made to fight day after day there until I could fight no more: my hands seized up and I was fucked for fighting. I had to lay off until I recovered. The syndicate only wanted winners. Their whole motivation was money, as I guess mine was by that time.

I had entered the world of extreme or reality fighting. These days that same circuit survives as Ultimate Fighting, only now it is a little more sophisticated and controlled. Ultimate has huge following capacities from state to state in the USA and has a pay-per-view contract with cable TV. The fight scene I had joined was pure sleaze, extortion, drugs and violence. I had joined a world I didn't understand and didn't like but I was making money. The crowd was aggressive, and they knew the game.

That's where I got the hammer in my head. A claw hammer came down out of the crowd as I headed toward the arena and knocked me completely sparko. The motive for the attack was revenge, I guess. The friends of a fighter I had injured badly had returned to settle the score. My assailant disappeared into the 500-strong crowd, leaving me with a fractured skull. My handlers rushed me to a private hospital where I was taken in the back door and patched up, but it took me almost five months to completely recover. By then, I had my own score to settle when I discovered that my American manager, who had claimed that my passport had been lost, had in fact got it all the time. I had been kept there like a prisoner. I really lost it after that, and I did his hands in the boot of a car and headed for the airport.

Leaving New York, I headed toward California, where I still live most of my life. It was there I found the cult circuit, and to really do the circuit justice, you will have to read my book; it would take forever to explain the complexity of the system there. A gay guy in San Francisco, just outside Roc Morais, ran the cult circuit. I lived then in Modesto, kept like a lord with everything I wanted. I fought in front of stars there, especially when we fought in Nevada, as the laws were more relaxed. I fought in front of Frank Sinatra, Jack Nicholson and even Joe Louis, the great boxer, who was then, I believe, working in the casinos of Las Vegas. The cult circuit was weird, a voyeuristic sport that could only come from the dreams of La La Land. There were events such as hang-fighting, where the two fighters hung from their ankles and fought at close quarters; The Tank, which was a little like the cage only it was a Perspex tank; and The Yard, where two men would be joined at the ankles by a yard of leather and then had to fight. It was all so weird and eventually killed my best friend.

Well, it isn't hard to work out that to fight in any of the ways I have described, you had to be off your nut, and I don't mean just mad, I mean drugs. Now drugs were a no-no to the gypsy way of life in those days. We never heard of drug abuse then, well I never had, anyway. That's the good thing about travelling: if you ever had bad neighbours, dad would just hitch up the trailer and pull away. My first close encounter with drugs was in the Canaries, long before the California scene and where I was involved in timeshare protection, but that was only someone else taking the stuff then, not me. Then I was introduced to Dexedrine to lose weight after a long spell of dossing around the beaches of Venice Beach, California. The Dexedrine had the effects of speed and I grew to like it. Now once I joined the stable of the gay feller, cocaine was laid on for all to abuse. It was in your house, at the parties, in the RV (recreational vehicle) that the company owned to ferry the fighters about all over the state. Everyone you fought would be on "charlie". Now I don't know if you have ever tried knocking someone out while they are on that stuff, but the fuckers just keep getting back up again, you can't hurt them. You had to be on charlie to just be equal, it wasn't enough to be good or brave, you had to be stoned.

My last real fight was in California. I fought in the sandbox [in which two opponents fight in a box that gradually fills up with sand, slowing their movements until they are virtually static – JD]. This was a particularly hard fight and a way I had never seen before. After my fight I found out that my greatest friend, Berrie, was killed. We usually fought on the same bill but this day I was the only man from our stable fighting in Nevada. When I returned to California, I telephoned the home we all shared and found that Berrie had died from internal bleeding after fighting a glass-fist battle [in which the bandaged fists are coated in resin and then powdered glass! – JD].

I was devastated and went up to Carmel to live for a while, then joined a commune. There I found salvation in the shape of a beautiful teenager called Sweetness. She was an angelic Jesus freak and she converted me, the little renegade gypsy, into a born-again, happy-clappy Christian. I admit that the "Jesus thing" saved my life. I joined the commune, which was based in Monterey, and lived with Sweetness. I prayed every day for my own salvation. I even stopped swearing, which sounds silly but was a real tough thing for me. But then I found out my teenage angel of mercy had began sleeping with another woman. I thought, *fuck that!* I just couldn't get the hang of the commune stuff and so I headed for the airport, taking the few dollars I had left after the commune had leeched most of my savings away. I flew to San Diego and got my head round counselling and psychology and became qualified to practise. I guess my faith hadn't been strong enough to maintain the religious thing. I felt sort of let down after losing Sweetness, although looking back now, I'm thinking how much more could the Lord have done for me? I was discovered as a wreck on a beach and was delivered back into society as a sound human being again.

It was when I returned from the States at the age of 30 that I met Lenny McLean [the infamous "Guv'nor" of the unlicensed boxing scene] at a venue in Ilford. It was during a time when the bareknuckle and unlicensed fight scene was having new life breathed into it from fighters like Roy Shaw, Donny Adams, Cliffy Fields, Danny Chippendale (the "Kangaroo Fighter"), etcetera. Lenny sat me down for a long chat. He was a real nice bloke, although we lost touch in later years. He convinced me that I should stay away from all the violence and use the skills I had learned in the States, and encouraged me to get involved with work in the boys' clubs round London's East End. He also introduced me to a comedian who was compère at the fighting events that Bob Wheatley was running. Lenny asked a man called Mike Pugh to help me out. I never looked back from that day. I became involved in the comedy circuit, which left me lots of time to work in the community on a voluntary basis, spend time with my family and enjoy my life. So I always say that it is thanks to Lenny and Pughie that my kids have a dad. I believe I may have got back into the scene that almost destroyed me and may have ended up a quivering basket case, banged up in the nick or dead.

Fighters today are fighting more for money than honour, so that takes the edge off it a bit. The heart is still there but the motive is not as strong. I have seen some great little fighters, however, but the whole sport scene is dominated by money, and bareknuckle is no different. It is more controlled by syndicates, groups or business and is not growing from the honour, culture and machismo that it stemmed from. I have to admit, however, that I have nothing to do with the UK scene any more but I am involved in the USA interest and trying to purify their Ultimate scene a little by creating an offshoot. Bareknuckle is far safer to fighters than gloved fighting. Punch-drunk syndrome was never identified until after Queensberry introduced the use of gloves. Gloves protect the hands, not the opponent. They allow the fight to go on for longer and more damage to be inflicted upon a fighter. Imagine hitting a wall with your bareknuckle: HURTS, DON'T IT? Now put on the huge gloves of today; they are almost like bubble wrap, you can punch away all day. You can knock someone around for ever until their brain goes to pulp, where bareknuckle, you would want to get it over quick before your hands went. The knuckles would get pushed up in to your hand or they would break or just hurt otherwise.

The worst thing a bareknuckle fighter can expect in a straightener is a few cuts and abrasions and his hands developing rheumatism by the time he is 40. Gloved fighters have the neurological system to take care of, becoming punchy or having the system destroyed through repeated blows to the head. Look at the pointless destruction of a great man like Ali. What a waste. My hands are fucked but my brain is strong. Remember, though, that professional bareknuckle is a little different to other forms of bareknuckle in that our hands would be strapped tightly to protect the small bones, unlike gypsy bareknuckle or streetfighting, where the hands would mostly be literally bare, although even some of those men have a rag wrap or wear thin leather gloves. Professional fighters would take more care of their hands and train harder, not like the spontaneous fighters I just mentioned that would not train regularly nor have a trainer to teach them to look after their hands.

I still love to watch the fights. There are some cabled in from Ireland to the States, you know. It's still that one-on-one that attracts most men, I think. Even if you have never fought or, like me, couldn't fight again, when you watch a fight you can fantasise that you are in there and every blow is yours. The smell and feel of the crowd evoke old memories. Things I miss the most are the comradeship of other fighters and the cheering of the people who appreciate what you have given them. I don't get to see real bareknuckle much any more because it is outlawed all over the place and I no longer belong to the scene of people that would be privy to the fight venue, so don't get invited.

The greatest gypsy fighter I ever saw fight was Hughie Burton, who I have mentioned before, also known as Uriah by some. Hughie was a brave and strong fighter and would never be hurried. He would take a challenge from any man and arrange the fight for the following morning, following a good breakfast. I took this advice from him: never fight angry, never fight without a good breakfast inside you and always make the man wait, never fight there and then. Unfortunately Hughie has passed away but he has been known to beat five men, even having had a hammer planted in his head during an ambush. This man always fought fair and never used a weapon in his entire fighting life. His family always filmed Hughie's fights, so if you were able to contact them, you would have a pot of gold.

Alongside Hughie and of equal quality was Tucker Dunn, a distant uncle to me and also to the fighter Bobby Frankham, related by marriage to Gypsy John Frankham: both boxers, of course, and subsequently bareknuckle fighters. I have never met Bobby, as we are very far removed in family terms. Bobby lost his licence after hitting the ref following his defeat by Billy Simms and turned to bareknuckle to earn his money. Bobby's greatest claim to fame was training Brad Pitt for the film *Snatch,* in which he played an Irish bareknuckle fighter. Tucker was a great fighter and even at the age of 76 knocked a man out for taking the piss while he was delivering some iron in a scrap yard. This was December 2000. The man is still a fighter today even after two heart attacks. I guess following the two men I mentioned – Hughie and Tucker are my absolute heroes – I would say the next bravest gypsy man I have seen fight would be Bartley Gorman. Bartley was a quietly spoken man who found the Lord and walked away from the violence of the bareknuckle arena. He had stories to tell that will spin your head, including the time he was macheted by several attackers after beating a man square.

What makes a *great* fighter? First of all, you mustn't fear pain. If you fear pain then you have lost already. You have to have a great belief in yourself, and a sense of pride in what you are doing. Be honourable, and show respect to your opponent, even if you think he is no good at the sport, because it takes a special kind of person to get in that fight arena and go one-on-one.

My life now is fantastic. I have my kids and grandchildren around me. I breed and sell thoroughbred horses which, after my family, is still my first love. I have my work as a comedy writer and author. I am active in the Roma National Congress, being recently invited to work with the scheme operated by the US Government. This is to locate Romany families regarding allocation of money held by the Swiss Government, part of the Nazi loot taken during World War Two during the Holocaust, in which the Germans murdered ninety per cent of the European Romany community. I live half of my time in the USA, in Windsor, California, which I love to death, and the rest of my time is spent home with the family. I would say that my life is perfect. No man could ask for any better. I have my lovely family, my health, the sun in my face and my work is also my hobby.

My story is a long one and the full version can be read in my own book *Tarmac Warrior* [available at major bookstores, priced £14.99]

JAMIE O'KEEFE

East London

Jamie has confronted his traumatic childhood in the same way he has confronted all other conflicts in his life: head-on. He has built on his traditional martial arts training and extended it to real life situations by developing his New Breed fighting system, which has won him acclaim the world over. Jamie can handle any situation, from a controlled environment to bedlam on the streets.

I WAS BORN in east London in 1961 and right from the start my life was a constant struggle. I come from a mixed background: my mother was Scottish and my father, as you might expect from my surname, was Irish. I have a sister two years younger than me and I was informed by my mother that I had a twin sister who was born disabled and was put immediately into care on my father's insistence. This was very much a taboo subject and as a result I've never ventured to find out the truth of the matter. My mother was an alcoholic and when I was four weeks old she took me out shopping and forgot about me, returning home alone before realising what had happened. Thankfully when she returned to the shop I was still there and she took me home. A similar thing happened a few years later, when I must have been about eight years old. My mother, sister and myself were travelling to Scotland on the train when my mother got off for a cup of tea at a station we'd stopped at and didn't get back on. I was old enough to realise what had happened and told the guard, who stopped the train at the next station for my mother to catch up with us.

My parents were always splitting up and getting back together, until I was about ten. It was then discovered that my father was sexually abusing my sister, which explained why he was always so nice to her but treated me so badly. It was me who accidentally discovered what was happening but my sister begged me not to tell anyone for fear of what he would do to her. However, the secret was cutting me up so badly inside that, in an act of sheer frustration and anger, I actually set fire to our house in the middle of the night. I could bottle it up no longer and told my mother what was happening. Shortly after, the police were involved and my father was sent to prison, but no time inside can compare to him having messed up the rest of my sister's life. That was the last we ever heard of the scumbag.

When all this was going on, my sister and myself were sent to live with our grandmother in Scotland. With us having English accents, this caused a few problems in our new Scottish school.

This was my first taste of the bullying which was going to make my life a misery for many years to come, but to look on it in a positive light, it was the bullying which was to ultimately change my life and led me to where I am today.

Despite the tough time I was having at school, I enjoyed my time in Scotland, but when I was around eleven both my sister and I were taken back to London to live with my mother and her new boyfriend. He was a crook who made his money by various forms of villainy: robbery, con-tricks, any way he could earn a dishonest pound. I have to admit that he always seemed to have plenty of it to flash around. Most of this would be blown on booze, with both him and my mother drunk most of the time. It was during these drinking binges that I would lie awake listening to him beating my mother up, and the beatings were getting worse and worse.

Around this time I was sent to a naval school and the bullying I was suffering reached its peak. I was picked on mainly because of my surname being Irish and also because, unlike most of the other boys, I came from a poor background. The worst times were the games lessons, when we used to play rugby, which usually consisted of the ball being thrown to me and then everyone else steaming into me. On one occasion it got so bad that the weight of everyone on top of me caused me to become unconscious, on the brink of being suffocated. The teacher saw that it was going too far and, after he revived me, said that I could be excused rugby and do swimming instead. This was no better and I nearly drowned on one occasion when I was thrown into the deep end by a gang of boys who jumped in after me to prevent me from scrambling to the edge of the pool.

Around this time, we moved home, which meant I had to leave the school, and I told my mother's boyfriend about the bullying, to which he replied, "Anybody can do anybody, you just have to find a way." This made a big impression on me and it is something that I have remembered over the years. In fact it has become my motto, and on many occasions I have passed this on to others.

In 1974 my mother and her boyfriend married and the physical abuse he dished out to us all got worse and worse. He was drinking more than ever and when he was drunk he was very violent. Around this same time, something happened at school which was to become something of a turning point in my life. I noticed that some of the boys at school were picking on my sister, and whereas I would normally take the beatings from the bullies, something snapped at the sight of seeing my sister getting hurt. I threw myself at the gang, throwing punches and kicking out at anyone who was within range. The feeling of knowing one of the kicks and punches had connected spurred me on and although I ended up getting a right old kicking, they left my sister alone to concentrate on me. In a way I had protected her, and I felt great.

I realised that I would have to learn to defend myself, from my stepfather and the bullies at school, so I started to learn judo. But after watching a junior karate champion on *Blue Peter*, I decided that was what I really wanted to learn. I threw myself into martial arts training and gained more and more confidence, until one day I was picked on by one of the school bullies – who got more than he bargained for. He probably had a go to impress his mates and certainly didn't expect me to turn into a screaming psychopath ready to rip his face off. The sheer aggression within me obviously showed and he backed down. In fact he absolutely shit himself. Years of bottled-up anger and frustration was now releasing itself upon this shit of a boy who was suddenly not feeling so big any more. This was one of the most important lessons I ever learnt – how to win a fight without actually fighting. It's all part of the psychology of fear.

My self-confidence took a huge leap with this one incident and almost at once my fear of fighting against the bullies disappeared. I now found myself fighting back more and more and actually started winning some of the fights I was getting into. I started to get a reputation as a fighter and had over 300 fights before I even left school. I quickly realised that the easiest way to win a fight was to strike first – and hard.

I left school and rented myself a flat, found myself getting into more and more fights and began hanging around with some lads who liked nothing better than a good ruck. We used to follow the Mod scene of the late Seventies and used to watch loads of bands such as The Jam, Secret Affair and The Chords. The highlight of the gig for us was the gang-fight which inevitably kicked off at some point during the night, usually involving tools of some description so that maximum damage could be inflicted. I look back at this time in my life and sometimes feel sick at the levels of violence I was enjoying. These fights attracted a lot of attention in the music papers and we became more organised. Our gang was known as "The Glory Boys".

My boyhood dream of achieving my karate black belt was soon to become a reality, but in strange circumstances. My instructor at the time was a right wanker who loved to show off if any young girls were in to watch. He was also known to be shagging some of his female students. One night he decided to use me as the mug for one of his demonstrations and went right over the top, landing heavy punches and kicking me full-force in the head. Karate etiquette would not allow me, as the student, to beat my master and I ended the exchange by bowing and going to change. He followed me into the changing room and tried to ridicule me and ended up offering to fight me on some waste ground. The alternative was for me to write a letter saying that I was afraid to meet him. I told him to fuck off, that I would be there and that I was going to beat shit out of him. My streetfighting ability plus my full-contact karate training gave me the confidence in myself that he would be on the receiving end of a right hammering.

I was at the agreed spot waiting for him but he didn't show and when I phoned his house it turned out that he was giving "private lessons" to a female student. I knew full well what that meant, and it turned out that she was the girlfriend of a mate of mine, another of the brown belts at the club. I phoned him at the girl's house and he was full of shit, saying that he didn't want to fight me and was sorry for what he'd said. Bollocks. To top it all, I received a phone call from the chief instructor saying that he'd heard I'd challenged my instructor to a streetfight. I arranged for the chief to visit me so that I could explain what really happened and when he arrived the following week, he'd already heard from other members of the club what went on and did not need an explanation from me. He saved the best until last, and invited me to squad training at his club with all the senior black belts, where I was awarded my black belt.

Something I haven't mentioned yet is that my sister had become heavily involved in the drug scene. This was particularly hard for me to accept, as I have always hated drugs and the way that they fuck people's lives up. She'd started by sniffing glue and had "progressed" to heroin. By this time she'd developed a serious habit and was living in a squat with a bunch of low-life druggies. It was killing me inside to see my little sister being dragged down so low and I decided to deal with her problem the way I dealt with all of my problems: physically and head-on. I found out where the squat was and got a little team together. I knocked on the door, pretending that I was looking for somewhere to score. The door was opened by a huge skinhead who looked as though he hadn't finished evolving. I hit him as hard as I'd ever hit anybody. Right on the snooze button. He went down like a sack of shit and we piled into the squat mob-handed. What followed was one of the biggest massacres I've ever witnessed. Everywhere you looked there were junkies with broken noses, ribs and arms lying in pools of their own blood. At one point I actually thought we'd gone overboard and killed one of them because he went into a coma. As we left, I told one of his mates to call an ambulance, and left thinking we'd be up on a murder charge. It turned out that he'd overdosed, which had caused him to go into the coma.

My sister was heavily into the drug scene and I called on her one day to find she'd been robbed. It was unusual how I'd come to visit her, but I was driving in my car and noticed some guy wearing one of my tracksuits that I'd kept at my sister's house. You may be wondering how I knew it was mine and not just a similar one, well, it had my club badge on it and my name embroidered on it! When I got to her house, she told me that the guy had beaten her up and nicked a load of stuff off her, including her wedding ring. She also told me the name of the guy and said that they'd argued after he'd ripped her off in a drugs deal. When he'd ripped off her wedding ring, he'd made a real mess of her finger and had also taken quite a bit of my stuff. He didn't know who I was and took the piss out of the owner of the tracksuit, mocking karate chops and kicks.

I found out fairly easily where he lived and decided to serve him up with one of my favourite ploys – an early morning wake-up call. If I had a particularly nasty situation to clear up, I would often call at 5am, when they were least expecting me. The element of surprise gave me an added advantage over them, plus the psychological effect it had on them was awesome. One rule I had, though, was that I never, ever, paid somebody a home visit if they had a wife or family. Unluckily for this wanker, he had neither.

A good lesson I had learned when dealing with druggies is that they always make sure they have plenty of locks on their door. Unfortunately the sad bastards are usually too stupid to work out that there is still only one pair of hinges holding the other side of the door, and this is the side I target. A well-aimed kick to the hinged side of the door and it flew off its hinges. I was in. In this type of situation, most druggies are expecting a bust, but this guy did not know what the fuck was going on. He just stood there terrified. I could already see my sister's wedding ring on his hand and let go with a right hand that connected well. He fell to the floor and now it really was fucking pay-back time. I hit him until he lost consciousness and tried to remove the ring from his finger. It wouldn't move. Remembering the state of my sister's hand, I got hold of a large kitchen knife and started to saw at his finger. I was not leaving without the ring and if that meant his finger had to come off, then so be it. The pain must have been so intense that he woke up and saw me cutting away at his hand. He struggled free and I got up with him and again battered him into a near lifeless state, breaking his jaw in two places along the way. I told him why I was there and warned him that if my sister's stuff was not returned by the end of the day, then worse was to follow – and it would have. I later found out that as well as his broken jaw, he had also lost my sister's ring, along with his finger. Guess what? The ring was anonymously returned to my sister.

Over the years, I have received numerous death threats. One of the few times that I have come close to one being carried out came when I was out walking near my sister's house and I was jumped and dragged into an alley by three guys. The way they set about me told me that they meant me serious harm. One of them had something around my neck trying to strangle me, while another slashed open my arm with a steel comb. All the time the kicks and punches were flying in, and it took all of my survival instincts just to keep conscious. I knew that if I got myself knocked out they would have finished the job. I somehow managed to dislocate one's knee with a kick, which put him out of action for a while, and repeated elbows into the face of the guy who was strangling me from behind eventually took their toll on him. I felt the ligature loosen enough for me to break free. The odds were now more in my favour and a combination of kicks and punches soon put the last man down. I found out that some guys from a local pub had paid them to do me, and although me and a few mates went to the pub that night, I never found out who or what was behind that one.

I was becoming increasingly disillusioned with my martial arts training, particularly how it never really prepared you for what can happen on the street. So I decided to open up my own club, which was not attached to any one particular style. This was a new concept and I intended right from the start to make it accessible to anyone who wanted to train there by keeping the costs down to a minimum. I called it the New Breed Academy. This coincided with me starting to write articles for *Fighters* magazine, and was the beginning of a new phase of my life. The idea of the Academy was not to teach people just martial arts techniques but to teach them in such a way that it prepares them for what can happen on the street, and traditional teaching methods did not take this into account.

To help bring some money in, I relied more and more on door work, and have, over the years, worked on some of the roughest, toughest doors around London. If I started to tell you about all of the fights that I had working on the doors it would fill a library, let alone a book. You really do see some of the worst kinds of people in this line of work. Don't get me wrong, the majority of people who go to the clubs are decent and polite, just out for a good time, but there is an element of tossers who get a few beers in them, or who are on the gear, and think they can take on the world. You have to be able to turn a deaf ear to a lot of the abuse and shit that you get when you turn somebody away from a club, but every so often they overstep the mark and you have to take them out. You get threatened almost every night and I've lost count of the number of losers who are going to come back and kill me. The trouble is, one day one of them might just try and do that. It helps if you've got a good little team working the doors and I've worked with some of the best, but there are also some doormen who I've worked with that I'd rather forget. When it kicks off they are nowhere to be seen, or they are doing drugs themselves, which means that they're just not switched on enough to notice the little things that can make a huge difference.

One of the worst situations I found myself in was when a fellow doorman who I had been working with came round my house and ended up trying to bloody shoot me. We initially fell out over his dealing in the club that we were supposed to be minding. It escalated and we arranged a meet where we were going to "sort it out". I didn't trust him and was expecting him to turn up mob-handed, so I went tooled up. He turned up alone, saying that he wanted to forget our differences. We went back to my place to talk things through and after a while he pulled out a gun, pointed it directly at me and fired. Whether it was a warning shot, or he just happened to be a shit shot, I don't know, but the bullet hit the ground beside me. [Jamie didn't say anything more about this episode, so if you want to know what happened, you'll have to ask him! – JD].

I hated the way my lifestyle was heading, with night after night of violence, but I had to keep working to pay the bills. One thing with door work is that your days are free-time and I started to work on a writing project that I'd thought about for a while. I had decided that there was a need for a book dedicated to female self-protection and, after what seemed like ages, I had a complete manuscript which I sent to my great friend Geoff Thompson [well-known martial artist and author – JD] for his opinion on whether or not he thought it was good enough to publish. Luckily he thought it was, and *Dogs Don't Know Kung Fu* was released. It turned out to be very successful and the standard reference text for female self-protection in this country, and yet to be equalled. I've since written a further five books, including my life story *Thugs, Mugs and Violence – The Story So Far*. Although my story revolves around violent situations, it's not the lifestyle I chose, it was thrust upon me.

My advice to everybody is to avoid getting into any situation that may progress onto the use of physical violence. I hate it if I am forced into a situation where violence needs to be introduced to bring the matter to an end, where all other alternative routes avoiding violence have failed. If I am ever in a confrontational situation, it will never be through personal choice, it will be because I have been forced into this situation and for that, somebody will pay a very high price. That somebody may even be me. Having been stabbed twice, shot and beaten to a pulp, I realise I do not have special superhero powers and that I do bleed and feel pain.

I will be happy if I never get into another situation involving violence for the rest of my life, because no matter how capable I or the other person may be at looking after ourselves, we will both be in a situation where either one of us may be taking a trip in an ambulance, police car or a hearse, and I don't want that person to be me. The only time I want my children to have to visit me in hospital, prison or a cemetery is if I have dealt with someone that has hurt one of them.

When it comes down to the laws of reality, *anybody can do anybody – you just have to find a way*. If I am capable of taking a life with my bare hands in a matter of seconds, there is no reason at all why somebody else cannot do the same to me. I teach people to protect themselves with their bare hands. Part and parcel of that is showing them how to take another human being to pieces if the need for survival arises. My own knowledge and teaching ability frightens me at times, in case this ability fell into the wrong hands, but if it saves just one young child or female from being sexually assaulted, raped, tortured or killed, then I will carry on transferring my knowledge in the form of my books, courses and personal tuition.

If I can back off or walk away from a situation and live to see my kids the next day, then I have succeeded. If I risk my life for a worthless incident that lasts for a few seconds and deprive my children and family from ever seeing me again, I will have failed. I do hope that people can see me for the kind, caring person that I really am, rather than the monster that people sometimes portray me to be. If you spill my beer in a pub then I would not see that as something worth fighting for. However, lay a finger on one of my children and I will not hesitate to come tearing through your door at 5am, before you can even wipe the sleep from your eyes, to serve you up. People will only treat you in the way that you allow them to. Unfortunately, though, children cannot do much about it when someone more powerful than them treats them bad or causes them harm. But I can. For most of the time I am the calmest person that you will ever have known in your life. But I will still turn into Hannibal Lecter if the need arises.

IVOR SMITH
Newport
As told by his daughter Paula

An extraordinary fighting man from yesteryear, the life story of Ivor Smith could easily form the basis of a great film. His rollercoaster life saw changes of fortunes that took him to the highest peaks and lowest depths a man could imagine. Renowned for his huge fists and massive punching power, he was equally at home trading it with travelling men or brawling in the bars of Tiger Bay.

259

MY FATHER WAS born in Newport, South Wales, in 1929. He was from a family of seven boys and one girl. His mother died from TB when he was young so he basically brought the family up. To get the kids fed my Dad would break into the Army camps at night. He would steal the supplies there, tins of ham, corned beef and the cigarettes. There was a war on so sometimes he would share with the neighbours, a bit of a Robin Hood he was. One night, he got caught in there and they sent him to Borstal for seven years. He moved to a couple of Borstals and in one he was forced to learn Welsh by the violin teacher there. Now my dad was a man's man who enjoyed a rough and tumble and didn't want to be listening to some idiot on the violin.

While in the Borstal kitchens he stole a carrot and one of the screws saw him. The next day, he was sent to have two strokes of the birch. This other boy was there for it as well and my dad let him go in first. Well, he said, "After hearing that twat scream, my arse was going like hell." It would have been better if he hadn't known what to expect. They made my dad drop his pants. The bastard who gave it to him run from one side of the room to the other and really gave it to him. Just for good measure they rubbed salt into the wounds as well.

When he left Borstal he was enlisted into the Army at 18. After having years of the screws shouting in his face he couldn't take to the drill sergeant. He was always onto my dad, so my dad gave him a right hiding and was straight off to the glasshouse. After nine months there, he had a dishonourable discharge, which made him happy as Larry. While there he met the Krays and they became good friends. Later in life I had many phone calls from Reg and he became a good friend.

He went into the merchant navy and met a girl called Clare when he was 21. He had learned to box in the Army so when he was home he would go to the fairground and fight in the boxing booths. My dad was six foot three and had a tremendous reach, which came in handy. If my dad hit them, they didn't get up and more often than not they were carted off to hospital. If he weren't at sea then he'd be fighting in the booths. Fighting came very easy for my dad, he was so tough and could punch so bloody hard.

Eventually he was fighting in bareknuckle scraps for good money. He did this from the age of 21 right up to the age of 35. My dad was a bugger for the women and Clare couldn't stick his ways so they got divorced. Once he was in a pub and a girlfriend was there. A Polish man made advances to her. Well, dad told him the score but the geezer made a bit of a stand, like. Dad pops him one and bang, he knocks the guy's eye out of the socket. You must understand my Dad had bloody huge hands with big mangled knuckles and one finger short on one hand that had gone through a mincer while in the ship's kitchen; he could wrap his hands around a man's head. Dad didn't hang around for the police and buggered off to sea again. He was always in big demand on board ship, being a good head chef, and for a bit extra would sort all the trouble out. When he came home the police nabbed him and he was sent down for four years.

My mother lived next door to my dad's sister, Grace. When he was inside, the girl who had my oldest brother John gave him to Grace to look after. Now Grace didn't have a clue with kids so my mum looked after him. Dad was happy knowing my mum was so kind to care for John, so when he came out he spent eleven months chasing after her until they became an item. When my sister and myself were born, my dad had taken over a pub called The Rupella, which was a bit rough, but my dad sorted it out. Dad would lift us onto the bar to sing songs for the customers. I remember on Sundays they would close early and put the barrels out in a circle and they would fight there for money. My Dad would fight some of the big Irish boys there and I watched some of his fights. There would be no kicking; it was sort of fair fights really. Some guys could really fight but once he stuck the big one on their chins, down they went.

One day I saw my old man in The Albert pub and he had an

argument with some Arab guys. There were some hookers there
and my dad didn't like that sort of thing. He also couldn't
understand why they had to give these Arabs most of their cash
and he told them. One of them pulled a knife on my dad, so dad
proceeded to strangle him. Dad took the knife off him and sliced it
across the geezer's face. He told him, "If you're going to pull a
knife on me, then make sure you use it." All the time I was
watching this and later he told me that this was how life sometimes
was, so always beware of twats like those guys.

To make some cash, my dad would go out collecting scrap
metal on the lorry. He would take me to all the gypsy camps as
well. He would know all the guys there. They would tell him to
come back at night sometimes because they had a fight on. It was
like a day's work for dad: he'd turn up, fight, then out later to
spend the money. Before and after the fight he treated them as
good friends and never held a grudge. Some of these travellers
were fighting all their lives and were as big as him. He loved these
fights because he said they were so hard he felt he had really
earned his money.

He was always coming home with black eyes, cut lips or stabbed
up. Sometimes he would come home and stitch himself up or pull
out a broken blade from his body. My mum couldn't bear to
watch him, she would be sick every time this happened. When he
had been stabbed he would tell mum to go get the axe because
now he had to take a trophy of his own. Many times he stuck an
axe in their heads.

After he earned good cash fighting, he would go out drinking
for days. Mam didn't mind so much but the house was always full
of murderers, robbers and all sorts, which she weren't happy
with. I didn't mind this because this was all I knew, but mam
didn't like it at all. When mam and dad were getting on okay,
things were great, but when they argued it was mental. She could
hit lumps out of him and he would never hit her back. Once she
made his dinner and he didn't turn up, so off she marched all us

kids down to the pub. She would bang on the doors and the landlord would let her in and disappear out of her way. She would march up to my dad and put his dinner over his head. She would even grab him by the scruff and pull him out of there. All the time he would be shouting that she was making him look a fool. Sometimes someone would comment that they wouldn't stand for that and dad should slap her back. Dad would walk up to them and tell them she was his wife and clout them one.

When the boys were playing up, mam would tell dad to get up stairs and use the belt on us, but he never did. He would strike the bed with belt and the boys would pretend to scream out. Well one day she caught him doing this so she hit everyone with the belt, even my dad. Sometimes when they argued she would be upstairs and she would call to him. Dad would come to the bottom of the stairs and she would drop a heavy wicker basket on his head. You'd think he would learn but she would catch him every time with that one.

One day he disappeared for a few days and we couldn't find him. Mam knew he was out drinking somewhere. It had been snowing real bad and dad caught a taxi home. His idea was to sneak upstairs when mam was watching TV. Well, next to the back door we had a big old china sink. Mam climbed up on it and when he was sneaking in banged him over the head with a wooden meat tenderiser. Dad was knocked out and mam pushed him down three steps out into the snow where he lay. Mam shouted to us to take dad's trousers off because that's where the rent money was. Mam left him there for ages in the snow and the neighbours phoned for the ambulance to take him away. He was in hospital for three days with hypothermia and concussion.

Sometimes dad would go out and pinch a safe. One day he dropped this big heavy safe on his toe. The bloody thing all but took his toe off. Well he had to go to the hospital and he told them he had dropped a bin on it. The police had witnesses to say they had seen him with the safe, and they didn't believe he had dropped the bin on it. Turns out the crafty bugger had rubbed his blood on the bottom of the bin, so he got off with that one.

Dad was going back to sea and was drinking heavy all the time; that and the fact that my dad was chasing every woman he could, split them up for good in the end. When I was about 15, I had a phone call saying he had been jumped up in Fishguard while drunk. I'd never seen my dad in any serious condition but this time two guys had shattered dad's jaw and stabbed him four times in the back. They even tried to cut his throat. From what I gather, one was found dead not long after. He had been tied up and thrown in the dock. The other was reported as missing at sea.

Dad was being nursed for about four months by mam but he hit the drink hard and went back to his old ways when he got better. This didn't help him and eventually his condition deteriorated and sadly he died. Even though he's gone now, I look at my older brother John and I see so much of my dad in him. John's a fighting man, just like Dad was.

ERNIE BEWICK

Sunderland

Hard as nails and afraid of neither man nor beast, Ernie has an easy-going nature that leads some to underestimate him. But beneath the relaxed exterior lies the heart of a lion. A legend on the streets of Sunderland, Ernie is both well liked and well feared – liked by most, but feared by those who cross the line.

I WAS BORN down what is known as the East End of Sunderland. My dad was a good fighter in his time and fought some very handy guys over the years. He brought us up to be able to handle ourselves but to never look for trouble. My great-grandfather was a professional boxer and in his first eight fights he knocked them all out. The story that I was told as a boy was that he had been beaten to death while he was in prison. I don't know the truth of it, but that's the story passed down over the years in my family.

I have two brothers and we never really had much. In fact none of the kids where we lived had a lot. It was a hard time for everyone, but what we never had, we never missed. We would always get into scuffles with other kids, winning some and losing some along the way. I got known as the toughest in the school, so I was always fighting. Looking back now, I realise that we all should have stuck to our schooling and got an education, but we look at our parents as role models, and my dad was a fighter.

I got it into my head that I was going to learn to box. It was just something that I wanted to do, so I got myself off to the gym. I found it all very exciting, and boxing held no fear for me at all. I was only a kid and was so impressed with the trainers and the gym. One of the trainers would tell all us kids, "When you leave this gym, I want you to be as good-looking going out as you were when you came in." They looked after us and taught us well.

I was back and forth to the gym a lot over the years but, of course, being young, I wanted to go to the disco and that. This was when, I guess, I really started to get into fights. I remember one lad telling my friends what he was going to do to me when we met up. My mate told him, "There's no way you're going to beat Ernie." A while later, I was in a nightclub when I see the lad coming over to me. He offers me into the toilets to sort things out. We both walk over to the toilets and all the while he's holding his pint glass, one of them old, heavy, chunky glasses. I guess he must have sensed how confident I was because he stopped just before the toilets and put the glass over my head. This didn't bother me and I just kept putting punches into him until I beat him. Thing is, no matter what they use against you in a fight, you have to keep going forward, keep attacking, and that's what I did.

When I was in the gym sparring, I liked to get into the fight and literally soak up my opponent's punches. I was so very game when I was young; even when I fought on the street, I loved a good tear-up. Once, in a fight, I got grabbed around the neck in a headlock. I just covered up my face and let the other guy wear himself out punching. He couldn't hurt me and was just getting tired trying. Before long, I managed to pull myself free and punched him down to the ground. Again he grabs me in a headlock and again I cover, absorb his punches and knock him down. His friends got between us because they knew he couldn't beat me. You could tell by looking at him that all the fight had left him, but me, I was still up for it. I guess it's because I idolized Rocky Marciano as a youngster and tried to base myself on him. I just thought the guy was the greatest fighter that I had ever seen. I just wanted to fight the same way as him and be as tough as him. Having Marciano as my idol helped me through all the fights I had when I was young. I wouldn't back down and would keep on fighting no matter what the odds against me were. My whole life was motivated by him.

I sometimes wish that I stayed with the boxing more than I did. You must understand I was drifting in and out of boxing all the time. I wouldn't train for, say, two years, come back, train for two weeks, and then fight in the ring. My trouble was that I treated boxing too much like a hobby, like some kids would have a game of football on a Saturday afternoon. One of my best wins in the ring was against big Viv Graham, who was murdered later on in life. I was a few years older than Viv and was told that he wasn't to be messed with, as he had knocked a few out. In the fight I kept throwing left hands into his face, not showing my right hand because I was keeping that back hoping to knock him out with it. I dominated the fight but couldn't get a knockout because he was defending himself quite well and had his guard up. I won the fight and felt it was a good fight for me, as I had handled myself quite well.

I never felt pain when I was actually in a streetfight, but later on, when I cooled down, I could feel every punch and kick that I had taken. I was out one night in a club called The Rink when I got into a fight with this lad called Harry. The fight moved to the centre of the dance floor with everyone around us. There were bottles and glasses raining down on us from everywhere. We didn't stop, just kept on fighting each other, both going for it. The doormen just stood around watching, they didn't want to get involved with it. I eventually got Harry onto the deck and, after hitting him a few times, he gave up, so I got off him and let him go. Now the bouncers came up to me and wanted to know if I was alright and that. I realised that I had at some time in the fight been kicked between the legs. I stood there acting as if I hadn't been hurt, but in fact my stomach and that were killing me.

I started drifting in and out of various jobs like working on the scrap wagon, just to get some money in. I wasn't making a lot and got involved in a wages snatch. Now don't get me wrong, I don't glorify crime and hope kids don't follow me down that road. Well, I left my fingerprint on the roof of a car; that and being identified, sent me away for a while. This is all something I never really talk about and I know that I did wrong. I wanted to change my life when I got out, and because I couldn't read or write, I decided that I wanted to better myself a bit. I started learning and spent a lot of time reading about different things. I would read about history and religion, about people who stood up for what they believed in. I would absorb everything from Socrates to the Romans. This all helped to strengthen me mentally and spiritually.

I was unemployed and looking hard for work but the only thing I was really cut out for was working the doors. First time I did door work was just because I needed a television; the second time was just to get money in for Christmas. It was the only real work I could find at the time, so eventually I got more and more door work. I was known as a handy lad, so the door work came easy. When you have no money and no job, the respect I had as a fighter did boost my self-esteem a bit. It was not just fighting I was respected for but for being a fair guy who would always help out the underdog. I've always been approachable and like to talk to people, so I got along with most folk.

I then got offered to sort this pub out on the Pennywell Estate. They were getting trouble there and offered me £100 to sort it. I went up to the pub on my own. I knew there would be guys waiting for me but I thought it best to go on my own. I walked up to the guys who I knew were causing all the trouble. "There'll be no more trouble here, I'm barring the lot of you," I told them. Now it may seem a bit dirty but I needed to really make my presence felt, so I lifted up the table and smashed it down on the floor. Well, that seemed to do the trick because when I offered them outside there were no takers. There were a good few guys there that could have a scrap. I knew I couldn't fight them all but I was willing to try. One guy said he was going to bring down a relative to sort me out. Well, when he said that I knew I had got them all beat. There was no more trouble in the place and I was getting paid good money to look after it.

One night a gang of lads burst into a club I was running. They are well-known guys, so I won't mention their names. They were looking for trouble, so I told them they had to leave.

"Are you daft?" the first one asked. "There are all of us here."

Now I had the other doormen with me and a load of back-up in the club if needed. "Look it's you that's outnumbered," I told him.

He looked around and said, "Yes, but we got guns."

Now I played a bit of a bluff here and told him, "Well, we got guns as well."

I pointed to one of the lads with me and told them that he had a gun. Funny thing is that one of the guys with us did have a gun; I was only trying to bluff them but he went to his car and told me he had a gun on himself. I spoke straight to the two main lads who were arguing with me. I offered to fight them both and they declined. I think the bluff with the gun worked because they turned around and went. Could have gone the other way and turned really nasty, mind you.

The benefit that I had in a fight was my heart. I wouldn't back down and would fight anyone who came looking for it. I have to admit, sometimes nerves would take hold of you, especially when you know you had to fight someone. It's not a nice feeling waiting for it to kick off, that nervous feeling in your stomach and the weakness you get in the legs. Even though you feel that way, there's just something inside you that wills you to go on. It's different when you go into a situation where you don't know it's going to happen, because you react without thinking, reflexes and instinct take over. I found the best way to get over the nerves, if I thought a fight would come off, was to keep light-hearted about it and relax. I'd think that maybe there wouldn't be a fight and things would work out fine. There are a lot of good men out there who have lost a fight through worrying about what may happen. Over the years I've walked into clubs on my own where I know some handy guys are waiting for me. I've walked up to them and told them if they want to have it, they can, even though I knew I could be jumped on by them all. It's better to face these things straight on. You tend to get respect off people for it.

I was working in a club called the Blue Monkey when I get told that someone was at the door and he wanted to come in without paying. We argued and he offers me round the corner and calls me a "little shit". All of a sudden he slaps me and I take a step forward to fight. He then throws a punch, which I ducked and, as fast as I could, I threw a right cross followed by an uppercut which puts him down. Now, most times this would be the end of things but I get a message that he wanted a return fight. He's a good fighter and quite a hard lad. These days we get on and I must say I do like him. Anyway, the fight was arranged and I travel down to the gym in Jesmond [an area of Newcastle-upon-Tyne], where we were to fight. My fight plan was to take everything he had, then wear him down. I knew he could fight and thought this would be the best way. I'm hanging around for about one and a half hours and at this stage nerves are starting to kick in a bit, it's the waiting that does it. I'm trying to stay focused and also staying as relaxed as I can, but it's hard when you're waiting for so long. While I waited I was made to feel comfortable, the gym owner Andy gave me a cup of tea to warm me up, as I was getting cold. My opponent turns up and we shake hands like gentlemen. We go around the back of the gym to get the fight started. I look around and at once I notice that the area is tailor-made for him, with him being bigger: there were corners that he could get me trapped in, and an embankment which later worked to his advantage a bit.

The fight starts and I'm flicking punches out, not hard shots, just enough for him to throw a few back. This way, I could then work my way in on him if he came forward. The guy was a big banger and I had to be careful and use my head a bit. The fight goes up against the wall and I cover and let him punch himself out a bit. He backs off up the embankment and I follow and trip on the way. He tries to get on top of me, but I manage to break free. The last thing I needed was his weight on me. I know I can catch him with a left hook, so I just throw rights for a while, then I throw a straight right and follow with a left hook. I feel that I can now finish the fight. Next thing I'm hit with an uppercut and I put my hand on the floor to steady myself. With that, someone gets in between us, and I'm thinking they are going to stop the fight, so I went mental and start to tear into my opponent. The fight is then stopped and I'm declared the winner. I'll be fair on my opponent: when I went back into the gym, he waited outside to shake my hand and to put it all behind us.

For a while later the whole town was full of excitement over the fight, there were so many stories going around about it. I had beaten a very hard, well-known fighter and everyone was talking about it. During the fight I had lost a false tooth and for some reason people were saying that big Viv Graham, who was watching the fight, had knocked one of my teeth out. I start getting told by people that Viv had thrown the punch that stung me just before the end of the fight. It dawns on me that was why I never saw the punch coming – I was struck by Viv from the side. I eventually confront Viv and he admits that he had struck me during the fight. He tells me it was because my opponent was like a father to him and he didn't want to see him beat. Now I'm not the type to hold a grudge and it was a daft thing for him to do, so I left it at that.

It was New Year's Eve [1993] and someone in a party told me that Viv had been shot dead. I didn't believe it at first but then the story went around that he had been blasted with a shotgun and was dead. I felt sorry for Viv. Nobody deserved that, no matter what he may or may not have done.

I was making the town safer by stopping the trouble in the clubs and that. I didn't want drugs in the pubs and clubs where I worked and kept them out. I had good lads working for me on the doors and felt I was doing a good service in the town. You must remember that at this time there was a lot of dangerous people around here, going around with guns and threatening to kill people. I was doing something that I liked and people knew I could do a good job.

Things came to a head one night when I got involved in a fight with this guy called Tony Waters and ended up doing three years for manslaughter. I've been out of prison for over a year now, and one of the conditions of my parole licence was that I stay away from door work. At the moment I'm working part-time with a building firm and just keeping my nose clean. Eventually, I will get back to running the doors again, maybe just taking a backseat and overseeing things. I'm just going to take life one step at a time and play whatever cards it deals me.